The Open University

Science: a second level course

ST240

OUR CHEMICAL ENVIRONMENT

BOOK 4
SENSATIONAL CHEMISTRY

The Open University

ST240 Course Team

Course Team Chair	Stuart Bennett
General editors	Michael Mortimer
	Malcolm Rose
Authors	Rod Barratt
	Alan Bassindale
	Stuart Bennett
	Michael Gagan
	Jim Iley
	Michael Mortimer
	David Roberts
	Malcolm Rose
	Peter Taylor
Course Manager	Charlotte Sweeney
Course Secretary	Sally Eaton
BBC	Cameron Balbirnie
	Sandra Budin
	Andrew Law
	Paul Manners
	Michael Peet
	Ian Thomas
	Nicholas Watson
	Darren Wycherley
Editors	Gerry Bearman
	Dick Sharp
Graphic Design	Sue Dobson
	Mark Kesby
	Mike Levers
	David Roberts
	Howard Taylor
	Rob Williams
Experimental work	Keith Cavanagh
	Ray Jones
	Pravin Patel

The Open University, Walton Hall, Milton Keynes, MK7 6AA

First published 1995. Reprinted 1997

Copyright © 1995 The Open University

Edited, designed and typeset by The Open University.

Printed in the United Kingdom by Bath Press Ltd, Glasgow.

ISBN 0 7492 51441

This text forms part of an Open University Second Level Course. If you would like a copy of Studying with The Open University, please write to the Central Enquiry Service, PO Box 200, The Open University, Walton Hall, Milton Keynes, MK7 6YZ. If you have not enrolled on the Course and would like to buy this or other Open University material, please write to Open University Educational Enterprises Ltd, 12 Cofferidge Close, Stony Stratford, Milton Keynes, MK11 1BY, United Kingdom.

1.2

ST240book4i1.2

In this part of Book 4, we aim to show you how chemistry contributes to the quality of all of our lives

PART 1
SEE, TASTE, SMELL

Prepared for the Course Team by Michael Gagan

Contents

Chapter 1
Introduction

So far in this Course, you have encountered chemistry at its interface with the necessities of life – materials, energy, food, health; but chemistry is also deeply involved in helping us to enjoy life more, in creating that ambience in our environment that enables life to be lived to the full. A large number of the chemists engaged in industry are concerned to make our world a brighter, more pleasant place to live. They use their skills to design and produce materials to delight our senses, rather than to meet our basic needs.

We experience the world through our five senses: sight, hearing, touch, taste and smell. All five senses rely on the *biochemistry* of nerve transmission, but sight, taste and smell have more particular chemical connections. The last two are actually called the 'chemical senses', as they are triggered at the molecular level by substances from outside our own bodies, which we perceive as having taste and smell. The sense of sight can most readily be linked to chemistry, through our ability to perceive colour. On the one hand, we can use chemical principles to explain why our world is coloured; and on the other, synthetic chemistry enables us to add to (and arguably improve upon) the colours of nature.

Colour is a well-understood phenomenon, and we hope to provide satisfactory answers to such questions as: 'How does colour arise?', 'Why are things coloured?', 'How can we design a dye to have a particular colour?', 'How do we perceive colour?', and 'How can this knowledge be utilized to bring us colour photography and colour television?'.

By comparison, our senses of taste and smell are still only partly understood. We can only hint at why substances taste the way they do, and we are quite unable to predict the fragrance of a newly synthesized compound with any degree of confidence.

Figure 1.1
Use of colour to enhance marketability.

1.1 Then and now

From prehistoric times, people have been fascinated by the colours of nature, and have attempted to duplicate these in their artefacts, usually for aesthetic, religious, or purely functional purposes. In more recent times, the economic benefits of colour have also been powerfully exploited. Colour makes a formidable, though largely subconscious, contribution to our everyday lives. Almost any product from industry is made more attractive by the use of artificial coloration, be it in textiles, furnishings, buildings, motor vehicles, or even food (Figure 1.1).

The marketability of all finished products can be enhanced by their presentation as an attractively coloured package. The psychological impact of colour is, of course, important in areas other than marketing, most notably in communication, safety, camouflage and design (Figure 1.2).

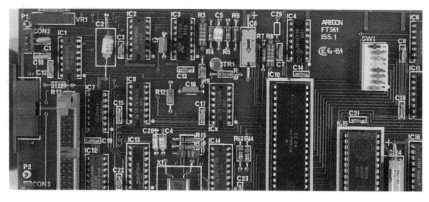

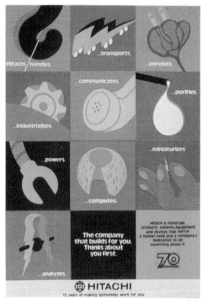

Figure 1.2
Human use of colour in communication,
safety and camouflage.

For thousands of years, humans could achieve the colour effects they so desired only by isolating the coloured materials that occur naturally in certain minerals, or particular plant and animal species. If you take a look at Figure 1.3, which shows Pieter Bruegel's well-known painting, *Children's games*, I have no doubt that you could tell immediately that it does not depict a modern scene.

Figure 1.3
Pieter Bruegel the Elder,
Children's games, 1560.

If asked why you were so sure, you would probably come up with a variety of answers, but I should be surprised if a comment on the general drabness of the children's clothing was not among them. You would only have to compare this scene with the recent photograph of a school playground (Figure 1.4) to see what I mean. The picture shown in Figure 1.3 was painted in the middle of the 16th century, and there are two reasons why such 'low key' colours are shown. The first is that the dyes available at that time differed significantly from those we use today.

Figure 1.4
Modern children at play.

They were mainly of plant origin, extracted by steeping, or boiling, the plant in water, so the range of colours available was limited to fairly dull reds, yellows, browns and blues; and the colours were **fugitive**, that is they faded quickly in sunlight or with washing, giving the clothes even more of a dull appearance.

The second reason is that even if Pieter Bruegel had wished to display a brighter selection of colours, the palette available to him was just as restricted as the range of dyes used to colour the children's clothes. The colours used by the artist will have faded even more since then.

Figure 1.5
Ancient wall painting of a bison from caves at Niaux, France.

Figure 1.6
Scribe's palette from an
Egyptian tomb of 1420 BC.

In the 10 000-year-old Ice Age cave paintings of France and Spain
(Figure 1.5), the artists used finely divided white chalk, yellow ochre, brown
and red haematite (iron oxide) and black manganese oxide, dispersed in
animal fat, to achieve their effects.

The 3 000-year-old palette of an Egyptian painter of the 18th Dynasty
(Figure 1.6), preserved in the Metropolitan Museum of Art, New York, has six
colours – terracotta, light yellow ochre, medium yellow ochre, turquoise, blue
and green – together with black and white. All of these colours are earth
pigments, derived from clays and minerals.

Until the Renaissance, this palette changed very little; Titian (c. 1487–1576),
for example, used only eight colours. From then on, new pigments kept
being discovered through simply performed chemical experiments. Some of
these colours could be incorporated into the newly developed oil paints –
dispersions of finely ground pigment in vegetable oils – which were
becoming increasingly popular with artists.

The choice steadily increased as more artificial colours were produced.
Renoir (1841–1919) used 11 colours (Figure 1.7), and Cézanne (1839–1906)
used 18 (Figure 1.8). By the time that Mirò died (1983), over 250 artists'
colours were available to the painter (Figure 1.9).

The world we inhabit shines with myriad colours of almost every conceivable
hue, but this is no longer the gift of nature alone. The dyes, pigments and
paints we take so much for granted are no longer just 'natural', but they now
include the products of a vast chemical industry that has grown up around
the production and use of synthetic dyes and pigments. It is now possible to
design to order any specified colouring material, and supply it in suitable
form for colouring the textiles of clothing and furnishing fabrics; to provide
the colour in enamel, gloss, matt or emulsion paint; or to colour cosmetics,
foodstuffs and the humble plastic bucket.

Figure 1.8
Paul Cézanne, *Still life with onions*, *c.* 1895–1900.

Figure 1.7
Jean Renoir, *Les parapluies*, 1881–1886.

Figure 1.9
Joan Mirò, *Dutch interior I*,
1928.

In the Chemistry Set Booklet Part 2, Experiment 4.2 is entitled 'Using nature's colours'. For this, you need to collect some raw wool, so bear this in mind on your next countryside walk.

Chapter 2
Where does colour come from?

2.1 Isaac Newton and 'A new theory about light and colour'

In the autumn of 1669, Isaac Newton was appointed Lucasian Professor of Mathematics at Cambridge, and for his inaugural series of lectures he took as his topic the theory of light and colour. He had acquired a triangular glass **prism** at Stourbridge Fair in 1666, intending 'to try therewith the celebrated phenomena of colours'. His researches must have been serious since 'in order to quicken his faculties and fix his attention', it is on record that he 'confined himself to a small quantity of bread, during all the time, with a little sack [sherry] and water, of which without any regulation, he took as he found a craving or failure of spirits'.

He had possibly become interested in colour through encountering the problem of chromatic aberration, which results in objects having 'rainbow-coloured' edges when viewed through the inaccurately ground lenses of a **refracting telescope**. This problem proved insurmountable, so he turned his attention to the development of the **reflecting telescope** (Figure 2.1).

Figure 2.1
A reconstruction of Newton's reflecting telescope.

Figure 2.2
Facsimile of the first page of Newton's paper to the Royal Society.

(3075)   Numb. 80.

PHILOSOPHICAL
TRANSACTIONS.

February 19. 16$\frac{71}{72}$.

The CONTENTS.

A Letter of Mr. Isaac Newton, *Mathematick Professor in the University of Cambridge ; containing his New Theory about Light and Colors : Where Light is declared to be not Similar or Homogeneal, but consisting of difform rays, some of which are more refrangible than others : And Colors are affirm'd to be not Qualifications of Light, deriv'd from Refractions of natural Bodies, (as 'tis generally believed ;) but Original and Connate properties, which in divers rays are divers : Where several Observations and Experiments are alledged to prove the said Theory. An Accompt of some Books : I. A Description of the* EAST-INDIAN COASTS, MALABAR, COROMANDEL, CEYLON, &c. *in* Dutch, *by* Phil. Baldæus. *II.* Antonii le Grand INSTITUTIO PHILOSOPHIÆ, *secundùm principia* Renati Des-Cartes ; *novâ methodo adornata & explicata.* III. *An Essay to the Advancement of* MUSICK ; *by* Thomas Salmon *M.A. Advertisement about* Thæon Smyrnæus. *An* Index *for the Tracts of the Year* 1671.

A Letter of Mr. Isaac Newton, *Professor of the Mathematicks in the University of Cambridge ; containing his New Theory about* Light *and* Colors : *sent by the Author to the Publisher from* Cambridge, *Febr.* 6. 16$\frac{71}{72}$; *in order to be communicated to the* R. Society.

SIR,

TO perform my late promise to you, I shall without further ceremony acquaint you, that in the beginning of the Year 1666 (at which time I applyed my self to the grinding of Optick glasses of other figures than *Spherical*,) I procured me a Triangular glass-Prisme, to try therewith the celebrated *Phænomena* of

G g g g   *Colours.*

Success in this endeavour resulted in his election to the Royal Society on 11 January 1672, and a week later he wrote a letter to the editor of *Philosophical Transactions*, the Society's learned journal. It was his intention, he said, to send an account of philosophical discovery 'being the oddest, if not the most considerable, detection, which hath hitherto been made in the operations of nature'. His communication was subsequently read to the Fellows on 8 February, and published on 19 February 1672 (*Philosophical Transactions*, **80**, 3075; see Figure 2.2).

Newton's discovery was the **solar spectrum** (Figure 2.3). This narrow band of **radiation**, in which we perceive the 'rainbow' colours – red, orange, yellow, green, blue, indigo and violet – is the only region in the whole of the electromagnetic spectrum (Book 2, Part 2) to which our eyes are sensitive. As you may remember, we call this the **visible region** of the spectrum.

Figure 2.3
The solar (or visible) spectrum: colours perceived over the range of wavelengths in the visible region of the electromagnetic spectrum.

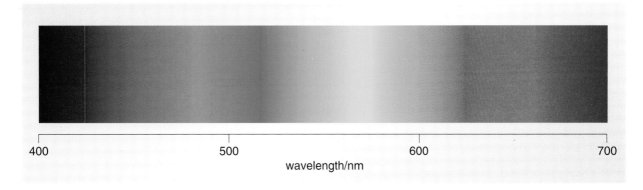

In the spectrum, the colours shade into one another but within it distinct 'pure' colours can be identified. These are the **hues** – colours that have familiar names (Figure 2.6). In addition, we recognize black, grey and white as 'colours' devoid of hue.

Like any type of radiation across the whole electromagnetic spectrum, the components of **white light** have *characteristic* wavelengths. They fall within a range that stretches from about 400 nm at the limits of violet, to about 700 nm at the limits of red. Radiation that we perceive as red has a wavelength in a small range either side of 650 nm. For green and blue, the ranges are centred on 530 nm and 460 nm respectively. You should now check these values on Figure 2.3.

Apple Computer

Figure 2.4
The Apple™ logo picks out the hues from the spectrum, but not in the order we observe them in the rainbow.

Box 2.1 The 'colour' of light

It is particularly important to note that although we talk about 'red light' or 'blue light', this is only a 'shorthand' terminology. Light itself has no colour. Instead, the impact of radiation of a certain wavelength on our eye is interpreted by our brain to produce the sensation we describe as red, green or blue. The correct expression is the light 'that we perceive as red'. However, we shall not use this extended form of words very often in this Book. When describing light, the terms 'colour' and 'wavelength' will be used interchangeably; e.g. 'blue light' or 'light with a wavelength of 460 nm'.

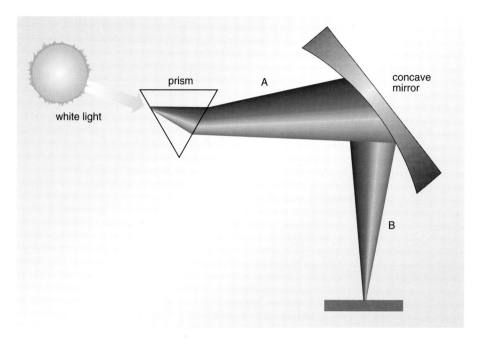

Figure 2.5
A prism splitting visible (white) light into separate colours, generating a **visible spectrum** (A). Recombination of colours, to give white light, using a concave mirror (B).

What Newton was saying to the Fellows of the Royal Society is that white light is not (as they had thought) a single form of radiation. It is actually composed of a mixture of distinct colours. To prove his point, he showed that white light can also be reconstituted from these separate colours. Newton did this using other prisms, but it can more easily be shown by reflecting the spectrum produced by a prism from a **concave** mirror (Figure 2.5).

2.2 Colour at source

Once Newton had split white light into its constituent colours, an interesting principle emerged. *All* the colours of the spectrum are needed to produce white light. So, if some of the colours are missing, the *residual* light will itself be coloured. By taking away selected coloured **bands of radiation** from the solar spectrum, it should therefore be possible to produce any required residual colour. There are two common ways in which we see this happening.

One way is exemplified by the projection of a colour slide when white light passing through a transparency emerges as light of different colours. For example, light passing through the red filter in your *Chemistry Set*, or through a patch of red on a slide, will appear as a beam of red light and give a red patch on the screen. It is a simple step to propose that in order for this to happen *all* the other visible radiation, i.e. that corresponding to yellow, green and blue light, must have been absorbed.

The other way is even more familiar. When white light shines on a coloured substance, only part of it is reflected back; the rest is absorbed. For example, when sunlight falls on a door painted blue, the paint must absorb the red, yellow and green components of the light, and reflect back *only* the radiation corresponding to blue.

■ What do you think happens when light falls on a black material, e.g. soot?

■ *All* the components of white light are absorbed, and so no light is reflected back at all.

This way of describing how colour arises is called the principle of **subtractive colour generation.**

If you are familiar with the idea of **complementary colours**, you have unwittingly encountered this principle already. A complementary colour (Figure 2.6) is simply the colour generated from the wavelengths left over when the band of wavelengths corresponding to one particular colour is removed from the spectrum. Hence, one way to generate a colour is to *remove* the band of wavelengths corresponding to its complementary colour from white light.

Figure 2.6
The complementary colours; colours on the top row are complementary to the colours below, and *vice versa*.

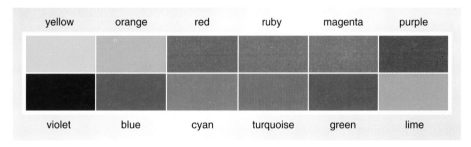

Table 2.1 puts Figure 2.6 on to a more quantitative basis by showing the wavelengths corresponding to each of the spectral hues. You should notice that the extent of the wavelength band corresponding to each different hue varies.

Table 2.1 Matching wavelengths (values in nm) to perceived hues.

Spectral colour	Violet	Blue	Cyan	Turquoise	Green	Lime	Yellow	Orange	Red
Light absorbed/ nm	400–435	435–480	480–490	490–500	500–560	560–580	580–595	595–605	605–700

Let us look at an example. If we wish to generate the hue *violet*, we must subtract its complementary colour, *yellow*, from white light. If you look at the spectrum (Figure 2.3) or Table 2.1, you will see that by absorbing the band of wavelengths in the yellow region (580–595 nm), bands of visible light from 400–580 nm (mainly blues) and 595–700 nm (mainly reds) are left. It is the mixing of the light in these two wavelength bands (red and blue) that our eyes perceive as violet.

Question 1 Which part of the visible spectrum (i.e. which complementary colour) must be absorbed to give these familiar objects their characteristic colours?

(i) An orange; (ii) blood; (iii) blue jeans.

There is one respect in which the spectrum and the table of complementary colours diverge. There is no colour *in the spectrum* complementary to green and its satellites lime (yellow–green) and turquoise (blue–green). It is a curious fact that red at one extreme of the spectrum appears to our eyes to have greater similarity to violet at the far end than it does to colours like yellow or green that are closer to it in wavelength. This anomaly has cleverly been resolved by bending the band of the spectrum round into a circle (Figure 2.7) and dropping the missing colours (magenta, and its satellites ruby and purple) into the gap between red and violet. Complementary colours are then to be found opposite each other on the **colour circle**.

- If magenta is missing from the spectrum, how then can we obtain magenta-coloured light?

- By absorbing the band of wavelengths corresponding to its complementary colour, green (500–560 nm), from white light.

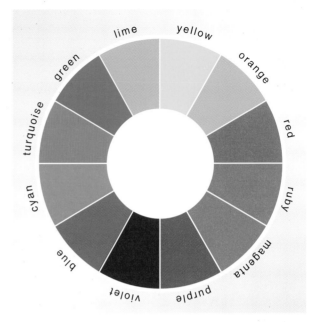

Figure 2.7
The colour circle used to describe hue.

Box 2.2   Beyond the eye – the visible spectrophotometer

Our eyes have an amazing ability to detect and interpret colour, but as a measuring instrument they have a basic flaw. They work in the opposite way to a prism. Instead of splitting light up into its component colours, they merge together the effect of all the wavelengths that they receive and present us with a composite colour. This is often sufficient; for example, we are able to blend and match the colour of a paint with a high degree of precision.

However, it does not allow us to define a colour in quantitative terms. For this we need an instrument called a **spectrophotometer** (Figure 2.8).

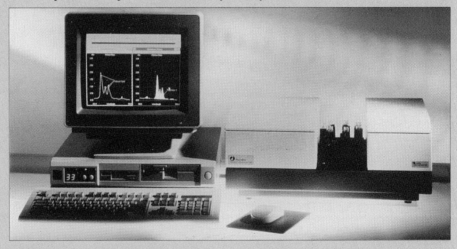

Figure 2.8
A modern *visible* spectrophotometer (i.e. one that operates in the visible region of the electromagnetic spectrum).

Inside the case, a beam of white light is spread out into a spectrum of wavelengths. This broad beam falls onto a screen in which there is a narrow slit. As the prism rotates backwards and forwards, only light of a particular wavelength is allowed to pass through the slit. This narrow beam falls on the sample and the spectrophotometer measures the proportion of the light that is absorbed (Figure 2.9).

The outcome of this procedure is a chart which shows how much

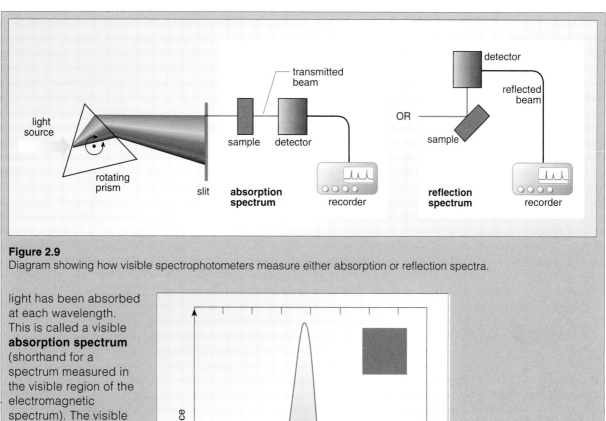

Figure 2.9
Diagram showing how visible spectrophotometers measure either absorption or reflection spectra.

light has been absorbed at each wavelength. This is called a visible **absorption spectrum** (shorthand for a spectrum measured in the visible region of the electromagnetic spectrum). The visible absorption spectrum of a dye (the indicator phenolphthalein) is shown in Figure 2.10.

Figure 2.10
The visible spectrum of the dye phenolphthalein in aqueous alkaline solution. Note that, in contrast to infrared spectra, the peaks indicating absorption point *upwards*.

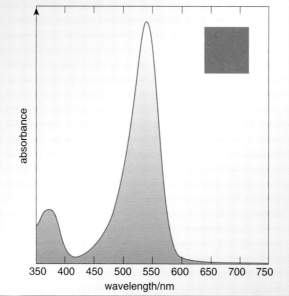

Figure 2.11 shows two more visible absorption spectra. The absorption spectra of a blue dye (Figure 2.11a) and a yellow dye (Figure 2.11b) measured by the spectrophotometer are shown as black silhouettes. The coloured background is the *solar* spectrum. Displaying the spectra this way shows which of the colours that constitute white light are absorbed by the dyes. As expected, the two dyes absorb light at different sets of wavelengths.

It is the combination of those wavelengths *not* absorbed by the dyes from the solar spectrum that the eye and brain interpret as blue and yellow respectively. This provides an answer to the question: 'How can we generate green if there is no complementary colour to absorb?' By absorbing both red and blue light at opposite ends of the spectrum, the residual colour is green.

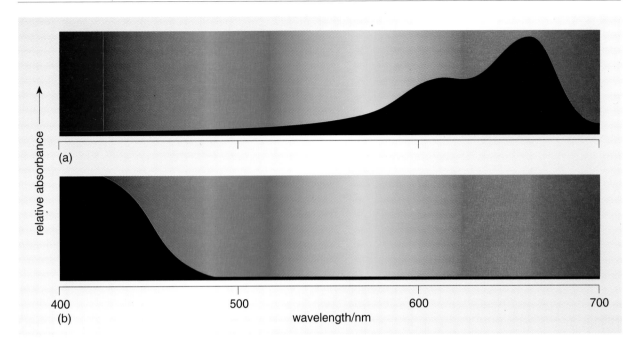

Figure 2.11
Absorption spectra (in the *visible* region) of (a) a blue dye and (b) a yellow dye, set against the solar (*visible*) spectrum.

It is also possible to measure the intensity (i.e. the proportion of light that is *not* absorbed) at each wavelength of light reflected from a surface. This gives a **reflection spectrum**. Reflection spectra from the skins of a ripe and an unripe tomato are shown in Figure 2.12. Not surprisingly, the former spectrum shows highest intensities in the red and orange regions of the spectrum, while the latter reflects mainly yellow and green light.

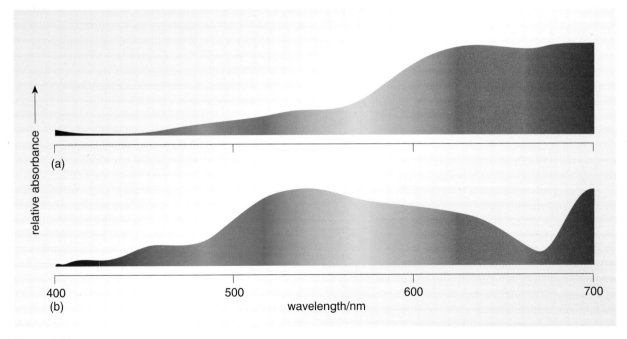

Figure 2.12
Reflection spectra from the skin of (a) a ripe tomato and (b) an unripe tomato.

Accurate colour measurement using a spectrophotometer is hardly necessary to distinguish ripe from unripe fruit, but it is extremely useful in the textile and paint industries. It is also being used in other fields such as medicine, where colour has been used from ancient times as an aid to diagnosis.

It is even more interesting to compare a reflection spectrum with the absorption bands of the coloured material we believe to be responsible for giving an object its colour. In Figure 2.13, the comparison is made between the absorption spectrum of carotene, an orange dye that can be extracted from carrots; the absorption at the surface of a carrot; and the reflection from the surface of a carrot.

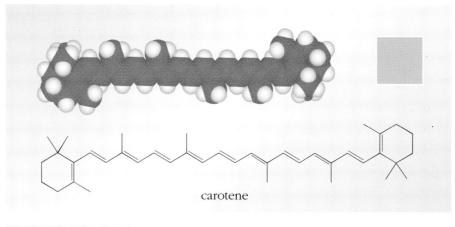

carotene

Figure 2.13
Structure of carotene and graph showing absorption spectrum of (A) carotene (C.I.Food Orange 5); absorption spectrum of the surface of a carrot (B); reflection spectrum from the surface of a carrot (C). *Note:* the initials C.I. stand for **Colour Index**, a classification scheme for dyes, jointly maintained by the Society for Dyers and Colourists (UK) and the American Association of Textile Chemists and Colorists. Indexing is applied both to natural colours and to the synthetic dyes (see Chapter 4).

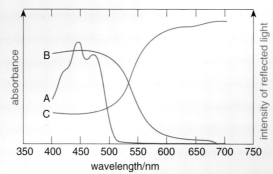

Note how the **absorption** shown by the carotene (A), although a narrower band, falls in the same region of the spectrum as the absorption of light at the surface of a carrot (B). This practical demonstration provides some evidence for the proposal that the *molecules* of dyes are responsible for absorbing light from the solar spectrum, and thereby generating the sensation of colour detected by our eyes and interpreted by our brain.

▨ How does the shape of the reflection spectrum from the surface (C in Figure 2.13) relate to the shape of the absorption spectrum (B in Figure 2.13)?

▪ Spectrum C is complementary to spectrum B, a high intensity of absorption in B corresponding to a low intensity of reflection in C and *vice versa*. This is to be expected, as the light absorbed and the light reflected should together add up to 100% of the light falling on the object.

Question 2 What colour would you expect to be exhibited by the dyes with the visible absorption spectra shown in Figure 2.14?

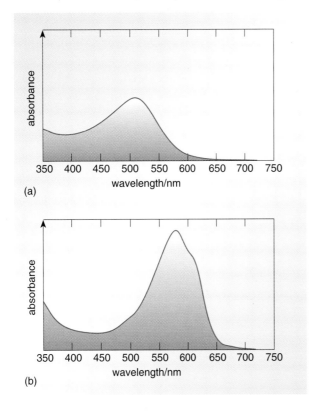

Figure 2.14
Visible absorption spectra of unknown dyes (a) and (b).

2.3 The interaction of light with atoms, ions and molecules

We must now go on to investigate the question 'Why and how is light absorbed?', which is perhaps better rephrased as 'What happens when light falls onto a material?'. The most obvious answer is that the radiation interacts with the material at the surface. To say that the radiation 'interacts' is a bit too vague. What really happens is that the radiation transfers energy to the surface material. How does it do this?

▨   Can you recall the way we chose to describe the structure of an atom?

◼   In Book 1, we developed a model of an atom as a small nucleus surrounded by a spherical cloud of electrons.

So, how then do you visualize a molecule? My guess is that you picture a molecule as either a 'ball-and-stick' model like the structures you made using your model kit, or possibly (after reading Book 3) as a skeletal framework with functional groups attached.

Another representation you have encountered earlier is the impression of a collection of spheres squashed together – the space-filling model. The outer surface of the model indicates approximately the distance the electrons extend from the nuclei of the atoms that make up the molecule. Framework and space-filling models of carotene are shown in Figure 2.13.

■ So, what will be the first thing the radiation encounters as it strikes the surface of a material?

■ It will encounter the outermost electrons of the atoms, ions or molecules of which the material is composed.

A fundamental characteristic of electrons is that they have energy. Before irradiation, the electrons are in their lowest energy condition, but they can acquire additional energy by absorbing radiation. In Book 2, Part 2, you were introduced to the **photon**, which was described as a 'packet of energy'. It is this photon energy carried by the radiation that can be transferred to the electrons.

You might reasonably expect that an electron could pick up energy from any photon that it encounters, but this is not so. Only photons with strictly defined energies are able to transfer their energy to an electron. On acquiring one of these packets of energy, the electron is raised (or **promoted**) to a higher **energy level** within the electronic system of the molecule. Each molecule has only a limited number of specific energy levels, and for each energy level there is a precisely defined energy gap between that level and the lowest energy level where the electrons were originally residing (Figure 2.15). *This idea that electrons are limited to a set of energy levels characteristic of a particular molecule is one of the fundamental concepts of chemistry.*

The set of molecular energy levels is like a ladder with electrons occupying the lowest rungs, and the higher rungs being empty. For each molecule, the size of the gaps between the rungs of this ladder, and hence the energy required to promote an electron from the rung it occupies to the next empty one, depends critically on the molecular structure. The promotion process is shown in diagrammatic form in Figure 2.15b.

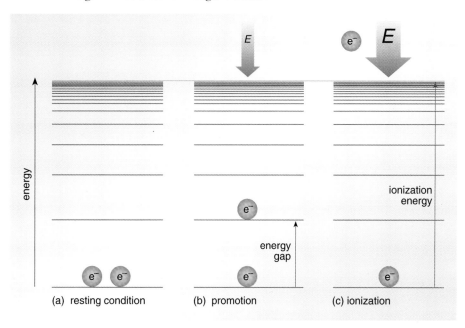

Figure 2.15
The promotion (b), and removal (c), of an electron from a low energy level (a).

- Look at Figure 2.15a, and suggest one way in which this model of energy levels is analogous to a real ladder; and also suggest one way in which it is obviously different.

- With both ladders, the higher up you go the more energy you need to expend; but the rungs of a real ladder would become very awkward if they became closer and closer together as you climbed up it.

You might imagine at first that a powerful beam of light would always be effective in transferring energy to electrons, but this is not so. The *intensity* of the light falling on the substance proves not to be significant; what matters is the *wavelength* of that light. When light with a range of wavelengths, e.g. white light, falls on a material, only certain wavelengths are absorbed. This must be the light that has photons with energies corresponding to the energy gaps on the electronic ladder.

So, in order to determine the sizes of these energy gaps, we need a method for relating photon energy to the wavelength of electromagnetic radiation that is absorbed (see Box 2.3). If the energy gap is such that the corresponding wavelength of the light absorbed lies in the visible region, or just outside it, the residual light will appear to us to be coloured.

Question 3 Calculate the energy of a photon which will promote an electron across the energy gap it must jump in order to absorb red light. Take this radiation to have a wavelength of 700 nm.

So, what happens to the energy that the electrons absorb? In the usual situation, after a very short time interval, the electron loses its energy and drops back down to its lowest level. A little of this energy may be re-emitted as radiation in the visible region, but most of it is converted into internal energy in the absorbing molecules. In other words, the absorbing substance warms up … but only very slightly! To cool down, the substance emits energy in the form of radiation. As the emission will be in the infrared region of the spectrum, it is invisible to our eyes.

- Where have you previously encountered this concept of absorbing light energy and re-emitting part of it as infrared radiation?

- You may recall that this phenomenon gives rise to the 'greenhouse effect' (Book 2, Part 2) after sunlight has been absorbed at the surface of the Earth. The infrared radiation that is subsequently emitted is not able to penetrate the atmosphere because it is trapped by the so-called 'greenhouse gases' (e.g. carbon dioxide and methane). As a result, the lower atmosphere becomes warmer.

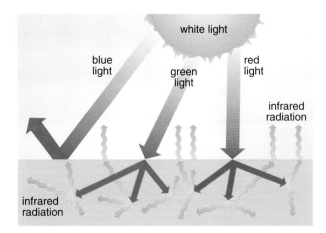

In Figure 2.17, white light is incident on a blue surface. Blue light is reflected, but light of other colours (shown here as green and red) is first absorbed and then re-emitted, mostly as infrared radiation.

Figure 2.17
Re-emission of previously absorbed radiation.

Box 2.3 The energy of radiation

We know from experience that different types of radiation have different energies. The ultraviolet radiation from a 'solarium' has a high enough energy to damage unprotected skin, whereas the infrared radiation from a physiotherapist's heat lamp is only comfortably warming.

Fortunately for us, it is easy to calculate the energy of a photon of radiation E, since it is related to its wavelength λ by the fairly simple equation:

$$E = hc/\lambda$$

Radiation travels at the speed of light, which is 3.00×10^8 m s^{-1} in a vacuum. It is given the symbol c. The symbol h is used to represent **Planck's constant**, in commemoration of Max Planck (Figure 2.16) who first recognized the link between energy and wavelength. It has the numerical value 6.63×10^{-34} and the unit joule seconds (J s).

Since h and c are both constants, the photon energy, E, is *inversely* proportional to the wavelength, λ. This shows why a photon with a long wavelength

Figure 2.16
Max Planck (1858–1947), a theoretical physicist who originated the quantum theory; i.e. that, at the microscopic level, natural phenomena do not occur continuously but in discrete steps. For this, he was awarded the Nobel Prize for Physics in 1918.

will have a correspondingly low energy (e.g. infrared radiation), and short wavelength radiation will have a high energy (e.g. ultraviolet radiation).

■ To get a feel for the size of these energies, calculate the energy associated with radiation having a wavelength of 400 nm, close to the limit of visible violet.

$$E = \frac{(6.63 \times 10^{-34}\ \mathrm{J\,s}) \times (3.00 \times 10^8\ \mathrm{m\,s^{-1}})}{400 \times 10^{-9}\ \mathrm{m}}$$

$$= 4.97 \times 10^{-19}\ \mathrm{J}$$

You should recall from Book 2 that the internationally agreed unit of energy is the joule (J), but to promote a single electron (as our calculation shows) only a tiny fraction of a joule is required. We shall therefore convert our energy values into the more convenient unit of joules per mole (J mol^{-1}).

■ How can this conversion be carried out?

■ We have to calculate the energy that *one mole* of electrons will need to obtain from the radiation for that number of electrons to be promoted from one level to another. Since a mole of anything consists of a number of units represented by Avogadro's constant, we must multiply the energy needed for *one* electron by 6.02×10^{23} mol^{-1}.

Our calculated value of 4.97×10^{-19} J *per electron* is therefore equivalent to:

$(4.97 \times 10^{-19}\ \mathrm{J}) \times$

$(6.02 \times 10^{23}\ \mathrm{mol^{-1}}) =$

2.99×10^5 J mol^{-1} =

299 kJ mol^{-1}

I hope you agree that this gives us a much more manageable quantity. This is the amount of energy *per mole* which must match exactly the energy gap between an energy level which has an electron resident in it and a higher energy level, in order for the radiation to be absorbed.

If an electron is given too much energy, it is removed completely from the molecule or atom with which it was originally associated – a process known as **ionization**. This is shown diagrammatically in Figure 2.15c. This too corresponds to our ladder analogy – if you go up high enough, you eventually drop off the end! *The important idea to appreciate here is that if an atom or molecule loses an electron, an ion is formed.*

This is not too serious for atoms, but for molecules this can initiate a chemical change resulting in reaction or decomposition, with deterioration of the material. This is why precautions need to be taken to prevent excessive ionizing radiation, like X-rays or even the ultraviolet light in sunlight, coming into contact with skin and other tissues.

2.4 Vegetable water, neon signs and fireworks

Anyone who has seen a pan of vegetables boil over on a gas cooker will probably have noticed the change in the gas flame from pale blue to a strong and persistent bright yellow. The colour in this instance cannot be the result of subtracting all wavelengths other than that corresponding to yellow from white light, so another explanation must be sought. Once again, electronic energy levels are involved; this time, it is the energy levels of the sodium of the salt (sodium chloride) dissolved in the vegetable water. The first step towards generating the colour is again the absorption of energy; in this case, the energy from within the gas flame.

To explore this process further, we first have to consider the electrons in a sodium atom. These electrons also have a ladder of energy levels they can occupy. The spectrophotometer enables us to discover that the yellow light has two slightly different wavelengths between 589 nm and 590 nm. From this observation, we can calculate that the first two energy levels to which electrons can be promoted are very close together with both energy gaps near to 203 kJ mol^{-1} above the bottom rung.

Above these levels are many more levels, getting closer and closer together, but all of them further away in energy terms (Figure 2.18). Eventually, if given an additional energy of 496 kJ mol^{-1} – the **ionization energy** – the outermost electron is lost from the sodium atom altogether (it is ionized) and the sodium atom becomes the positively charged sodium cation.

Now consider what might happen to a sodium cation from the vegetable water. As the water evaporates in the hot flame, the sodium cations will enter the gas phase. Can you recall from Book 2 the 'chemical turmoil' in the flame in which the hydrocarbon fuel is 'literally torn apart'? Along with the 'highly reactive species' that are formed in the heat of the flame, there will be many 'energy-charged' free electrons generated during the combustion of the gas. When one of these becomes attached to the positive sodium cation, it converts it into the neutral sodium atom. This electron may at first enter an energy level high up on the ladder, and from here it may drop straight down to the lowest level. However, it is more likely that it will fall from level to level, a process called **cascading**, like water running down the steps of a waterfall (Figure 2.19).

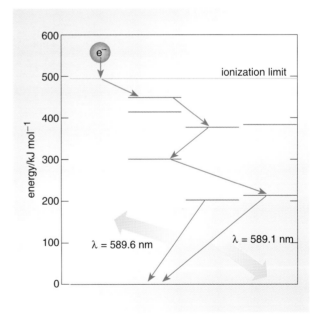

Figure 2.18
Energy levels in the sodium atom.

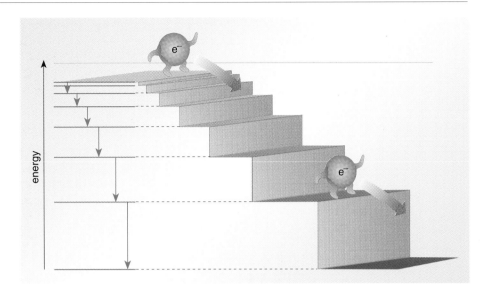

Figure 2.19
Electron cascade analogy.

When the electron reaches the next to bottom level, it has only one more step to go down the cascade. Just as electrons need to *absorb* energies close to 203 kJ mol^{-1} to raise the electrons across the gap to the first two closely spaced higher levels, when they fall from these levels they will *emit* radiation with the same energy values. Photons with these energies correspond to light with wavelengths between 589 nm and 590 nm, right at the centre of the yellow part of the spectrum. These two emissions are responsible for the colour of the flame.

> **Question 4** Why do we not observe light emitted as a result of the electron dropping down the steps higher up on the cascade?

In subtractive processes like the reflection of light from a coloured surface, or the partial transmission of **coloured light** through a transparency, the intensity of the light is always reduced. By contrast, an emission process is sustained by inputs of energy, so light of high intensity can be generated.

The emission process is a much less common source of colour than the reflection process (discounting the emission of light in the first place from the Sun, or a light bulb). However, it should not surprise you to learn that the sodium street lamp produces its light in this way. The red glow of neon lighting is similarly the result of an emission process from neon atoms at wavelengths of 649 nm and 641 nm. Again, check the expected colour at these wavelengths on Figure 2.3. You may have wondered why sodium lamps glow red just after they are switched on. This is because the lamp is filled with neon, which is ionized more easily than sodium (it is a gas already) and in effect 'starts off' the sodium emission.

A regularly observed example of the emission of light is to be found in the coloured stars and sprays of the firework display (Figure 2.20). In Book 2, the burning of a firework was given as an example of a chemical reaction that generates a lot of heat. This heat is sufficient to vaporize the inorganic compounds that are included in the firework mixture to provide colour.

Figure 2.20
Chrysanthemum shells
create perfect patterns in
the sky.

The strongest colours are usually obtained by using metal chlorides, because they are amongst the most volatile of metal compounds and generate a vapour rich in metal ions. Chlorine-containing materials like polyvinylchloride (PVC) are sometimes added to the mixture to bring about the formation of metal chlorides as the firework burns. The ions of strontium (which emit red light), copper (blue), barium (green) and sodium (yellow) pick up electrons generated in the combustion processes and the cascading electrons are responsible for the 'oohs' and 'aahs' of the spectators.

This might be a suitable point at which to try Experiment 4.1 'Coloured flames'.

Experiment 4.1 Coloured flames

Question 5 The noble gas krypton can be used instead of neon in advertising displays. Account for the generation of colour in a krypton discharge tube. What colour would you expect the light to be? *Note:* krypton has two levels of similar energy at 204 and 215 kJ mol^{-1} above the lowest level.

We have now looked at the two main sources of colour generation and we have discovered that colour is the result of either absorption or emission of light energy by electrons. Apart from sodium lamps, neon signs and fireworks, coloured light generated by the emission process is not a very commonly observed phenomenon. When most people think about colour, they imagine coloured objects or fabrics coloured by dyes and pigments. It is this branch of colour chemistry we shall move on to discuss next.

Summary of Chapter 2

In Chapter 2, you have seen how Newton was the first person to disperse white (or visible) light with a prism. This produced a solar spectrum over the wavelength range from 400 nm (violet) to 700 nm (red). An individual colour from the solar spectrum is characterized by its hue; this also determines its location on the 'colour circle'. Each hue corresponds to a specific band of wavelengths.

The principle of subtractive colour generation states that colour is the result of a material absorbing certain wavelengths from white light, and allowing the remainder to be reflected or transmitted. The colour that is perceived when wavelengths corresponding to a particular hue are removed is called the complementary colour of that hue.

An absorption spectrum shows the light absorbed from an incident beam, and a reflection spectrum the light reflected, at every wavelength. The measuring instrument used is a spectrophotometer. Spectra arise when electrons in atoms and molecules absorb energy from radiation. These electrons are confined to a limited number of specific energy levels on an 'energy ladder', and energy may only be absorbed if photon energies in the radiation exactly match the gap between two electronic energy levels.

The energy E of a photon of electromagnetic radiation is related to its wavelength λ by the equation: $E = hc/\lambda$; c is the speed of light and h is Planck's constant. Absorption of energy promotes an electron to a higher energy level, and light of a corresponding wavelength is absorbed from the reflected or transmitted beam.

The ionization energy is just enough energy to remove an electron from a molecule, atom or ion. If instead an electron is added to an ion in the vapour state, it cascades down the energy levels. Visible light is emitted if the energy gap between the bottom rung on the energy ladder and the lowest level, or levels corresponds to a wavelength in the visible region.

Chapter 3
A short history of colours

3.1 Dyes and pigments

Most people would not make a distinction between the terms dye and pigment, considering that both terms apply equally to any intensely coloured substance. However, there is a specific technical difference.

A **dye** is a coloured substance that has, either naturally or by design, an affinity for the material to which it is applied. In particular, this means an ability to become attached to one or more of the polymer molecules that are the chemicals that make up textiles, leather or wood. You should recall from Book 2 that these include polyamides, like wool, silk, and nylon; cellulosics like cotton and viscose; and other synthetics like acrylic and polyester. Dyes, or sometimes their precursors, are nearly always readily soluble in water, or else they are water-dispersible substances. Only rarely are organic solvents used. In the dyeing process, individual molecules of the dye migrate, from solution, to specific sites along or between the polymer chains.

By contrast, a **pigment** has no affinity for the molecules of the material that it colours. Instead, it is a highly insoluble material, which is applied as minute crystalline particles (Figure 3.1). Pigments are used principally in the coloration of plastics, in artists' materials and in surface coatings (e.g. paints and inks). Their permanence does not depend on any specific interactive forces between the pigment molecules and the paint or plastic in which they are trapped. Instead, they rely on the general insolubility of the pigment particles and their supporting matrix to make them weather- and solvent-resistant.

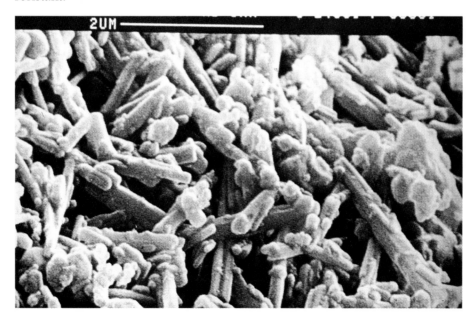

Figure 3.1
Electron micrograph of crystals of the pigment lead chromate.

So, although the colouring matters found in plants and animals are often referred to as 'pigments', largely for historical reasons, most of them should more accurately be described as dyes.

The colours of the plant and animal kingdoms nearly always have a function, even though they are often not essential to the basic life processes of the organism. In the progress of natural selection, colours that camouflage predator or prey, that attract pollinating insects or a mate, or that warn off an impending attack, offer obvious advantages (Figure 3.2). Coloration frequently results from natural dyes, complex chemicals that are present at or near the surface layers of the animal or plant.

However, some colours are due to purely physical effects; the iridescent colours of beetles, butterflies and some birds' feathers, for example, are analogous to the colours shown by a thin layer of oil on water. Other natural colours, such as the 'fire' of an opal, result from the microscopic structure of the material. We shall not consider colours generated in these ways any further in this Course.

(a)

(b)

(c)

Figure 3.2
Use of natural colours: (a) leopard (camouflage); (b) flounder (camouflage); (c) bee orchid (to attract pollinating insects).

3.2 The colours of leaves and flowers

It is one of the most commonly known facts of science that the green colouring matter of plants is called **chlorophyll**. Many people also know that it is the catalyst for the process of photosynthesis, but fewer people (even chemists!) know its chemical structure (Figure 3.3). Chlorophyll is localized within the plant's cells in small bodies called chloroplasts (Figure 3.4).

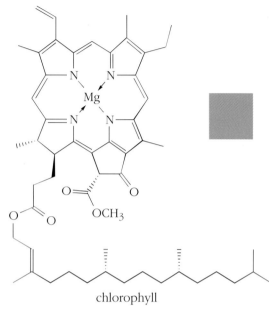

chlorophyll

Figure 3.3
The structure of chlorophyll
(C.I.Natural Green 3).

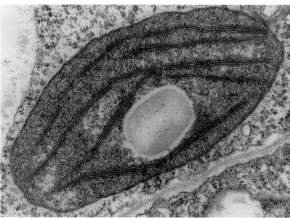

Figure 3.4
Electron micrograph of a chloroplast in the leaf of a pea plant.
(Magnification × 47 000.)

Box 3.1 A note on molecular structures

It is important in reading this Book that you are not put off by the complex structures used to represent the molecules of coloured compounds. You are not expected to remember them – indeed, few practising chemists are able to do that! You will, however, need to learn how to look at them in order to pick out structural features, chiral centres and functional groups, and to make comparisons between different molecules. As you will see, making quite small changes in structure, like introducing an extra functional group, can result in a considerable difference in colour.

Chlorophyll is not the only coloured substance in the chloroplasts. There are also compounds with long hydrocarbon chains – like carotene (Figure 2.13), and similar compounds which have oxygen-containing functional groups attached – like the xanthophylls.

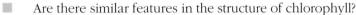

a xanthophyll (lutein)

■ What is the common structural feature in the carbon chains of carotene and xanthophyll?

■ You should have noticed that both chains possess *alternating* single and double bonds. The structural system in which single and double bonds alternate is called **conjugation**. We shall find it is particularly important when discussing the structure of coloured compounds. Carotene and xanthophyll are **conjugated molecules**. They are also called **polyenes** (poly = many; ene = double bond).

■ Are there similar features in the structure of chlorophyll?

■ Chlorophyll is also a conjugated molecule, although its series of alternating double and single bonds runs round rings rather than along a chain, and it also includes doubly bonded oxygen and nitrogen atoms.

Figure 3.5
Autumn colours.

Plants stop making chlorophyll in the absence of light. The yellow xanthophyll, however, is still produced and under these conditions becomes the principal colouring matter of the leaves. This explains why the leaves of Christmas hyacinth bulbs or forced rhubarb are yellow, but quickly turn green when exposure to light provides energetically favourable conditions for the further production of chlorophyll.

At the end of the growing season, when photosynthesis diminishes, chlorophyll and carotene break down first. Yellow xanthophyll and the red substance rhodoxanthin, which is found in higher proportions in ornamental shrubs, both increase, giving rise to the glorious colours of autumn (Figure 3.5). As winter approaches, further decomposition processes generate the dark brown colours of the dead leaves.

rhodoxanthin

Xanthophyll is also the yellow colouring matter of both egg yolks and canary feathers but birds are not able to synthesize this compound using their own metabolism. Instead, they have to obtain it from their diet. It *is* therefore true that if you want your canary to stay yellow (as well as to sing), you should feed it on sweetcorn!

Box 3.2 Carbonyl groups – ketones

The two hexagonal structures in the molecule of rhodoxanthin both include a functional group you have not so far encountered on its own. This is the **carbonyl** group, which is characterized by a double bond between carbon and oxygen.

■ In what other functional groups have you come across carbonyl groups?

■ They are present in ester groups (−COOR), acid groups (−COOH) and the amide groups (−CONH₂) of proteins, and fibres like wool and nylon.

■ How do the carbonyl groups in rhodoxanthin differ from those you have met already?

■ Esters and acids have an oxygen atom attached to the carbonyl group; amides have nitrogen. In rhodoxanthin, *carbon* atoms are attached at both sides of the carbonyl group.

In this molecular environment, the functional group is called a **ketone**. Systematic names of molecules containing the ketone group have the suffix '**one**'. As it must have carbon atoms at both sides, a ketone group can never be located at the end of a carbon chain. Ketone groups are very common in naturally occurring molecules.

Another whole family of colouring materials is based on the fairly simple structure, benzopyran.

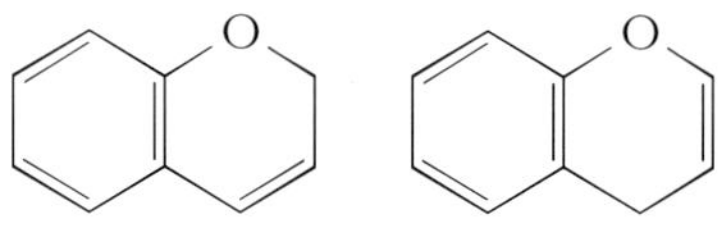

two isomers of benzopyran

■ Look at the two structures shown below and identify the functional groups that are present in these molecules in addition to the benzopyran framework.

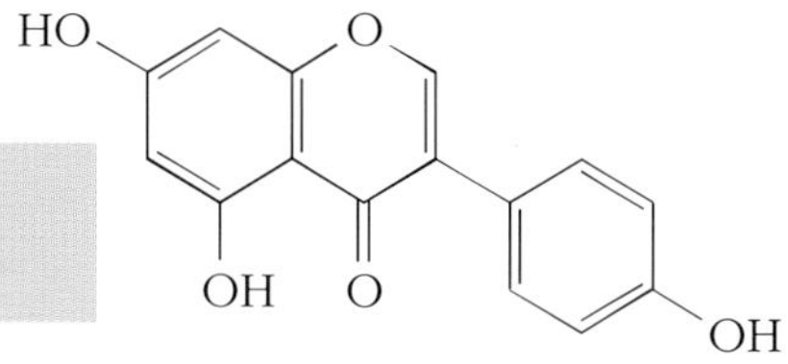

genistein (from dyer's broom) 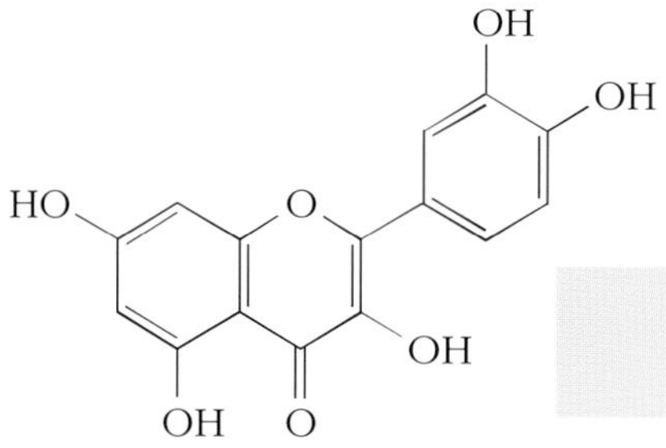   quercitin (from dyer's oak)

■ They both have an extra benzene ring attached and several other oxygen-containing functional groups (−OH, C=O) are also present. These features are always found in the colouring materials of this group.

Box 3.3 The anthocyanidins

X =

pelargonidin (geraniums,
raspberries, strawberries)

cyanidin (roses,
blackberries, cherries)

delphinidin
(delphiniums, hydrangeas)

Sir Robert Robinson (Figure 3.6), winner of the Nobel Prize for Chemistry in 1947, carried out extensive synthetic work in the 1920s on the colouring materials of flowers. He isolated the compounds responsible for the striking colours of the pelargonium (geranium), rose and delphinium, and found that they belonged to a very closely related chemical group, the anthocyanidins.

- How is the structure of the anthocyanidins related to benzopyran?

- The dye molecules still have the two rings consisting of 1 oxygen and 9 carbon atoms, but an extra carbon–carbon double bond and a positive charge have been introduced.

Imagine his surprise when he discovered that he had isolated exactly the same compound, cyanidin, from both the red petals of poppy flowers and the blue petals of the cornflower (Figure 3.7 overleaf). He was able to show that the different colours largely depended on whether the sap in the plants was acid, neutral or alkaline. This brings about a change in the structure of the molecule as a hydrogen ion (H^+) is *added* in acid, or *removed* in alkaline, solution.

Figure 3.6
Sir Robert Robinson (1886–1975), an organic chemist whose particular interest was the study and laboratory synthesis of the chemicals that occur in plants. His Nobel Prize for Chemistry in 1947 was awarded for research in plant *biology*.

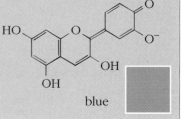

red

violet

blue

Figure 3.7
Coloration in poppies and cornflowers.

Question 6 Starting with the structural formula of the violet-coloured compound (overleaf), has a hydrogen ion (H^+) been added or removed to generate the structure of (a) the red compound and (b) the blue compound? Which colours will thus be present in (a) plant sap that is acid and (b) sap that is alkaline?

In living systems, the molecules of the coloured compounds are incorporated into a much more complex molecule, so the observed colours are not *solely* determined by the acidity of the sap. Nevertheless, it is interesting to see how, by simply adding or taking away a hydrogen ion, a dramatic colour change is brought about.

Another surprise was to find that the colour of both pink and blue hydrangeas arise from the same chemical substance, delphinidin. It is the soil conditions that lead to the different colours; acid soils favour blue flowers, and alkaline soils favour pink flowers (Figure 3.8). However, this is not the whole story. In 1871, Joseph Busch, gardener to the Czar of Russia, stated that to obtain blue flowers, hydrangeas should be treated with alum water (an aqueous solution containing aluminium ions). About 120 years later, analysis of blue hydrangea flowers showed that they contained almost twice as much aluminium (250 ppm) as did the pink flowers. It seems that an aluminium-containing acid is readily taken up from the soil by the hydrangea plant. The gardener's hunch has been vindicated!

(a)

(b)

Figure 3.8
(a) Pink and (b) blue hydrangeas.

3.3 Useful colours from plants and animals

This Section and the next provide an historical background to the Chapters on modern synthetic dyes that follow. Once again, you are not expected to memorize the complex structures and the historical details.

Two of the most ancient dyes are of animal origin. The famous **Tyrian purple** (C.I.Vat Blue 35), known since Phoenician times and used to dye the robes of Roman emperors, was produced from small molluscs (*Murex brandaris* and *Murex trunculus*) native to the eastern end of the Mediterranean (Figure 3.9). Since it required 8 500 of these molluscs to produce a single gram of the dye, it is not surprising that its use was limited to the rich and famous. A whole hill of discarded shells was discovered in 1864 at an ancient dyeworks near to the Phoenician city of Sidon.

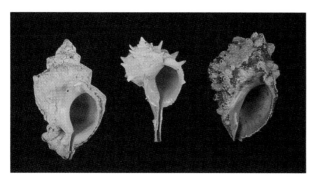

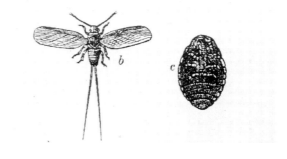

The molecule responsible for the colour of Tyrian purple

Figure 3.9   Shells of some species of *Murex*.

Figure 3.10
Coccus male (b) and female (c), living on *Opuntia* cactus (a).

The second of these dyes is **cochineal**, C.I.Natural Red 4. When the Spaniards arrived in Mexico in 1518, they found that the Aztecs were dyeing cloth with a substance that had already been in use for 2 500 years. They extracted it from the female scale insects, *Coccus cacti* (*Dactylopius coccus*), that live on the *Opuntia* cactus (Figure 3.10). More than 150 dried insects are required to produce each gram of dye.

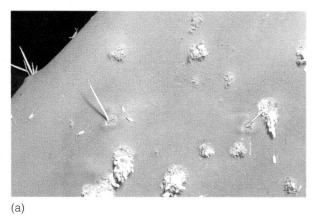

(a)

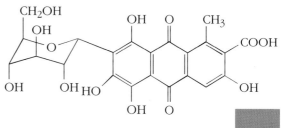

The molecule responsible for the colour of cochineal

Cochineal is a bright red dye, beloved for its
'hunting pink' by those who go fox hunting. It was
also used to dye the red jackets of the Brigade of
Guards until 1954. It is still used as a food colorant,
for example in cake icing, and in Mentadent™
toothpaste (Figure 3.11).

The Spaniards established a lucrative monopoly in
the cochineal trade throughout Europe, reputedly
shipping in one year (1785) almost 65 tonnes of
the dried insects. Only in Italy, where a European
insect, *Kermes vermilio* (which surprisingly yields essentially the same
substance) was already being exploited, was the triumph of this New World
dye incomplete.

Figure 3.11
Food colours, including
cochineal.

However, until the middle of the 19th century, most dyes were obtained from
plants, which were gathered from the wild, or cultivated like grain or
vegetables. At one time, half a million acres of arable land were used for
growing the madder plant (see opposite).

There are many natural yellow dyes, but most of them have only weak
colours and do not survive washing or exposure to sunlight. This contrasts
with the performance of the red and blue natural dyes which have structures
closely similar to modern synthetic dyes. The most important yellow dye of
the Middle Ages was **weld** (**luteolin**, C.I.Natural Yellow 2) obtained from the
plant dyer's rocket or wild mignonette (*Reseda luteola*) (Figure 3.12). It was
used, mixed with woad, to produce Lincoln green, made famous by the
legend of Robin Hood and his merry men.

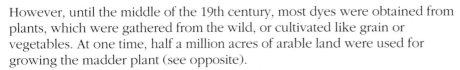

luteolin

■ Looking at the functional groups of
luteolin (weld), can you suggest
why it is easy to extract the dye
from plant material by steeping or
boiling it in water?

Figure 3.12
Dyer's rocket.

■ The four −OH groups and the two other oxygen atoms in the luteolin
structure are able to participate in extensive hydrogen bonding with
water molecules, favouring its solubility. This is a very important
observation to keep in mind.

*This might be a suitable point at which to try Experiment 4.2 'Using the
colours of nature'.*

Experiment 4.2 Using the colours of nature

Figure 3.13
(a) The madder plant;
(b) the alizarin molecule
(C.I.Natural Red); and
(c) cotton cloth dyed using
the Turkey red process.

The roots of the Middle Eastern madder plant (*Rubia tinctorum*) yield a red dye, **alizarin**, C.I.Natural Red (Figure 3.13), which was used to dye cotton fabric using the Turkey red process. This technique has been known for thousands of years, and involved treating the material with a witches' brew of rancid olive oil, lime or potash, and one of a variety of inorganic metal compounds. Lastly, a fine suspension of the root extract was added. In order to dye silk, it was even necessary to add a cowpat to the mixture.

(a)

(b)   alizarin

(c)

Figure 3.14
William Frith, *Ramsgate sands* (detail), 1854. A Victorian scene showing the different colours available just before the discovery of synthetic dyes.

The Turkey red process was introduced into Britain in 1785, and Manchester and Glasgow became centres of the industry. In 1859, one factory alone produced nearly $6\frac{1}{2}$ million metres of cloth, and nearly 340 tonnes of yarn dyed with Turkey red. Red was used as a background colour, and it had to be bleached away and filled in with yellow, blue and black to create patterned cloth. In 1868, 70 000 tonnes of madder root were processed, yielding about 750 tonnes of alizarin. When different metal ions are used in the dye mixture, alizarin gives different colours. The traditional bright red requires aluminium salts, but tin produces pink cloth, chromium brownish-red, and iron a violet-brown.

The other commercially important plant extract was **indigo** (indigotin, C.I.Natural Blue 1), obtained from the leaves of the East Asiatic plant *Indigofera tinctoria*; 100 kg of plant material yields 150–200 g of the pure dye. The blue dye from woad (*Isatis tinctoria*), used as a body paint in ancient Britain, is chemically identical, but present at a much lower percentage of the plant material by mass. Indigo has a structure very similar to Tyrian purple, but neither dye occurs naturally. Instead, they are formed during the processing of the natural material (Figure 3.15). This dye is still used to produce the famous faded colour of blue denim jeans. It is remarkable that the way it fades in sunlight, which originally caused it to be superseded by synthetic dyes, is now considered to be a credit factor.

Alizarin and indigo are both fairly simple molecules, but until 1868 their structures were completely unknown. In that year, alizarin was shown chemically to be derived from the hydrocarbon anthracene, a minor component of coal tar.

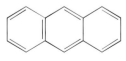

anthracene

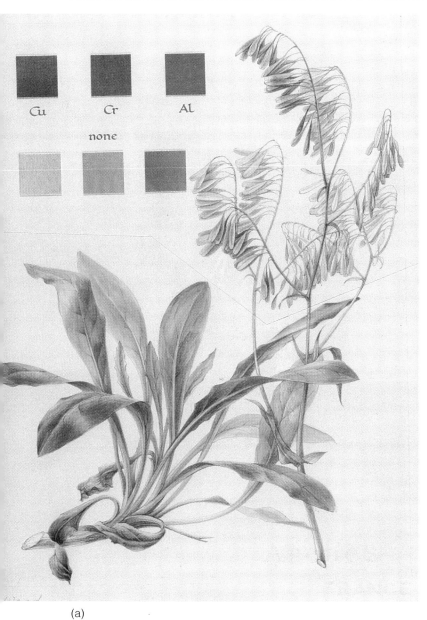

(a)

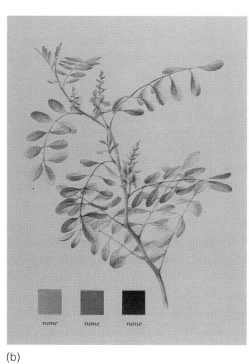

(b)

(c)   indican (colourless)   indigo (blue)

Figure 3.15
(a) The woad plant *Isatis tinctoria*; (b) the indigo plant *Indigofera tinctoria*; and (c) the chemical change that converts the natural substance to the dye, indigo (C.I.Natural Blue 1).

Although the structure of anthracene itself was not known either, a starting material was now available, and in June 1869 the rivals BASF in Germany and William Perkin's dye company in England filed patents for the same synthetic route to alizarin just one day apart. Within five years, the madder industry had disappeared, and Perkin's company alone was producing over 400 tonnes of alizarin a year. Having killed off the madder industry, Perkin proved to be an environmentalist before his time, because he grew a patch of madder near to his factory 'lest the breed should become extinct'.

- Compare the structure of anthracene with that of alizarin. What functional groups are present in the dye that were not in the starting material? So what sort of chemical processes will be needed to convert anthracene to alizarin?

- The functional groups —OH and C=O have been introduced. Remembering that each angle of the carbon framework in the anthracene structure represents =CH— (except at the ring junctions where there is no hydrogen atom attached), then *overall* two hydrogen atoms have been lost and four oxygen atoms introduced. The process is therefore an *oxidation*.

The demise of natural indigo was equally dramatic. Bayer synthesized indigo in 1897, but it took almost £1 million of research at BASF to produce a commercially viable synthetic route. A few years later, the Indian indigo trade was dead. Almost all the indigo used from that time until now has been synthetic material. Only for a short time during the First World War was trade in the natural dye revived, but it succumbed almost immediately in the post-war period.

> **Question 7** Pure synthetic indigo sold well from the start, even though at first it cost 15–25% more than the natural product. Can you suggest some reasons why dyers might prefer the more expensive material?

3.4 William Perkin and the foundation of the chemical industry

The 'high-tech' industry of the later part of the 19th century was the dye industry, and the acknowledged founder of that industry was an Englishman, William Perkin (Figure 3.16). In a pre-run of Open University tradition, it all began with a home experiment.

Perkin's achievement was not just in his discovery, but in its development and exploitation. He showed that chemical research can give rise to useful and valuable materials; that it is possible to produce specialized chemicals on a large scale in a process that requires several reactions to be carried out in succession; that co-operation between manufacturers and users is necessary for progress; and that with the right product, chemical manufacture could be commercially viable. He really does deserve the title of 'the father of the British chemical industry'.

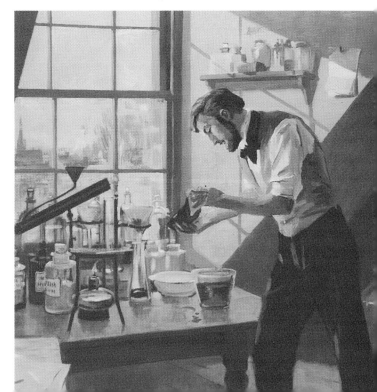

Figure 3.16
An artist's impression of the young William Perkin in his home laboratory.

Box 3.4 William Perkin and mauve

William Henry Perkin was the son of a builder, and it was his father's dearest wish that his talented child should become an architect. Fortunately, William was introduced to chemistry by a friend at the City of London School, which was one of the first schools to teach experimental science. So he persuaded his family to allow him to study chemistry, and at the age of 15 enrolled at the Royal College of Chemistry in London. His tutor there was the outstanding German chemist, August Wilhelm von Hofmann (Figure 3.17).

At Eastertime in 1856, Perkin was 18 years old and on vacation, working in his home laboratory. In a speculative attempt to make the antimalarial drug quinine (Book 3, Part 2), he mixed a minor component of coal tar, allyltoluidine, with a warm aqueous solution of potassium dichromate in sulfuric acid. It was a bold try, since at that time not even the structure of benzene was known. An exothermic reaction

Figure 3.17
A. W. von Hofmann (1818–1892). Hofmann was the first Director of the Royal College of Chemistry, now the Imperial College of Science, Technology and Medicine, in London. On his return to Germany, he became one of the co-founders of the German Chemical Society in 1867.

gave him a brown powder. Nevertheless, this intrigued him, so he turned his attention to the simplest coal tar amine, **aniline** (originally pronounced 'an-il-yne' (see Box 3.5), but now pronounced 'an-il-inn').

This time, he obtained a black precipitate. In testing its solubility, he discovered that alcohol extracted a purple colour, which readily dyed silk, and was much more stable in sunlight than any other purple dye then in use. Indeed, some of his original dyed samples are still in existence and remain purple to this day.

Surprisingly, Hofmann showed no interest, but Perkin persisted. After consulting commercial dyers, especially Robert Pullar of Perth (a dyeing company still operating as a dry cleaners today), he patented his dye in August 1856 and decided to go into manufacture. Perkin had to develop large-scale chemical production methods for his starting materials, and to do this he built his own factory at Greenford Green in Middlesex (Figure 3.18). *(continued overleaf)*

Figure 3.18
A contemporary sketch of Perkin's dye factory at Greenford in 1858.

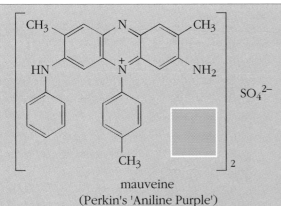

mauveine
(Perkin's 'Aniline Purple')

He made his own aniline from rather impure coal tar benzene, and he even made his own nitric acid. At first he called the dye aniline purple, but, following its success in France, it was renamed mauve, after the French word for the mallow flower.

Mauve was a sensation. Empress Eugènie wore a dress dyed with mauve, and it was one of Queen Victoria's favourite colours. A technique was developed to use the dye with cotton fabrics, and soon everyone was using it. From 1881–1901, the British 'penny lilac' postage stamps were coloured mauve (Figure 3.19).

Figure 3.19
A 'penny lilac' postage stamp.

In 1874, at the age of only 36, Perkin sold the business and retired to enjoy private research and family life, over £100 000 better off! Among his later successes was the synthesis of coumarin, the first natural *perfume* to be made in a

Figure 3.20
Perkin in later life.

laboratory. However, it was not until 50 years later, in the year before he died, that his momentous discovery was recognized with a knighthood (Figure 3.20).

coumarin

Unfortunately for Britain, these lessons were better learned by the German companies AGFA, BASF, Bayer and Hoechst, all of which grew up about this time. Ironically, several of the chemists employed by these companies were Hofmann's students, who had learned their trade with British dye manufacturers before returning to Germany. The British Government chose to neglect the infant dye industry, and concentrated their support on the well-established textile industry instead. By 1913, Germany was exporting about 135 000 tonnes of dyes compared to Britain's 5 000 tonnes. At the outbreak of the First World War, the only khaki dye available for British army uniforms was manufactured in Germany and had to be imported secretly!

Box 3.5 The importance of aniline

*Oil and ointment, and
wax and wine
And the lovely colours
called 'aniline'
You can make anything
from a salve to a star
(If you only know how),
from black coal tar*

benzene $\xrightarrow{HNO_3/H_2SO_4}$ nitrobenzene $\xrightarrow{HCl/Fe}$ aniline

This bit of doggerel from *Punch* records the amazement of the general public of the day at the unexpected versatility of what had been treated as a useless and filthy by-product of the coking and coal gas industries. In Book 3, we have already discussed the uses of one product – the phenols, of value in 'ointment' and 'salve'. The coal tar bases, of which aniline is the most prominent, were to prove even more significant as starting materials for the production of 'the lovely colours called "aniline"'.

Aniline is named after the Portuguese word for indigo (*anil*) because it can be obtained by heating the dye strongly until it decomposes and then condensing the vapour that is given off. Although it was originally extracted from coal tar, it is now made on a vast scale in the two-step reaction sequence shown above.

The first step explains why Perkin needed to make his own nitric acid.

Aniline is a key intermediate for the dye industry. Most of us are used to the acronyms for the giant German chemical companies AGFA and BASF (Figure 3.21), but not everyone

Figure 3.21
The AGFA and BASF logos.

realizes that they refer to the **A**ktien **G**esellschaft **F**ür **A**nilin**fa**brikation and the **B**adische **A**nilin und **S**oda **F**abrik. In the UK, the former dye company, Clayton *Aniline*, similarly reflected the importance of this starting material.

Question 8 As well as mauve, the dye magenta which gives its name to the missing colour in the colour circle (Chapter 2) was also a product of the crude aniline from coal tar. From the molecule of magenta, pick out the structural elements of *three* molecules of aniline that are incorporated into the structure. What extra component does the structure have that could not have come from aniline?

magenta

aniline

Summary of Chapter 3

In Chapter 3, you have seen that dyes are technically water-soluble colouring materials, and pigments are insoluble colouring materials. The colouring materials of leaves (chlorophyll and long conjugated molecules) are present in different proportions at different seasons. The dyes colouring many flowers are based on the benzopyran structure with attached benzene rings and oxygen-containing functional groups. The same dye may generate different flower colours in acid and alkaline sap. This is a result of changes in structure brought about by adding or removing a hydrogen ion (H^+). Most natural dyes are obtained from plants, but notable exceptions were Tyrian purple (from shellfish) and cochineal (from insects). Natural alizarin and indigo were the products of huge agricultural enterprises that collapsed when the dyes were synthesized during the 19th century.

The earliest products of the European chemical industry were dyes discovered by accident by William Perkin. The key industrial starting material was aniline, made by nitration of benzene, and the subsequent conversion of the nitro group to an amino group. By the beginning of the 20th century, Britain's manufacturing lead had been overtaken by Germany.

Chapter 4
All the colours of the rainbow

4.1 Designing a textile dye

Perhaps nowhere in our lives is colour more important to us than in the clothes we wear. Natural fibres are relatively easy to dye but the development of synthetic fibres has posed many problems for the dyer and colour chemist. Although most of these have been solved satisfactorily, the search for new and improved dyes goes on constantly. There are two main goals to achieve in designing a dye, even before it is subjected to detailed testing for commercial viability:

1 The structure of the dye must possess the correct characteristics of light absorption, to exhibit the specified hue and intensity of colour.

Hue is usually the first target. This generally depends on the wavelength of the most intense absorption peak in the dye spectrum. However, you have probably noticed that some colours are bright, but others are more subdued or subtle. Usually, bright colours are associated with narrow absorption bands that have sharp peaks (Figure 4.1). By contrast, the duller non-spectrum colours like brown or khaki result from a fairly evenly spread absorption over a wide wavelength range.

Colour intensity depends on how efficiently the material absorbs photons. Some textiles are rather reluctant to incorporate dye molecules into the spaces between the polymer strands. Under these circumstances, molecules that are able to absorb energy efficiently give a better chance of producing a strong colour in the dyed material. A weakly absorbing molecule would need to be present in much greater quantity.

If most of the light is absorbed at some wavelengths, the colour due to the residual light will also be very intense (Figure 4.2b). If little light is absorbed, the residual colour will be much diluted with white light to give a pale **tint** (Figure 4.2a). If the material absorbs strongly across the spectrum, this is equivalent to mixing black with the colour to produce a deep **shade** (Figure 4.2c).

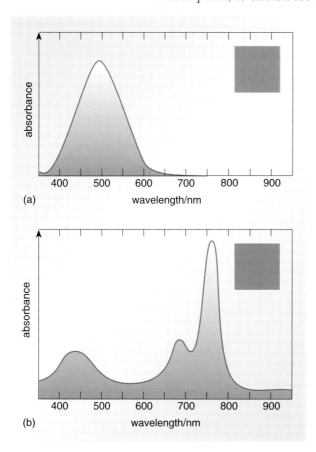

Figure 4.1
The visible absorption spectra of (a) khaki C.I.Mordant Orange 1 and (b) Monastral blue C.I.Pigment Blue 15.

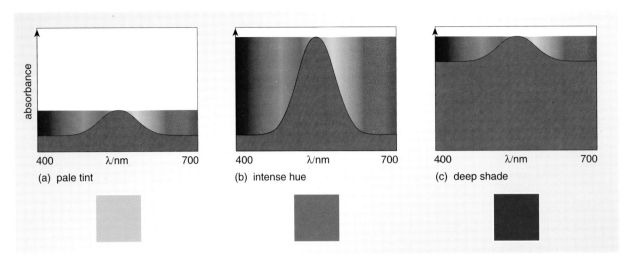

Figure 4.2
Absorption generating (a) tints, (b) hues and (c) shades.

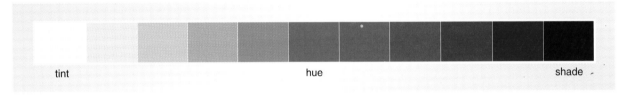

Figure 4.3
A scale of shades and tints.

2 The functional groups built into the molecule must ensure that the dye has a suitable degree of solubility, and a natural affinity for the polymer to which it will eventually be applied.

▫   From Book 3, recall which functional group was used to give detergents their water solubility.

▪   The sulfonate group, $-SO_3^-$, was found to be the most effective.

In the same way, introducing sulfonate groups (preferably more than one) into complex organic dye molecules makes them readily soluble in water.

▫   Suggest why the presence of sulfonate groups might improve the water solubility of a dye.

▪   Probably the most important reason is that sulfonate groups readily form hydrogen bonds with water molecules.

You should recall from Book 2, Part 1, that fibres are composed of bundles of polymer molecules held together by molecular interactions. Table 4.1 reminds you of the chemical structures of some important fibre molecules.

Table 4.1 Chemical structures of fibre molecules.

1 Cellulosic fibres

flax, $n = 18\,000$; cotton, $n = 5\,000$; viscose (rayon), $n = 175$

acetate (**cellulose acetate**), $n = 100$–250

2 Polyamide fibres

$$H \left[NH-\underset{\underset{R^1}{|}}{CH}-CO-NH-\underset{\underset{R^2}{|}}{CH}-CO \right]_n OH$$

wool (constituted from 20 amino acids)
silk (constituted from 16 amino acids)

$$H \left[NH-(CH_2)_6-NH-CO-(CH_2)_4-CO \right]_n OH$$

one form of nylon, $n = 50$–80

3 Polyester fibres

$$HO \left[CO-\bigcirc-CO-O(CH_2)_2O \right]_n H$$

from ethylene glycol (1,2-ethandiol and terephthalic acid)

4 Acrylic fibres

$$H \left[\left(CH_2-\underset{\underset{CN}{|}}{CH} \right)_m \left(CH_2-\underset{\underset{X}{|}}{CH} \right)_n \right]_x OH$$

$m = 85\%$ minimum; $n = 15\%$ maximum
X = Cl (Teklon), $OCOCH_3$, $CONH_2$ (Creslan),
CO_2H, $C_6H_5SO_3^-$ Na^+, 2-pyridyl (Acrilan)

■ Look at the structures in Table 4.1 and pick out some of the functional groups that could be involved in molecular interactions. Which groups will be involved in which interactions?

■ $-OH$ and $-NH-$ groups will provide hydrogen atoms for participation in hydrogen bonding. Oxygen and nitrogen atoms will also act as the receiving end of hydrogen bonds. The $-CN$ groups, which are polar, will be able to undergo permanent dipole interactions, and the SO_3^- and CO_2^- groups will show ionic interactions. All groups will also experience London forces.

If the dye molecules have similar groups 'built-in' during synthesis, they too will participate in molecular interactions with the polymer molecules of the fibre.

Commercial dyes must also satisfy other criteria, generally referred to as **fastness** properties. The same affinity that sets up the original association between dye and polymer also prevents subsequent removal of the dye from the fibre even after repeated washing. This is termed **wash-fastness**. The resistance of the dye to fading when exposed to sunlight – **light-fastness** – is also particularly important.

4.2 How do dyes work?

The Liquors that Dyers employ to tinge are qualified to do so by multitudes of little corpuscles of the Pigment or Dyeing stuff, which are dissolved and extracted by the Liquor and swim to and fro in it. These Corpuscles of Colour (as the Atomists call them) insinuating themselves into, and filling all the Pores of the Body to be Dyed.

(Robert Boyle, 1627–1691)

The polymer system of a fibre has distinctly crystalline and amorphous phases (Figure 4.4). Each polymer chain extends through several amorphous and crystalline regions, and this assists in the cohesion of the polymer system. Crystalline regions occur whenever several polymers are closely packed and aligned in approximately parallel order; amorphous regions occur where polymers are not well oriented but more loosely tangled together. Amorphous and crystalline regions will occur at random throughout the polymer system of the fibre.

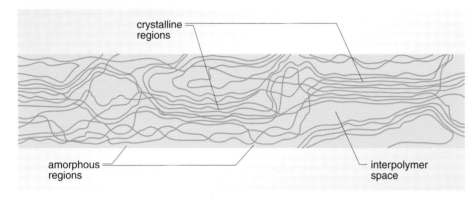

crystalline regions

amorphous regions

interpolymer space

Figure 4.4
A simplified representation of a segment of a fibre's polymer system, to show amorphous and crystalline regions, and the spaces between polymer strands.

Activity 1 Models of indigo and alizarin

For both these models, you should begin by making up two benzene rings. There is no need to add the white hydrogens. Look at the structure of indigo (Figure 3.15c) and construct a model which has the two five-membered rings joined by two flexible bonds.

Make sure that the blue nitrogens are on opposite sides of this double bond. There is no real need to attach the carbonyl oxygens because this will not alter the overall shape of the model. How would you describe this 'overall shape'?

Recover the two benzene rings and build a model of the alizarin molecule (Figure 3.13c) attaching the two oxygens to the central ring with pairs of flexible bonds.

Now look at this model, and see if there are common features of *shape* with your model of indigo.

It is not known how dye molecules enter a fibre. Once the dye molecule approaches the fibre surface, its functional groups will begin to interact with the constituent polar groups of the fibre molecules. The flattened shape of dye molecules should give them the best chance of penetrating the polymer system. A long flat dye molecule will also be able to align itself with linear sections of the polymer molecules within the amorphous regions of the fibre, helping to maximize the forces of attraction between the polar groups (Figure 4.5).

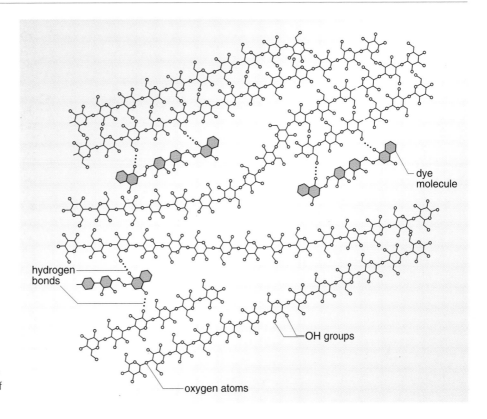

Figure 4.5
A possible arrangement of cellulose polymers in a cotton fibre, showing the dye molecules present only in the amorphous regions of the polymer system.

It is not therefore surprising that cotton and wool are both easy to dye. Although the polymer system in cotton is only about 65–70% crystalline in form, its many −OH groups readily form hydrogen bonds with dye molecules. The −OH groups also interact with molecules of water, which causes cotton to swell in aqueous dyebaths. This disrupts the crystalline structure and gives dye molecules easier access.

▨ Would you expect **acetate**, a chemically treated natural cellulose, to be more or less easily dyed than cotton? (*Hint*: how well will acetate groups form hydrogen bonds?)

▨ In the acetate fibre molecules, many of the oxygen atoms, which were present as −OH groups in the original cellulose, do not now have hydrogen attached. The acetate molecules are therefore considerably less well equipped than cotton fibre molecules to participate in hydrogen bond formation. As a result, there will be much less attractive force between fibre and dye molecules, making acetate difficult to dye. (Polyester fibres are similarly difficult to dye.)

The complexity of the chain of the wool polymer, keratin, results in strong interaction between its functional groups (Figure 4.6). However, the large number of different amino acids found in wool makes it very difficult to align the fibre molecules, so only about 25–30% of a wool fibre is crystalline. Dye molecules penetrate the highly amorphous structure and readily bond to the many interactive groups.

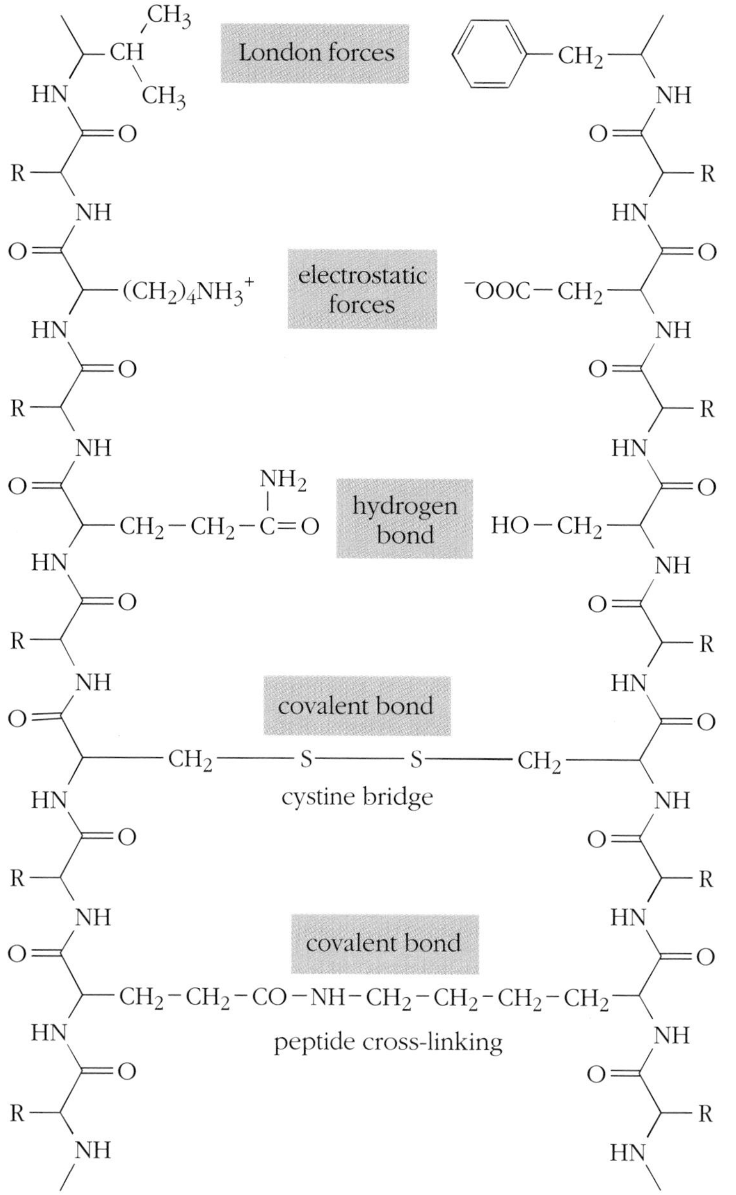

Figure 4.6
Interactions between fibre molecules in wool.

By contrast, silk fibres, although chemically very similar to wool, are 65–70% crystalline, making it more difficult to dye. The structure of the synthetic polyamide nylon (Figure 4.7) makes it a highly crystalline (85%) fibre held together by strong uniform hydrogen bonds. Nylon molecules prefer to form hydrogen bonds to each other, so neither water nor dye molecules penetrate easily into the fibres.

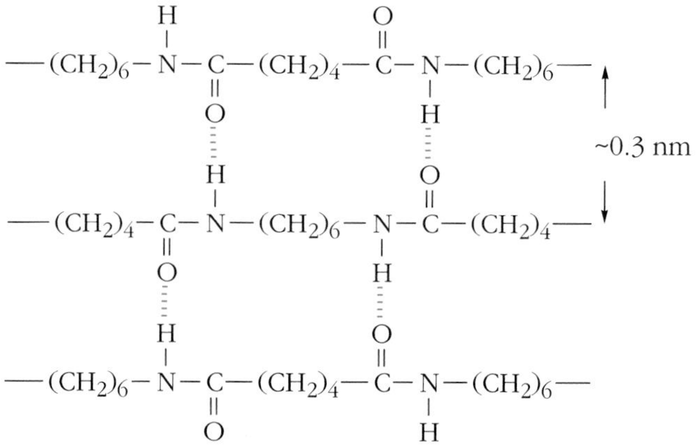

Figure 4.7
Hydrogen bonding in nylon.

4.3 The dyer's paintbox

The largest and commercially the most significant group of dyes are the **direct dyes**, used primarily for dyeing cellulosic fibres, but occasionally used to dye polyamides. Direct dyes offer a host of cheaply made bright colours (Figure 4.8).

A feature of direct dyes is their ease of application – the fabric is simply dipped into an aqueous solution of the dye – but unfortunately dyers have a saying: 'Easy on, easy off', which implies only too accurately that they are also easy to wash out. Washing water, which also is able to hydrogen-bond with molecules, is in competition for the dye with the attractive forces of the fibre polymer; wash by wash, the water gradually wins.

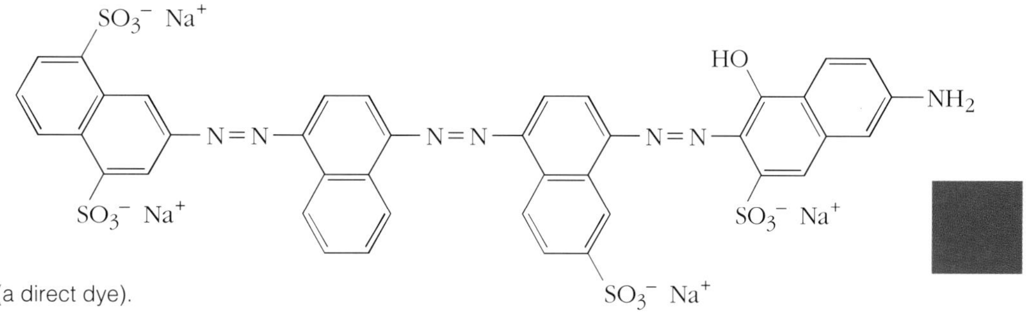

Figure 4.8
C.I.Direct Blue 71 (a direct dye).

Box 4.1 The diazotization and coupling reaction

You will have noticed in C.I.Direct Blue 71 that the structural unit —N=N— appears three times. This is the **azo** group (strictly **di**azo – two nitrogens) named using the old word for nitrogen, *azote*. It is surprisingly easy to introduce this group into a molecule using a simple chemical reaction.

Aniline treated with nitrous acid, formed *in situ* from sodium nitrite and a strong acid (like hydrochloric), keeping the temperature near to 0 °C, yields a colourless solution of the **intermediate** benzene diazonium chloride. This is the **diazotization** step.

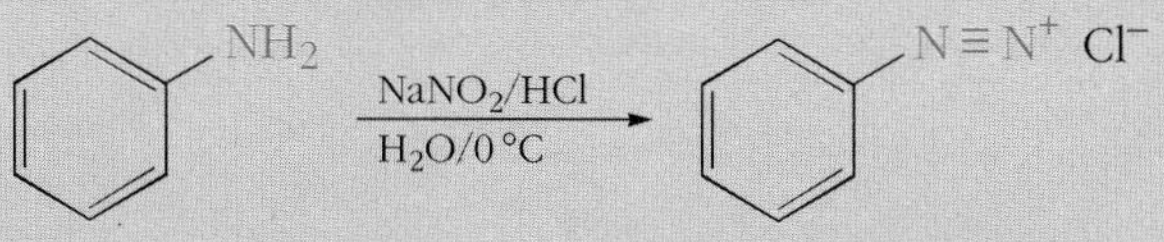

benzene diazonium
chloride

Benzene diazonium chloride reacts with a host of compounds (also described as intermediates) which have one or more benzene rings. This step is called **coupling** and is particularly easy if the benzene ring has —OH, —NH$_2$, or —OCH$_3$ groups attached:

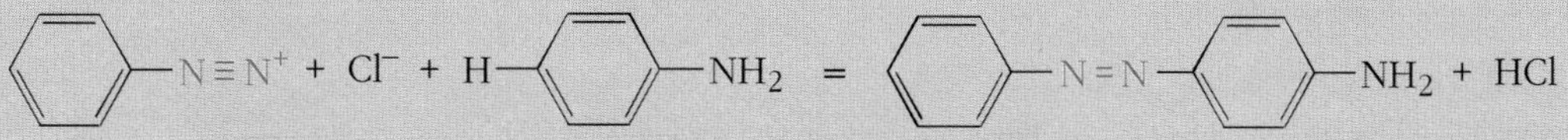

This sequence of reactions was discovered in 1859 by Peter Griess, who was working at the Ind Coope Brewery at Burton-on-Trent. It was to become the springboard for the rapid development of the dye industry in both Britain and Germany. Note once again the key importance of aniline.

The **azoic dyes** are the water-insoluble counterpart of the direct dyes. The difficulty of applying *insoluble* materials to the fabric is overcome in a most ingenious way. Both the components that react to form the dye are soluble in water, so the fabric is first dipped in a solution of the **coupling component**, and then dipped into dye liquor that contains the **diazo component**. A reaction takes place in the fabric and the product is a large and insoluble azo dye, which is trapped in the amorphous region of the polymer system (Figure 4.9). This *in situ* preparation of the dye also overcomes some of the problems of dyeing processed or synthetic fibres like acetate or acrylic that lack interactive functional groups.

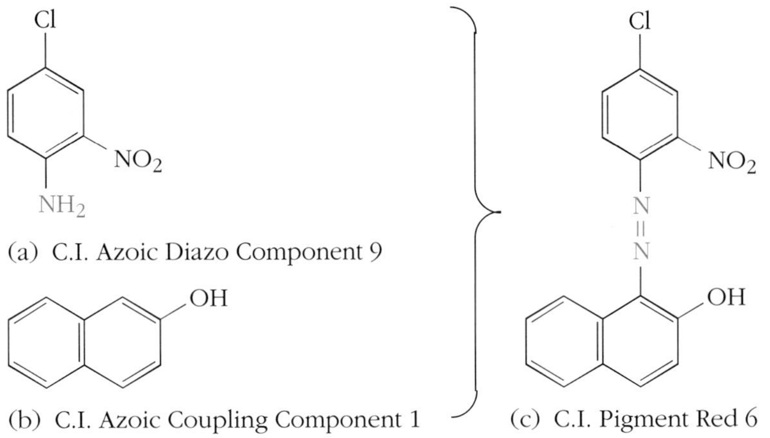

(a) C.I. Azoic Diazo Component 9

(b) C.I. Azoic Coupling Component 1

(c) C.I. Pigment Red 6

Figure 4.9
The formation of an azoic dye. (a) Diazo component (C.I.Azoic Diazo Component 9). (b) Coupling component (C.I.Azoic Coupling Component 1). (c) C.I.Pigment Red 6.

Since the dye liquor has to be kept ice-cold in order to prevent the spontaneous decomposition of the diazo component, the azoic dyes are sometimes called the '**ice colours**'.

▢ Why do you think that washing in water has little effect on these insoluble molecules?

◼ They are large molecules with few functional groups that can hydrogen-bond with water molecules; so they are not dissolved out of the fibre.

For printing, the fabric is impregnated with the coupling component in the required pattern before it is dipped in the diazo bath. If the pattern is applied using different coupling components, a multicoloured print can be formed by a single pass through the dye liquor.

Vat dyes are also large, highly water-insoluble molecules that become entangled very effectively in the amorphous regions of a fibre. They have always been very expensive to produce, and so are only used when good fastness properties are essential.

Another ingenious method is used to transfer vat dyes from the dyebath to the fabric. The dye is first reduced to its **leuco** (Greek for 'colourless') form, which is soluble in aqueous alkaline solution because it exists as ions. Once this intermediate is absorbed, the fabric is dipped into a vat containing a mild oxidizing agent which will convert the leuco form back into the original insoluble dye within the fibres (Figure 4.10). Indigo dyers still use this technique (Figure 4.11).

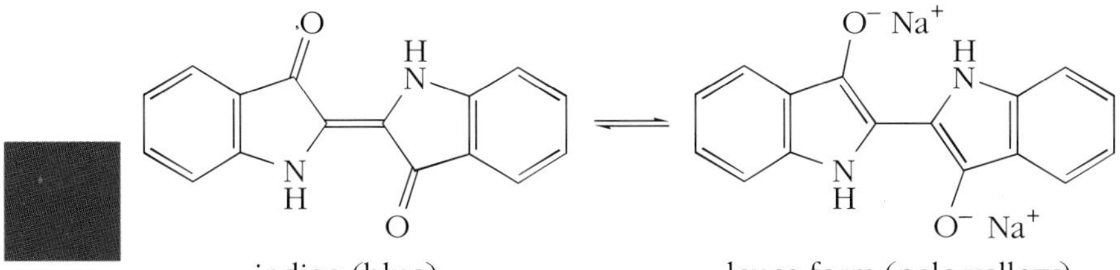

Figure 4.10
The coloured and leuco form of indigo.

indigo (blue)   leuco form (pale yellow)

Figure 4.11
Indigo production in the early 1900s.

Many vat dyes are based on indigo or alizarin. They are much more effective with cellulosic fibres than with synthetics. They have very high light-fastness ratings, probably because sunlight is unable to break down the particularly stable benzene rings in their structures.

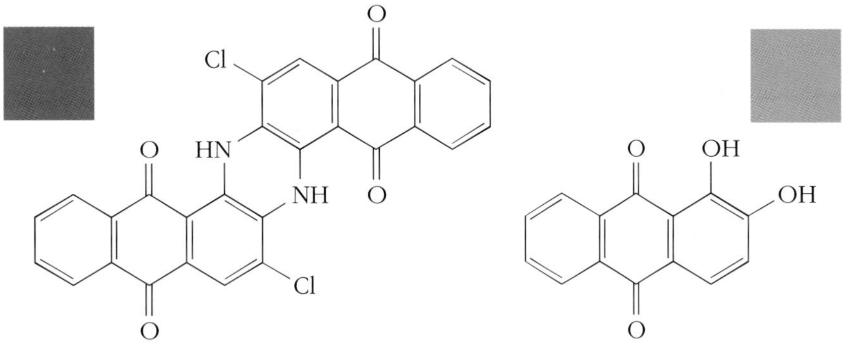

C.I. Vat Blue 6 (compare with alizarin)   alizarin

Since ancient times, substances have been known that seem to have the property of making a dye stick more tenaciously to a fabric. These are called **mordants**, from the Latin word *mordere* meaning to bite, or to grasp. The mordant is applied to the textile first.

Usually, the mordant is a soluble ionic metal compound. The Stockholm Papyrus, a 'dyers' handbook' from Egypt of the 3rd or 4th century AD (but undoubtedly recording skills acquired over many centuries), lists identifiable aluminium, iron and copper compounds for use as mordants. An ancient practice in Northern Europe was to include club mosses (e.g. *Lycopodium complanatum*) in the wool-dyers' brew. Modern analysis has shown that such plants have a particular ability (like hydrangeas) to extract and accumulate aluminium from the soil. Today, chromium compounds, introduced during the 19th century, are the most commonly used.

Mordants act in two similar but distinct ways; one with silk or wool, and one with cotton. When dye is applied to mordanted wool or silk, it combines with the metal cation to form a much larger structure called a **lake**. Their large size causes lakes to be trapped in the fibre, and they are also able to bind to charged sites in protein fibres by ionic interaction (Figure 4.12).

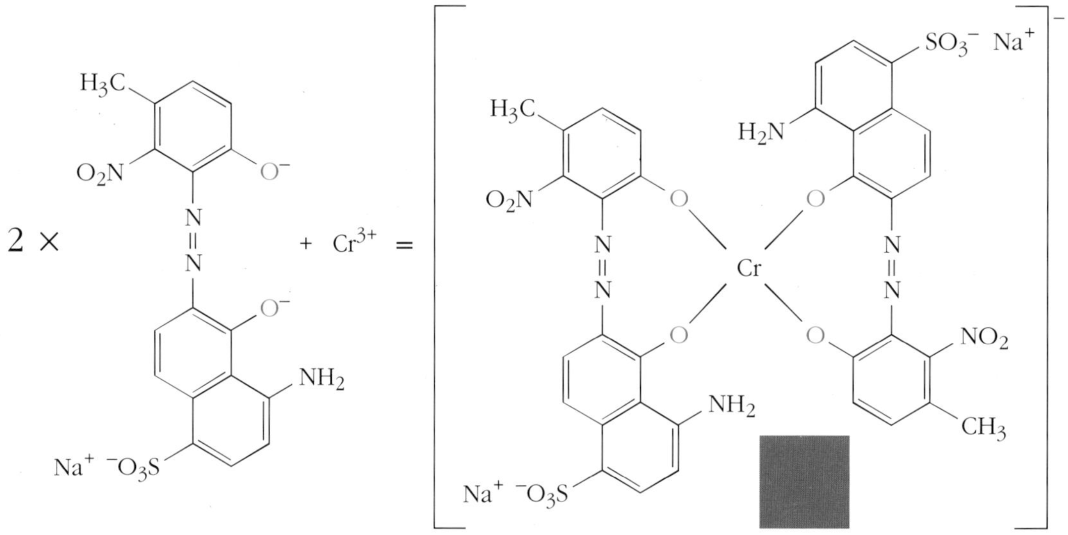

Figure 4.12
A mordant dye and lake (C.I.Mordant Green 30).

Alizarin is a mordant dye for cotton. With cotton, the —OH groups of the fibre molecules, polar groups on the dye, and even hydroxide anions from the alkaline dyebath can all become attached to the metal cation. In this second mode of action, the fibre molecules thus become a component part of the lake, with the metal cation linking the dye and the fibre together (Figure 4.13).

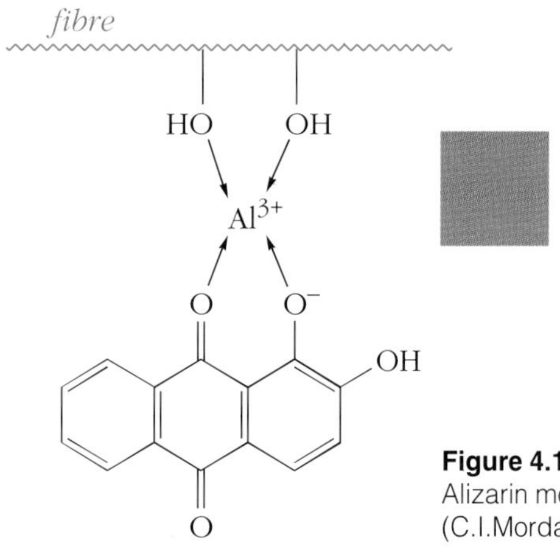

Figure 4.13
Alizarin mordanted with the metal ion Al3+
(C.I.Mordant Red 11).

The presence of the metal ion therefore improves the wash-fastness of the dye either by effectively increasing the size of the dye complex or by strengthening the binding between dye and fibre. It seems to have a stabilizing effect, too, because the light-fastness is also enhanced. Alizarin was notable as one of the few colours to withstand the bleaching effect of tropical sunlight.

Artificial fibres are not easily dyed with the traditional dyes used for cotton, wool or silk, because they have fewer polar groups, and are more highly crystalline than the natural fibres. **Disperse dyes** have been developed to exploit their non-polar character. These insoluble dyes are applied as an aqueous dispersion in the presence of a detergent. They are generally much smaller molecules than other classes of dyes, and they usually lack the functional groups that would assist their solubility in water.

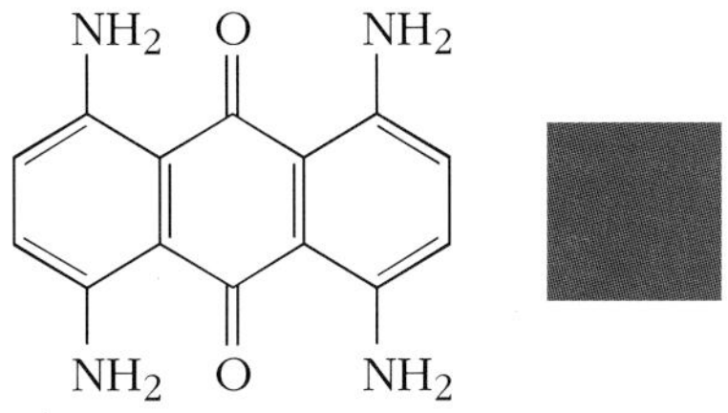

C.I. Disperse Blue 1
(a disperse dye)

Disperse dyes have more affinity with the non-polar polymer than with the dye liquor, and since they are relatively small, the molecules can penetrate the spaces between the polymer strands. However, only pastel shades are obtained unless pressure-dying techniques are used at elevated temperatures.

In the final class for consideration are the commercial **pigments**. These may be organic structures or inorganic compounds like red cadmium sulfide, or violet cobalt ammonium phosphate. The only characteristic they share is their complete insolubility, and lack of affinity for any fibre. They can be introduced only by mixing into fibre solutions, or into molten polymer before extrusion. They are valuable colouring agents for synthetic fibres, and also plastics like polyethene and polypropene.

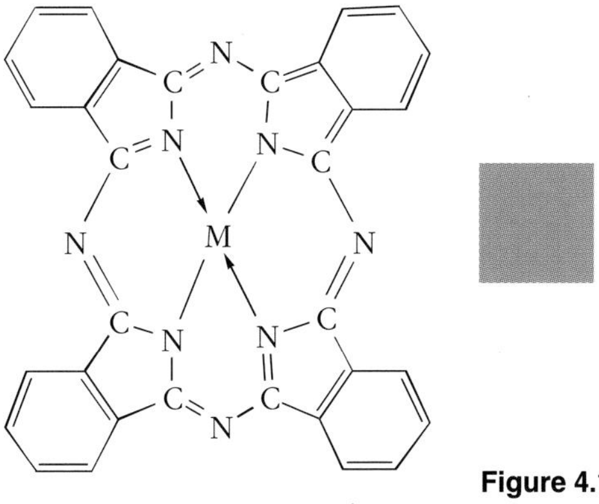

an organic pigment colour

Figure 4.14
An organic pigment (M = a metal cation).

One of the best pigments ever made is **Monastral blue** – C.I.Pigment Blue 15 (Figure 4.14; M = Cu^{2+}), which is widely used in printing inks, plastics and paints. The paint of most blue cars contains this pigment. Monastral blue is stable in molten potassium hydroxide and boiling hydrochloric acid. It can even be vaporized at 580 °C in an inert atmosphere, and on condensing it gives lustrous purple crystals up to 1 cm long.

It was developed after a chance discovery, in 1934, at Scottish Dyes Ltd. A batch of a colourless chemical was being prepared in a glass-lined iron vessel, but where it had come into contact with a part of the iron vessel with a damaged lining, the reaction mixture was seen to be coloured blue. The blue substance was isolated and analysis showed it to contain 12.6% of iron by mass (Figure 4.14; M = Fe^{2+}). Researchers soon found that a whole range of metal ions could replace the iron, the best proving to be the copper ions that give Monastral blue.

It is interesting to note that nature got there first. Looking back and comparing Monastral blue with the plant pigment chlorophyll (Figure 3.3), you should be struck by the similarity in the structures.

> **Question 9** Go back through this Chapter and summarize it by listing in Table 4.2: (a) suitable types of dyes opposite each of the fibres; and (b) the interactions between dye and fibre molecules.

Table 4.2 Suitable dyes for use with natural and artificial fibres.

(a) Fibre type	Suitable dyes
cellulosic (cotton, viscose)	
protein (wool, silk)	
acetate	
polyamide (nylon)	
acrylic	
polyester	

(b) Dye	Type of interaction
direct	
azoic	
vat	
disperse	
mordant	
pigment	

Summary of Chapter 4

In Chapter 4, you have seen how commercial dyes must have the appropriate characteristics of hue, colour intensity, an affinity for fibre polymers, water solubility, and wash- and light-fastness. Colour intensity can be related to the absorption spectrum of the dye, and water solubility is often achieved by incorporating sulfonic acid groups into the dye structure.

Fibres consist of long chain molecules packed together to give amorphous and crystalline regions. As dye molecules have flat extended structures, this allows them to penetrate the amorphous regions of fibres. Natural fibres are generally more easily dyed than synthetics, because they have more functional groups capable of molecular interactions with dye molecules. A key reaction in forming dye molecules is diazotization and coupling. The azoic dyes are prepared this way in the fabric. Direct dyes are too water soluble to be very wash-fast; the insoluble azoic and vat dyes, formed by chemical processing on the fibre, endure better. Vat dyes are produced by *in situ* oxidation of a leuco form.

Ionic metallic compounds can act as mordants by forming lakes between functional groups on the dye or polymer molecules, and the metal cations. Disperse dyes are small non-ionizable molecules that can infiltrate synthetic fibres. Pigments are insoluble organic or inorganic materials, which are often mixed with polymers before extrusion.

This might be the most suitable point at which to try Experiment 4.3 'A coat of many colours'.

Experiment 4.3 A coat of many colours

Chapter 5
Another country

The text so far may have given you the impression that colour is the realm of the organic chemist; but a moment's reflection should surely dispel this impression. In the field of dyes, the organic chemist reigns supreme, but the bright colours of pigments, the sparkling colours of minerals and gemstones, and the glowing colours of pottery glazes and stained glass, are produced by inorganic materials.

5.1 Rubies, emeralds and sapphires: strangers in the crystal

If you were to look at a tray of engagement rings in the window of a jeweller's shop, the diamonds would probably be the first to catch your eye. Almost certainly the rubies, emeralds and sapphires would also attract your attention. These so-called 'precious' stones have long been admired and treasured for their durability, for their brilliance, but above all, for their dazzling colour. You may be tempted to believe that such different colours must have originated in quite different ways but a true explanation shows that it is the similarity rather than the difference that is remarkable.

Ruby (Figure 5.1) is basically a faceted crystalline form of the hard abrasive aluminium oxide, corundum, regularly to be found on the surface of grinding wheels and emery paper. It differs from the pure chemical compound by having a tiny amount (only about 0.05% by mass) of chromium ions (Cr^{3+}), in place of the usual aluminium ions (Al^{3+}). Note that the balance of the positive and negative charges in the crystal is not disturbed since one cation with a charge of 3+ is replaced by another with the same charge. The regular aluminium cations and the chromium infiltrators are both surrounded in the crystal by six oxygen anions arranged roughly in an **octahedron** (Figure 5.2). The distance between the chromium and oxygen centres is about 0.19 nm.

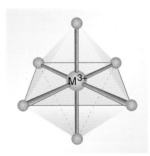

Figure 5.2
Octahedral array of oxygen anions (red) around a tripositive metal cation (grey).

Figure 5.1
Ruby.

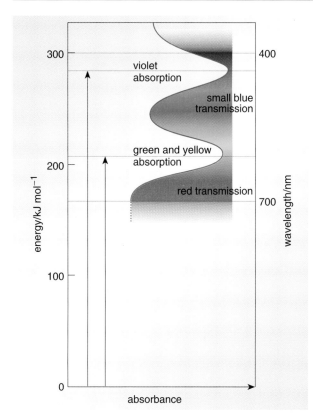

Figure 5.3
Energy levels in ruby.

Figure 5.4
Emerald.

Just as we saw in Chapter 2, the colour of these gems results from the absorption of light, as electrons associated with the 'stranger' chromium cations are promoted from their lowest energy level to a higher one. In these inorganic crystals, it is the electrical environment created by the electrons of the surrounding oxygen atoms that determines the levels on the energy ladder that are allowed to the electrons of the chromium cation. For Cr^{3+} in ruby, there are two energy gaps that correspond to wavelengths in the violet and yellow–green regions of the visible spectrum (Figure 5.3).

White light passing through the ruby becomes depleted of the violet and yellow–green components, leaving almost all the red and a small amount of blue. The result is to give the ruby its characteristic and attractive deep red colour with a slight purple cast.

Today, more synthetic rubies are used than natural stones. They may readily be made by fusing aluminium oxide powder with a trace of chromium in a hydrogen/oxygen flame at 2 050 °C, and slowly cooling the melt. The physical and optical properties of natural and artificial rubies are almost indistinguishable, but there is still a market for natural stones even though they are up to a thousand times more expensive!

Emeralds (Figure 5.4) were mined in Egypt at the time of Cleopatra, but the best gemstones come from South America. The Incas, and other pre-Columbian civilizations, used them for ornamentation.

Tradition has it that the world's most prolific mine, at Muzo in Colombia, was discovered in 1594 by accident. A Spanish cavalryman found that his horse was limping, and was surprised to find an emerald embedded in its hoof. By retracing his route, he came across the concealed entrance to the mine.

Emerald is a beryllium aluminium silicate, that is, a crystalline structure containing the elements beryllium and silicon as well as aluminium and oxygen. Once again, the colour results from a small proportion of chromium cations which replace some of the regular aluminium cations. As with the crystal of ruby, each rogue chromium cation is surrounded by an octahedral array of oxygen anions, again at a distance of about 0.19 nm.

The presence of beryllium and silicon in emerald changes the electrical environment of the Cr^{3+} cations. This slightly alters the corresponding energy gaps on the chromium cation energy level ladder. As a result, the first two levels above the lowest rung are both lower in energy than they are in the ruby crystal (Figure 5.5).

■ What effect will this have on the wavelengths of the light absorbed?

■ The wavelengths of the light absorbed will both be slightly longer (Figure 5.5). Instead of absorbing light from the green and yellow region, emerald absorbs light from the red and yellow region. This leaves the light that is transmitted or reflected from the gemstone rich in green and blue, giving the characteristic emerald green.

In Figures 5.3 and 5.5, you can see that the absorption bands are quite narrow, which explains why the colours of these gemstones are so clear and bright.

Many other gemstones have beautiful colours resulting from the random inclusion of a few metal cations. Since cations of different metallic elements have different sets of energy levels, this leads to minerals showing a very wide range of colours. Aquamarine, jade and citrine are basically quartz (silicon dioxide) but the absorption of light by the electrons of a few stray cations of iron (not chromium this time) within the structure gives rise to their respective delicate blue, green and yellow colours.

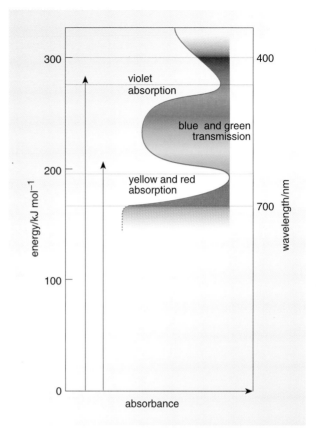

Figure 5.5
Energy levels in emerald.

Numerous minerals in which the metal cations are not impurities, but major constituents, also show strong colours because their electrons can be promoted across energy gaps corresponding to wavelengths in the visible region of the spectrum. These include azurite, turquoise and malachite, in which the blue and green colours result from the presence of copper cations; and garnet, which owes its red colour to cations of iron.

However, it is not just natural minerals that derive their colour from the presence of metal cations. A great many metal compounds produced in laboratories are strongly coloured. These range from the tiny quantities of precipitates generated while testing analytical solutions for the presence of certain metal cations, through intermediate quantities prepared for artists' materials, to the tonnes of some metal compounds manufactured for use as pigments by the paint industry.

This might be a suitable point at which to try Experiment 4.4 'Coloured compounds from metals'.

Experiment 4.4 Coloured compounds from metals

Figure 5.6
Sapphire.

Like ruby, **sapphire** (Figure 5.6) is another modification of the aluminium oxide, corundum, but secreted within the crystal structure this time there are two types of rogue cation.

Instead of a straightforward exchange of Cr^{3+} for Al^{3+}, sapphire has equal numbers of *di*positive iron, Fe^{2+} (i.e. cations with *two* positive charges) and *tetra*positive titanium, Ti^{4+} (i.e. cations with *four* positive charges) occupying centres where there ought to be aluminium cations. Once again, the electrical balance is maintained, but the electrons can now employ a different mechanism for absorbing energy from the white light that falls on the crystal.

Up until now, you have only encountered ions that have a fixed charge. All sodium cations for example are Na^+, calcium and magnesium are always Ca^{2+} and Mg^{2+}, and chloride is always Cl^-. The cations of some metallic elements (e.g. tin, chromium, copper, and mercury) have different numbers of positive charges in different compounds. Iron and titanium similarly can both exist in different ionic states.

In the sapphire crystal, it is relatively easy to transfer an electron from Fe^{2+} to Ti^{4+}. As you know, an electron carries a single *negative* charge, so this transfer process generates the two *tri*positive cations Fe^{3+} and Ti^{3+}:

$$Fe^{2+} + Ti^{4+} = Fe^{3+} + Ti^{3+}$$

All it needs is for an electron on an Fe^{2+} ion to absorb the equivalent in molar terms of about 200 kJ of energy, and it will jump from its place on the electronic energy ladder of iron across to the bottom rung of the titanium ladder. As we have previously noted, this will deplete the reflected or transmitted light in the red–yellow region of the spectrum. The result of this electron transfer, usually termed 'charge transfer', is to produce the beautiful sapphire blue. As this results in a higher energy situation in the crystal, the electron very soon jumps back again, dispersing its energy as infrared radiation.

Question 10 The deep blue crystals of the pigment Prussian blue C.I.Pigment Blue 27 (used in our grandparents' time as washday 'Dolly Blue', Figure 5.7) have the empirical formula $KFe[Fe(CN)_6]$, and the crystal structure shown in Figure 5.8. As we have seen, cations of iron (Fe) can have charges of either 2^+ or 3^+, and in crystals of Prussian blue there are equal numbers of Fe^{2+} and Fe^{3+} ions. Account for the colour of Prussian blue.

Figure 5.7
Advertisement for Dolly Blue.

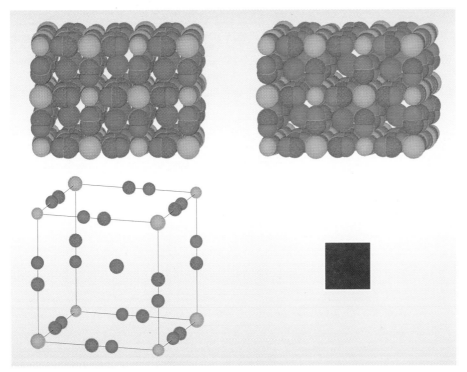

Figure 5.8
The crystal structure of Prussian blue. (Potassium ions, K^+, are at the centre of every other cube.)

5.2 Church windows and ornamental vases

Among the creations handed down from the past, the stained glass of cathedrals (Figure 5.9) and the glazed pottery of ancient artisans (Figure 5.10) must be included in a list of those we most admire. Both of these art forms were developed through the process of trial and error, and the handing on of craft secrets from generation to generation. However, using the principles discussed so far, a scientific explanation can be given to account for their glowing colours. The benefit to the artist of this scientific scrutiny has been an increase in purity and brilliance of colour; better control of the process, leading to a more accurate prediction of the outcome; and the discovery of totally new colours.

Figure 5.9
A 19th century stained glass window from Lincoln Cathedral showing David and Goliath.

You may recall from Book 2 that glass is a chemical material composed mostly of silica (silicon dioxide) with small quantities of other metal oxides like sodium, boron and lead. It is not a crystalline material, but really a liquid that has solidified, because it has cooled too rapidly to allow an ordered structure to form (Figure 5.11a). Pottery glaze is just a thin film of glass coating the ceramic surface. To add colour to glass (Table 5.1), traces of metallic compounds are incorporated into the melt, and become widely dispersed within it (Figure 5.11b).

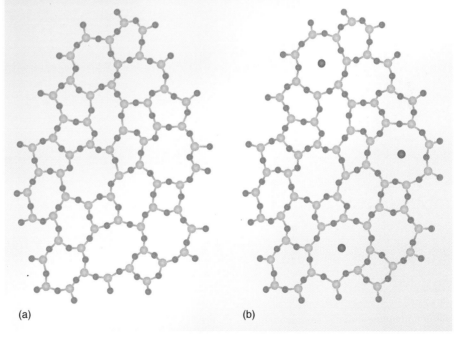

(a)   (b)

Figure 5.10
Chinese pottery.

Figure 5.11
(a) The structure of glass. (b) Metal cations (shown in blue) in glass.

Table 5.1 The effect of incorporating metal cations into glass. (Part of Table 3.1, Book 2, Part 1.)

Metal cation	Chromium	Cobalt	Copper	Iron	Manganese	Selenium
Associated colour	Green	Blue	Red, or blue–green	Brown, or green	Purple	Red

■ Look back at Figure 5.2 and suggest a similarity between the location of the metal cations in ruby and in glass.

■ If you imagine the glass structure extended in three dimensions, in both materials the metal cation will be surrounded by oxygen atoms.

■ What effect might you expect this to have on the electronic structure of the metal cation in glass?

■ It would not be surprising to find that the oxygen atoms of glass determine the energy levels of the surrounded metal cation. This would correspond to the way that the energy level ladder of each chromium cation in ruby is determined by its surrounding oxygens.

■ What other electrical characteristic of a metal cation would you expect to make a difference to the environment of its electrons?

■ Since electrons are negatively charged, you would expect the number of positive charges on the cation to have a significant effect on the energy levels of the electronic ladder.

You may have wondered why, in Table 5.1, copper and iron cations generate more than one colour in glass. This is another consequence of metal cations being able to exist in differently charged states: e.g. iron (Fe^{2+} and Fe^{3+}) and copper (Cu^+ and Cu^{2+}). Although the potters of antiquity did not know this, they did know that by varying the conditions in the kiln they could change the colour of a glaze. The atmosphere inside a pottery kiln can be made oxidizing or reducing, just like the different regions of the blast furnace used in steel-making (Book 2). Under oxidizing conditions, iron exists as the ion Fe^{3+}, which gives rust its brown colour; under reducing conditions, the green Fe^{2+} ion is favoured.

> **Question 11** Now see if you can propose an explanation for how the colours of the borax beads that you investigated in Experiment 2.3 in Book 2 might be generated? Recall that borax is sodium borate tetrahydrate ($Na_2B_4O_7.4H_2O$).

Summary of Chapter 5

In Chapter 5, you have seen that ruby and emerald are slightly impure crystalline minerals, which owe their colour to the absorption of energy by the electrons of contaminating chromium cations (Cr^{3+}). In the crystals, Cr^{3+} is surrounded by six oxygen anions. The electrical environment they create determines the ladder of energy levels available to the electrons of the chromium cation. Sapphire crystals contain traces of both iron and titanium. The blue colour is generated when absorption of energy brings about the transfer of an electron from Fe^{2+} ions to Ti^{4+} ions, to form Fe^{3+} and Ti^{3+} ions. Colours in 'stained' glass and pottery glazes are generated in essentially the same way as the colours of gemstones.

Chapter 6
Why are dyes coloured?

As our understanding of molecular structure progressed, it became interesting to try to identify the system within a molecule that caused a substance to be coloured. Nature and the dye industry offer a vast range of coloured materials with a host of different structures, but is there a unifying theory that could explain the origin of colour?

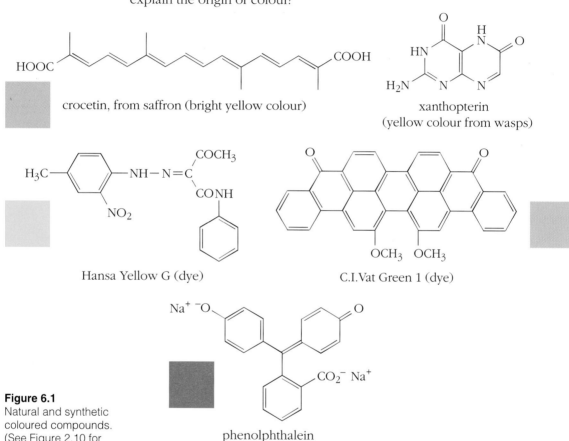

crocetin, from saffron (bright yellow colour)

xanthopterin
(yellow colour from wasps)

Hansa Yellow G (dye)

C.I.Vat Green 1 (dye)

phenolphthalein
(magenta form, an indicator dye)

Figure 6.1
Natural and synthetic coloured compounds. (See Figure 2.10 for phenolphthalein.)

Look at the molecular structures of the coloured materials in Figure 6.1, and also at some of the structures for coloured compounds encountered earlier in this Book. See if you can pick out some common characteristics.

A first impression must be that all have large complex molecules, and ring systems occur frequently. Another feature is the presence of a great many double bonds, most of which are part of the alternating single and double bond pattern of conjugated systems. Most of these molecules also have several nitrogen or oxygen atoms, either as part of their structure, or in attached groups. Lastly, some of the structures carry charges, positive or negative.

In 1875, a Swiss chemist, Otto Witt, was making dyes for a British company at Brentford using the diazo coupling reaction (see Box 4.1). He observed that when aniline (*mono*aminobenzene) was used as the coupling agent, a yellow compound was obtained, but with *tri*aminobenzene the colour produced was brown. He reasoned that if he used *di*aminobenzene, the product should have an intermediate colour. So he tried it; and produced the orange dye, **chrysoidine**, the first **azo dye** to be marketed.

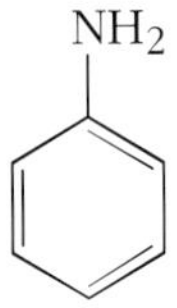

aniline 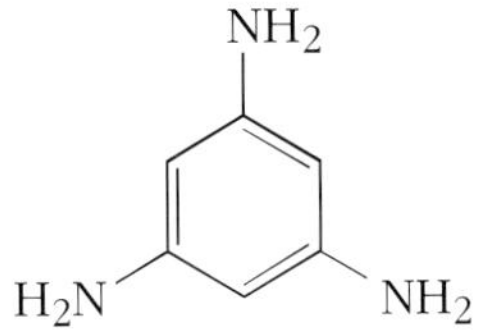   triaminobenzene 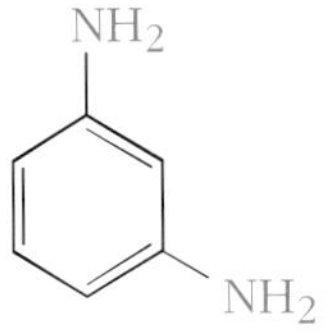   diaminobenzene 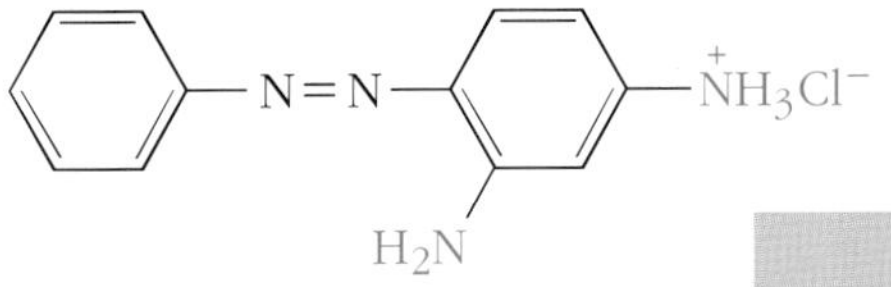   chrysoidine
                                                                  C.I. Basic Orange 2

Witt's experiment had consequences that reached much further than commercial success. He went on to put forward a theory of colour in dyes which is still used today. Witt had noticed, as we did in Figure 6.1, that certain structural features appeared regularly in the molecules of coloured compounds. He first proposed that the molecules of any coloured substance must contain a structural unit that is responsible for it being coloured. In Witt's three dyes, this unit would be the two benzene rings linked by the azo group. These structural units are called **chromogens** (colour producers). However, as compounds with the same structural chromogen are found to exhibit a range of colours, he further stated that the actual colour observed will depend on subsidiary groups which are directly attached to the chromogen. These he called **auxochromes** (colour boosters). Table 6.1 shows a number of contributors to chromogenic systems, and also some auxochromes that occur frequently.

▨   Looking at the list in Table 6.1, what seem to be the features of an effective auxochrome?

▮   Groups carrying positive or negative charges seem to be effective; so do groups containing oxygen or nitrogen atoms, and also those containing double bonds. It appears that both singly and doubly bonded oxygen and nitrogen atoms give rise to auxochromic effects.

Question 12

Table 6.2 shows the effect of adding substituents to the azobenzene chromogen:

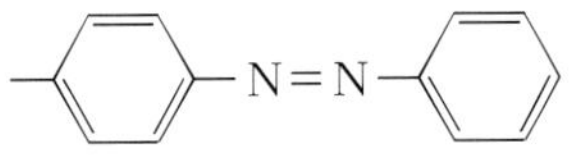

Complete the column of difference in wavelength of substituents in Table 6.2 and place the substituents in a quantitative order of auxochromic effectiveness.

Table 6.1 Common components of chromogens and functional groups that act as auxochromes.

Chromogen components   *Auxochromes*

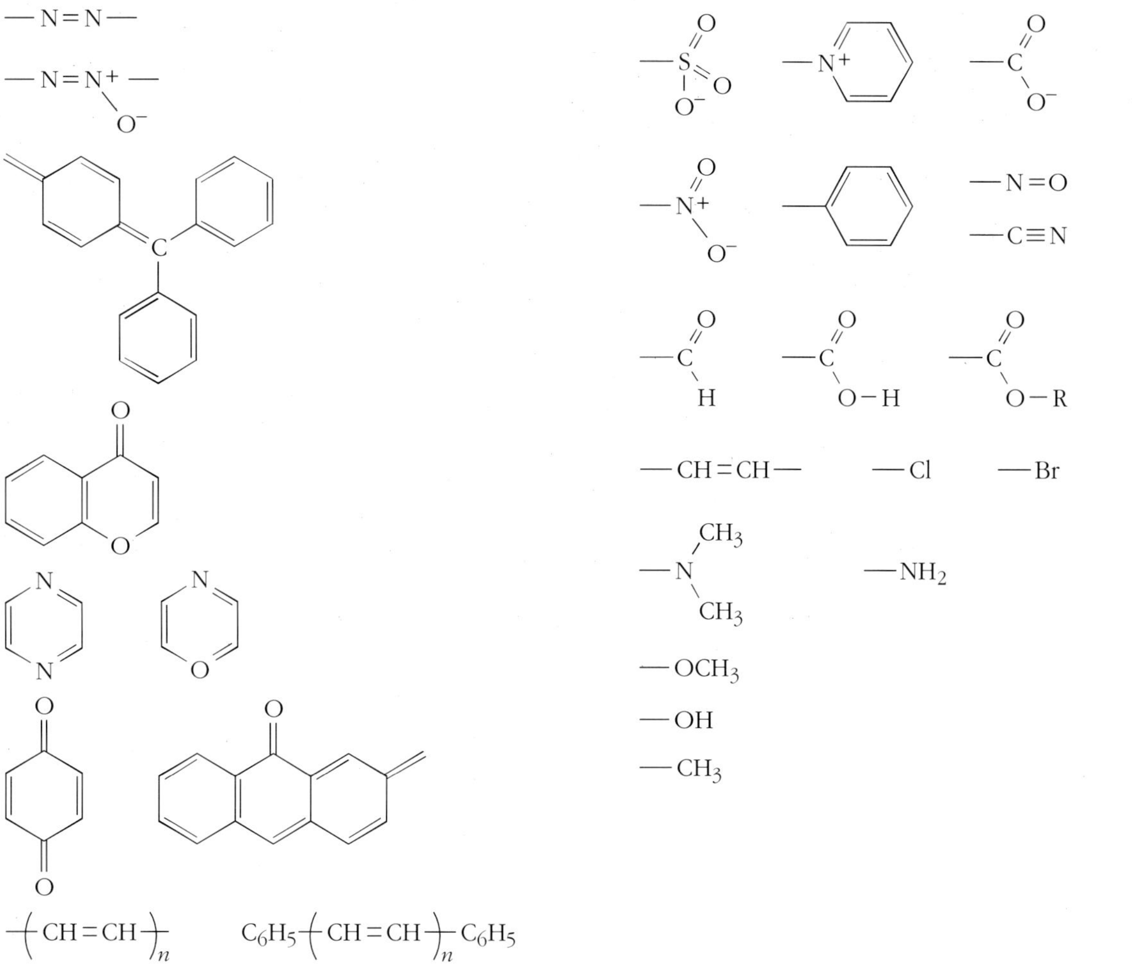

Table 6.2 Auxochromic effect of substituents in the series of dyes: $A-\langle \rangle-N=N-\langle \rangle$
Visible spectra measured in ethanol solution.

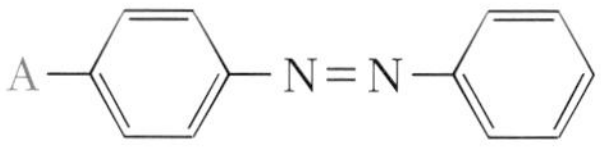

Substituent A	λ_{max}/nm	Difference/nm	Substituent A	λ_{max}/nm	Difference/nm
H	318	0	NH_2	387	
CH_3	333	15	SO_3H	329	
NO_2	338		Br	329	
$(C_2H_5)_2N$	415		COOH	325	
CH_3O	346		OH	350	
NC	324		$COCH_3$	329	

Witt's theory leads us immediately to ask two questions: 'Why does the presence of a chromogen in a molecule give rise to colour in a material?' and 'How does an auxochrome change the colour?'.

From earlier discussion, we know that colour is a consequence of absorption of some of the wavelengths from white light, and that absorption occurs by a photon transferring an appropriate quantity of energy to an electron and promoting it to a higher energy level. So the questions become: 'What is the relationship between chromogenic structures and photon energies that correspond to wavelengths in the visible region?' and 'How do auxochromes affect energy levels?'.

In singly bonded organic molecules, the bonding electrons are essentially confined to the space between the atoms that they bind together. However, if a molecule has double bonds in it, the electrons are not so tightly restrained. The most effective way to give the electrons freedom is to include a conjugated system in the molecule.

All the electrons associated with the double bonds of a conjugated system are then described as being **delocalized** over the whole system between its two end atoms. These electrons should no longer be regarded as 'belonging' to particular bonds but as 'spreading' throughout the entire conjugated system. Instead of being limited to a series of energy levels associated with single atoms (like sodium or neon), or cations (like Cr^{3+} or Fe^{2+}), they are able to occupy energy levels associated with the conjugated system as a whole.

Figure 6.2 shows the effect on the wavelength of most intense absorption as double bonds are added into a system; i.e. as conjugation increases.

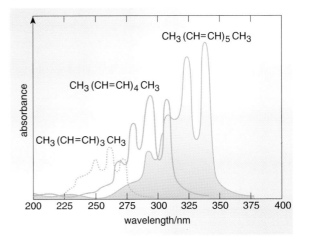

- From Figure 6.2, deduce the way the gap between molecular energy levels will change as conjugation increases.

- As more and more double bonds are added to the conjugated chain, the wavelength of absorption becomes longer and so the gap between molecular energy levels gets progressively smaller.

- What will be the consequence of this change for the molecules in Figure 6.2?

- Eventually, part of the absorption pattern falls just within the visible region of the spectrum. The absorbing system becomes a chromogen, and the compounds will then show a yellow colour (complementary to violet – see Figure 2.6). As the conjugation increases and the energy gap becomes smaller, the colour will become orange, then red.

Figure 6.2
The effect on wavelength of absorption on increasing the length of a conjugated chain. Although the absorption pattern is complex, it moves *as a whole* to longer wavelength as the conjugation increases.

There is a useful 'rule of thumb' that says: 'The greater the extent of the delocalization, the smaller the energy gap; and therefore the longer the wavelength of absorption'.

The simplest form of chromogen is therefore a long conjugated system. The orange dye from carrots, carotene, with 11 conjugated double bonds (Figure 2.13) is the prime example of a molecule containing this type of chromogen.

Other long chain, conjugated molecules are the plant colours crocetin (Figure 6.1) and rhodoxanthin. Chromogens of this type are called **polyene chromogens** because they are made up of systems that have many double bonds.

The double bonds need not be in a chain; they can also be in ring systems. An array of benzene rings, joined by single bonds or fused together, is a particularly effective contributor to chromogenic systems. Several of the vat dyes, like C.I.Vat Green 1 (Figure 6.1) which has *nine* rings fused together, are classified as polyene chromogens.

Box 6.1 The role of nitrogen and oxygen in auxochromes

You may be wondering why oxygen and nitrogen atoms feature so prominently in the table of auxochromes. Unlike carbon, neither of these atoms uses all its outer electrons for forming bonds. These 'leftover' electrons are not as tightly confined as the bonding electrons and so they too can be delocalized. Any oxygen or nitrogen atom attached by a single bond to a double bond can share electrons with a conjugated system. As a result, the gaps between the molecular energy levels are reduced further. An oxygen atom carrying a negative charge does this even more effectively.

In addition, recall that both nitrogen and oxygen have a greater attraction than carbon for electrons. It is, after all, this attraction for the hydrogen electrons of —OH and —NH— groups that gives rise to hydrogen bonding. The attraction is most effective when the nitrogen or oxygen atoms are doubly or triply bonded because the electrons of these **multiple bonds** are held more loosely in the molecule than the electrons of single bonds. The result is that functional groups like nitro ($-NO_2$), carbonyl ($C=O$) and cyano ($-C\equiv N$) attract electrons out of a conjugated system. If the nitrogen bears a positive charge, this effect is increased.

Both feeding electrons into a conjugated system and attracting them out of it produce an auxochromic effect.

So Witt's ideas about the origin of colour have been refined, but the value of his approach towards designing a dye with a specific colour is undiminished. Starting with a material with an observed colour, and with a known chromogen, the colour of the dye can be 'tweaked' by introducing or removing auxochromic groups until the system absorbs just those points of the visible spectrum that will leave the exact colour required.

When we are making comparisons between two similar molecules that show different colours, the *whole of the common structure* is considered to be the chromogen. The different attached groups, however big, small, simple or complex they may be, are the auxochromes.

> **Question 13** Figure 6.3 (overleaf) shows how the colour changes as auxochromes are added in two series of commercially important dyes. Identify the chromogen in each of the two series of dyes. Into what category of dye (Section 4.3) would you place the dyes in Figure 6.3? Would you expect dyes with this classification to be appropriate for use with acetate fibres?

Summary of Chapter 6

In Chapter 6 you have seen how certain structural elements characterize molecules that give rise to colour. Their structures are found to incorporate conjugated double bonds, benzene rings, oxygen and nitrogen atoms, and positive and negative charges – often in combination.

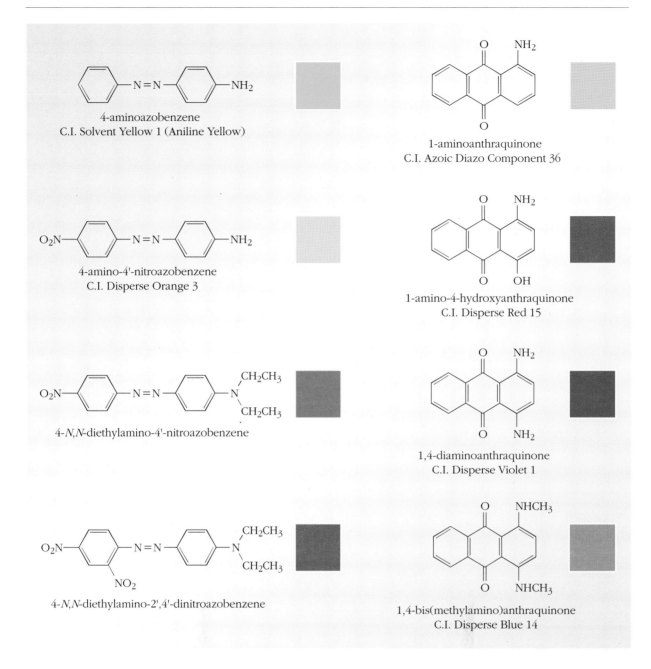

4-aminoazobenzene
C.I. Solvent Yellow 1 (Aniline Yellow)

4-amino-4'-nitroazobenzene
C.I. Disperse Orange 3

4-*N*,*N*-diethylamino-4'-nitroazobenzene

4-*N*,*N*-diethylamino-2',4'-dinitroazobenzene

1-aminoanthraquinone
C.I. Azoic Diazo Component 36

1-amino-4-hydroxyanthraquinone
C.I. Disperse Red 15

1,4-diaminoanthraquinone
C.I. Disperse Violet 1

1,4-bis(methylamino)anthraquinone
C.I. Disperse Blue 14

The molecular colour-generating system consists of a chromogen with additional auxochromes. The principal chromogenic structure is the conjugated polyene chain or multiple ring system. The electrons in conjugated systems are delocalized over the whole system. Extending conjugation, and increasing delocalization, reduces the energy gaps between electronic levels in a molecule, and therefore increases the wavelength of absorption. Singly bonded oxygen and nitrogen have non-bonded electrons that can also be delocalized; multiply bonded oxygen and nitrogen atoms not only extend conjugation, but also attract electrons. Both these features are auxochromic.

Figure 6.3
Colour changes brought about by auxochromes.

Chapter 7
The trichromacy theory

It was more than 100 years after Newton's light-splitting experiment before any further progress was made towards the understanding of colour perception. Then, in 1790, Thomas Young demonstrated that if red, green and blue light are mixed together, white light is obtained (Figure 7.1).

However, it is not just white light that can be produced in this way. By varying the relative intensity of the overlapping spots, *any* colour across the spectrum can be reproduced. This phenomenon is known as **trichromacy**.

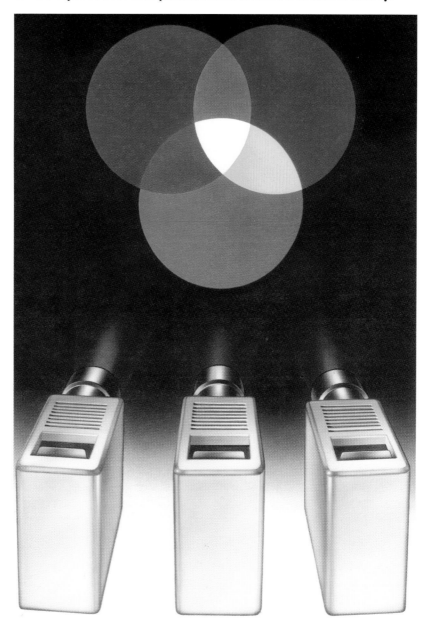

Figure 7.1
The mixing of red, green and blue light.

Activity 2 Spinning colour discs I & II

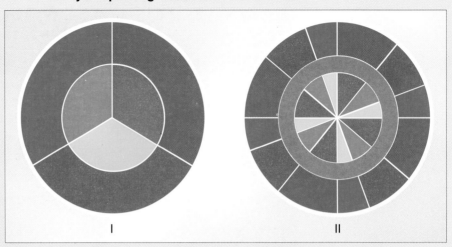

An alternative way of blending colours is spinning a multicoloured disc. Young also used this technique. You can carry out a similar experiment to his by using the coloured discs of the *Chemistry Set* (Figure 7.2). When we spin the disc, we are genuinely blending the different colours of light reflected from the coloured surfaces. However, in comparison with coloured lights, printed colours have a much reduced brightness and a combination of the three colours on a spinning disc will generate grey rather than white.

Carefully cut discs I and II from the card using a pair of sharp scissors. Pierce the centre of the discs with a skewer, and push a pencil stub, or golf tee, carefully through the hole. A little Blu-Tack™ will fix the disc more firmly in place.

Spin disc I, and observe the blend of colours obtained.

Equal areas of the three printed primaries do not mix by spinning to give a grey entirely devoid of colour. The brighter hues, red and green, dominate. Thus, the rotated mix of red, green and blue gives a yellowish-grey.

Now spin disc II. This disc shows that it is possible to get closer to a neutral grey (inner band) by altering the proportions of the colours in the mixture.

Figure 7.2
Colour discs I and II (also printed at a larger size on a separate card).

7.1 Colour perception

Thomas Young had introduced the trichromacy theory to try to explain **colour vision**, on the assumption that our eyes contain **receptors** that are sensitive to light of different wavelengths. If we had different receptors in our eyes for every colour, the number of receptors responsive to any particular colour, say orange, would be low. We would expect the eye's sensitivity to orange light to be very much less than that to white light. In practice, however, our sensitivity to separate colours is almost as good as it is to white light.

Young suggested there were just three types of colour receptor in the eye: one sensitive to red, one to green and the third to blue. The colour we see will then depend on the relative extent to which each of these colour receptors is stimulated. Thus, colour is 'synthesized' in the eye and brain. This is the **Young–Helmholtz theory of colour vision**, because Hermann von Helmholtz further refined the idea of trichromacy.

Box 7.1 How our eyes respond to colours

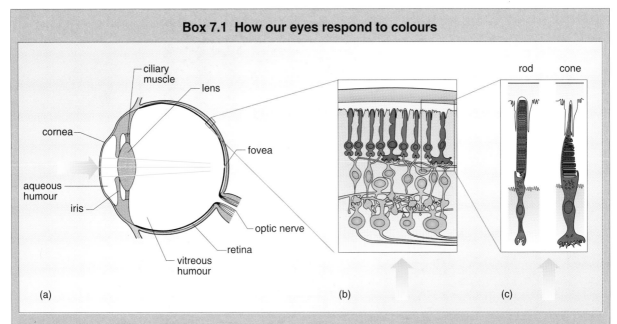

Figure 7.3
(a) Diagrammatic cross-section of a vertebrate eye. (b) Cross-section of retina. (c) Rod and cone cells.

The reason that we perceive colours is that the energy corresponding to wavelengths of light lying between 400–700 nm causes a chemical change to take place in the **retina**, the light-sensitive lining at the back of the eye (Figure 7.3a, b).

If the light has wavelengths shorter than 400 nm, it is filtered out by the cornea; if the wavelengths exceed 700 nm, the corresponding energy is insufficient to bring about the chemical change. The three receptors postulated by Young must therefore be located in the retina. Microscopic examination of the retina shows that there are two kinds of light receptor at the back of the eye – **rod cells** and **cone cells** (Figure 7.3c). Rods are sensitive to low levels of light, but are not colour-sensitive. Bright-light vision and colour perception occur through cone receptors.

By very careful experimentation, James Bowmaker at Queen Mary College London was able to measure the absorption spectrum of individual cone cells. A beam of white light was narrowed to a width comparable with that of a single cone cell (2 micrometres). A specimen of frog retina was mounted on a microscope stage and manipulated until the beam passed through a single cone cell. The fraction of the light absorbed by this cell was then recorded between 400 nm and 700 nm. When the process was repeated with other cone cells in the specimen, Bowmaker found only *three* types of absorption (Figure 7.4 overleaf).

The cones absorbing at the shortest wavelength – i.e. those most sensitive to light in the blue region of the visible spectrum – are known as blue cones. They show maximum absorbance at a wavelength of 420 nm. Similarly, the other two types are known as green cones (maximum 534 nm) and red cones (maximum 564 nm). Note that the response ranges of the three cones overlap. It was Helmholtz who predicted that this *must* happen if trichromacy were to explain colour vision.

The Young–Helmholtz theory appears to be a satisfactory model. It explains, for example, how a yellow colour sensation can arise in two ways:

- light with a mixture of wavelengths in the red and green regions of the spectrum activates the separate receptors near to their peaks of absorption; or

- monochromatic light with a wavelength of about 590 nm (e.g. a sodium lamp) activates both red and green receptors by falling in the spectral region where their absorption bands overlap.

As our eyes respond to simultaneous stimulation of the red and green cones, the brain interprets the sensation as yellow.

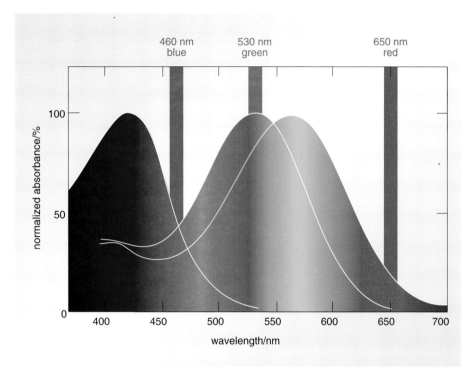

Figure 7.4
Absorption spectra (response curves) for the blue, green and red cone cells. For ease of comparison, the maxima of all three response curves have been set at equal heights (normalized absorbance). The coloured bands show typical wavelengths used in additive mixing experiments (Section 7.2).

The trichromacy theory also provides an explanation for colour blindness. Men (approximately 8%) are much more likely than women to suffer from this disability, especially its commonest form: red/green colour blindness. If the red cones are lacking, the eye will still *respond* to green, yellow, orange, and even orange–red light using the green cones, since the absorption band covers all these wavelengths (refer to Figure 7.4). However, it will be impossible to *distinguish* red from green, as there are no red cones offering a response to contrast with the signals from the green cones. Similarly, an eye lacking green cones will again see all the colours, but will have nothing to contrast with the red cone response.

Figure 7.5
John Dalton (1766–1844). In his *New System of Chemical Philosophy* (1808), Dalton gave the first clear exposition of the atomic theory. This enabled chemists for the first time to express chemical behaviour, both qualitatively and quantitatively, in terms of formulas and equations.

Question 14 The most famous colour-blind chemist was surely John Dalton (Figure 7.5). Colour blindness is still called *Daltonism*. He wrote in 1798:

I had not attended much to the practical discrimination of colours owing in some degree to what I conceived to be a perplexity in their nomenclature. With respect to colours that were white, yellow or green, I readily consented to the appropriate term. Blue, purple, pink and crimson appeared rather less distinguishable; being according to my idea, all referable to blue.

With what deficiency of vision do you conclude Dalton to be afflicted?

7.2 Trichromacy theory and colour mixing

The three colours Young selected – red, green and blue – are now known as the **additive primaries**. They do not correspond exactly to the colours that stimulate the retina, but they are quite close (Figure 7.4). If we select violet as a primary, because this is where the maximum wavelength of the blue cones' response falls, the additive primaries are found at equal distances from each other on the colour circle (Figure 2.7), forming an equilateral triangle (Figure 7.6a).

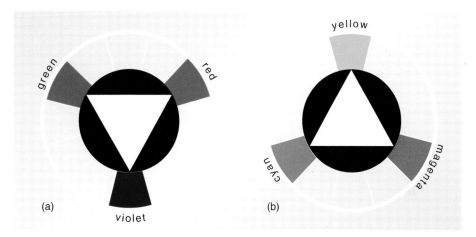

Figure 7.6
The colour circle showing (a) the additive and (b) the subtractive primaries.

Activity 3 Spinning colour discs III, IV and V

Carefully cut out discs III–V (on a separate card), and then mount and spin each on a central spindle as before.

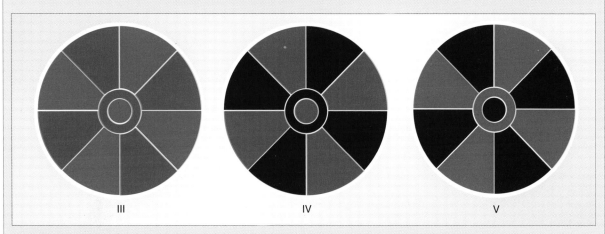

Figure 7.7
Disc designs with the additive primary colours.

Note down your observations below:

Disc	Colours on disc	Colour observed on spinning
III		
IV		
V		

This Activity shows that overlapping Young's additive primaries in pairs generates a second threesome – yellow (red and green), cyan (green and blue), and magenta (red and blue). This is equivalent to removing completely the wavelengths corresponding to the additive primary colours *in turn* from white light. For example, if blue is removed from white light, red and green remain. This is the combination that generates yellow. This set of colours – yellow, cyan and magenta – is known as the **subtractive primaries**. They form a complementary equilateral triangle on the colour circle (Figure 7.6b).

At last we can resolve the anomaly of the absent complementary colour in the spectrum. Our eyes will interpret a combination of red and blue as equivalent to the missing colour, magenta, opposite green on the colour circle. In the same way that the coloured *lights* of the additive primaries combine to give white light, a combination of yellow, cyan and magenta lights will do the same (Figure 7.8a).

However, when it comes to *pigments*, a red pigment will absorb green and blue, a green pigment will absorb red and blue, and a blue pigment will absorb red and green. So a pigment mixture of all three additive primaries will not reflect any light at all, and be black. A mixture of yellow, cyan and magenta pigments will give a similar result (Figure 7.8b).

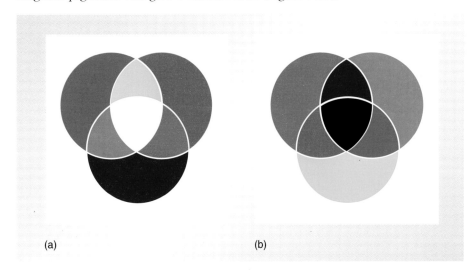

(a)   (b)

Figure 7.8
(a) Additive primaries and their combinations (coloured lights).
(b) Subtractive primaries and their combinations (pigments).

The response of the three primaries to white incident light is shown in Figure 7.9. You will certainly have seen how colours look quite different in the light from a sodium lamp. Yellow light has no blue component (blue is its complementary colour) and so it is a mixture of red and green. Red objects will still appear red because red is reflected and green absorbed; and green objects will still appear green. However, blue objects will absorb both red and green light and reflect no component of yellow light. As a result, they will appear black (Figure 7.10).

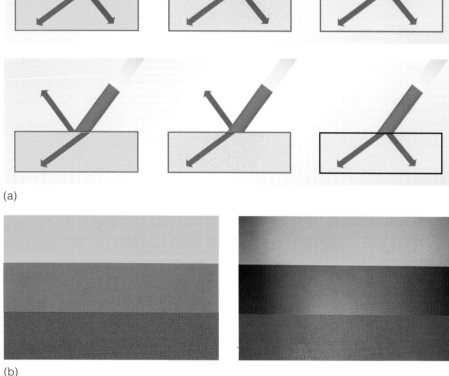

Figure 7.9
Absorption and reflection of light.

Figure 7.10
(a) Diagram showing the effect of yellow light falling on the three additive primaries (red, green and blue); (b) the three subtractive primaries (magenta, cyan and yellow) photographed in daylight (left) and sodium light (right). As expected, the cyan (rather too blue) absorbs all the red, and most of the green therefore appears greenish-grey; magenta absorbs all the green and relects only the red; yellow reflects yellow (i.e. the red and the green).

(a)

(b)

Activity 4 Using colour filters

Look at Figure 7.8 through the red and blue colour filters in the *Chemistry Set* and note down the colours you observe in Table 7.1.

Table 7.1 Appearance of primary colours through red and blue filters.

Primary colour	Viewed through red filter	Viewed through blue filter
red	red	black
green	black	green
violet (blue)	black	blue
yellow	orange	green
cyan	black	blue
magenta	red	purple

magenta = red + blue
cyan = blue + green.
yellow = red + green

Question 15 (a) Magenta light falls on a chess board that in daylight appears to have blue and yellow squares. What colours will it appear to have with this source of illumination? *red + blue* *blue reflects blue, absorbs red (blue)* *yellow reflected red & green, absorb blue (red)*

(b) What colour pattern would you detect if you were to view the board through a red filter? *red filter will only pass red light (blue reflected light will appear black) so red/black squares*

7.3 Applications of trichromacy

The concept of trichromacy has been exploited in three very familiar ways: colour photography, colour printing, and colour television. If ever there was a need to justify the value of a theoretical concept in relation to its potential for practical application, this surely must be the prime example!

7.3.1 What a picture, what a photograph!

In the 1850s, James Maxwell took three photographs of the same scene through separate red, green and blue filters. He then projected them simultaneously through separate filters, and claimed to have produced a full colour picture on the screen. This experiment has proved very difficult to reproduce, but at least it encouraged the development of colour photography.

This might be a suitable time at which to try Experiment 4.5 'The basis of photography'.

Experiment 4.5 The basis of photography

Black and white photography depends on the observation that when light falls on certain colourless silver compounds they become black through the light-induced formation of metallic silver. These silver compounds are very sensitive to blue light, but if we want full colour photography it is necessary to find substances that are selectively sensitive to red and green light, too.

As early as 1873, Hermann Vogel found that adding a yellow dye to the emulsion made the silver layer more sensitive to yellow and green. This idea was developed into the modern photographic film which is a sandwich of three emulsion layers, each with a different dye, and so each differently sensitive to the light falling on it (Figure 7.11). A yellow filter is also included. Since yellow is complementary to blue, the filter absorbs all the blue light and prevents it from penetrating to the bottom two layers, which then only respond to green and red light, respectively.

Figure 7.11
Cross-section through a developed piece of 'three-layered' photographic film.

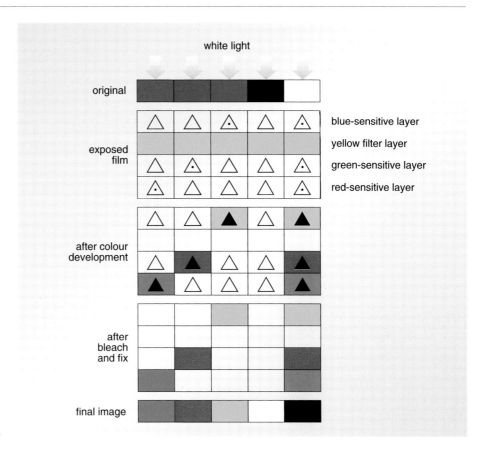

Figure 7.12
The colour-negative system.

A diagram of the exposure and development processes that take place to produce colour-negative film is given in Figure 7.12.

In order to see what happens when light of a particular colour strikes the film, we could take green light as an example. Green light will not affect the blue-sensitive layer (as it contains no blue); it then passes through the yellow filter (as yellow will not absorb red or green); it activates the green-sensitive layer where it is absorbed; and does not pass through to the final red-sensitive layer. A black dot in a triangle shows that incident light has activated the silver compound in that layer. The black dot therefore appears in the green-sensitive layer. As this is a colour-*negative* process, on development this activated area will produce a patch of magenta dye (complementary to green) in the green-sensitive layer.

> **Question 16** Using the approach in the paragraph above, describe how cyan light would interact with three-layered colour-negative film. Begin by deciding what are the components of cyan that will affect the blue-, green- and red-sensitive layers; and what effect the yellow filter will have on these components.

7.3.2 Coloured spots before the eyes

Four-colour printing by the CMYK process, like colour photography, uses the subtractive primary colours cyan (C), magenta (M) and yellow (Y), rather than the additive primaries (K stands for black, or, in printers' jargon, 'key'). If you examine coloured pictures in most newspapers, books or magazines using a magnifying glass, you will see they are made up from tiny dots printed in these four colours. Where the dots are overprinted, additive primaries can be seen. Even black can be produced in this way, but printers prefer to have black as a separate 'colour'.

If you have never looked at a coloured illustration through a magnifying glass, try it now. It is a revelation!

All the hues on the colour circle, and thousands more, can be produced from the right mixture of these three subtractive primary colours (Table 7.2 and Figure 7.13) simply by altering the proportions of each colour present.

Table 7.2 Proportions of the subtractive primaries used in 'half-tone' colour printing.

	Yellow	Magenta	Cyan	
yellow	100	0	0	
orange	100	40	0	
red	100	100	0	
ruby	40	100	0	
magenta	0	100	0	
purple	0	100	40	
violet	0	100	100	
blue	0	40	100	
cyan	0	0	100	
turquoise	40	0	100	
green	100	0	100	
lime	100	0	40	

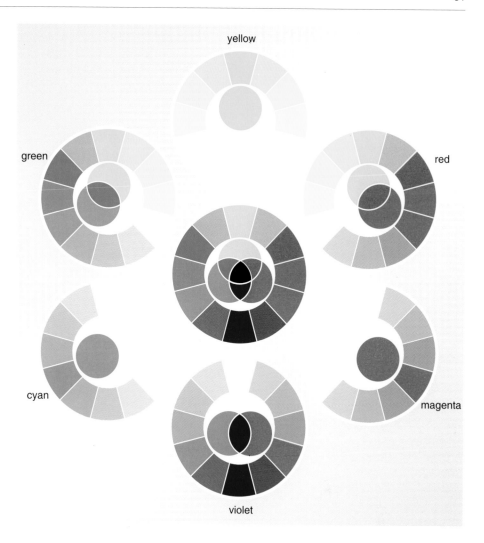

Figure 7.13
The colours produced by using three printing inks of pure subtractive primary hues.

Question 17 Examine the structures of the magenta and cyan dyes (Figure 7.14) designed to survive the high temperatures generated in the dye-sublimation colour printers of electronic publishing systems, and suggest reasons for their difference in colour using the chromogen–auxochrome theory.

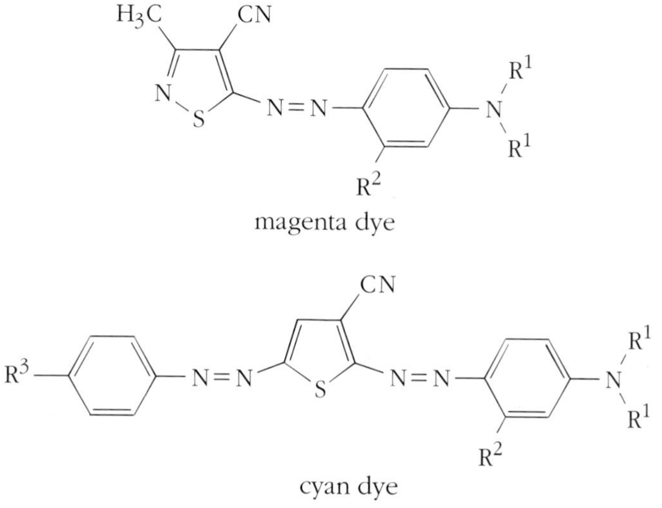

magenta dye

Figure 7.14
Dyes designed for dye-sublimation colour printers (R^1, R^2, R^3 represent alkyl groups).

cyan dye

7.3.3 Excitement on the TV screen

We are reminded of the trichromacy theory every day that we watch BBC television, for the familiar logo (Figure 7.15) has each of the three initials underlined by an additive primary colour – blue, red and green.

Figure 7.15
The BBC logo.

In a TV camera, there are three mirrors. One is transparent to all but red light, and reflects the red component of the light coming through the lens. Two other mirrors similarly handle the green and blue components (Figure 7.16). This reflected light is picked up by an electron tube detector, which translates the light signal into an electric current. The current varies according to the intensity of the light at each point of the recorded picture. The signal is transmitted and received as radio waves, but at the receiver the signal is retranslated into beams of electrons inside the TV tube.

The inner surface of a TV tube has a coating of 200 000 precisely spaced spots of three different kinds of phosphorescent compounds, called **phosphors**. One type of spot glows red, one green and one blue, when a beam of electrons falls on it. The signal from the red reflections sweeps the screen, lighting up the red phosphors; the green and blue phosphors are activated similarly. The overall glow from the screen then regenerates the original picture. The colour-generating process is therefore an *emission* process.

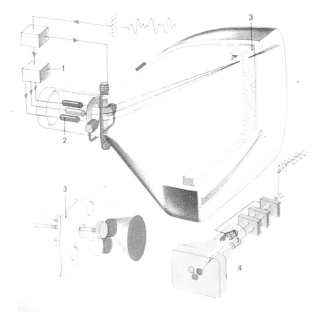

Figure 7.16
Schematic of television receiver.

Summary of Chapter 7

In Chapter 7, you have seen that our eyes have three types of colour receptor (cones) sensitive to radiation bands with wavelengths centred on 420 nm (blue), 534 nm (green), and 564 nm (red). The response ranges of the three cones must overlap to explain colour vision. Red, green and blue light (the additive primary colours) mixed together in the correct proportions give white light; so do yellow, cyan and magenta (the subtractive primary colours). This phenomenon is known as trichromacy. The subtractive primaries are obtained by subtracting in turn a single additive primary from white light. A mixture of either set of primary pigments gives black.

A colour photograph results from the selective sensitivity to different colours of light by a three-layered photographic film. Printing also uses yellow, cyan and magenta dyes (together with black) to build up a full range of colours by varying the proportions of each dye. A television camera uses the electrical response to the proportions of red, green, and blue light to build up a picture. In the television tube, beams of electrons corresponding in intensity to these three primary colours activate red, green and blue phosphors to regenerate the picture.

Chapter 8
Overview of colour

We have looked at a variety of mechanisms for the generation of colour: promotion of electrons in free atoms and ions, electronic transitions between atomic and molecular energy levels, and electron transfer from ion to ion. Kurt Nassau, writing in *Scientific American*, made this general observation:

> *It may seem an extraordinary coincidence that such a diversity of phenomena is encompassed in a band of wavelengths that is not even a full octave wide; it may seem still more remarkable that this narrow band happens to be just the one to which the human eye is sensitive.*

> *Actually, it may not be a coincidence at all. So much of interest happens in this narrow region of the spectrum of radiation because these are the wavelengths where interactions of light with electrons first become important. Waves of lower energy mainly stimulate the motions of atoms and molecules, and so they are usually sensed as heat. Radiation of higher energy can ionise atoms and permanently damage molecules, so that its effects seem largely destructive. Only in the narrow transition zone between these extremes is the energy of light well tuned to the electronic structure of matter.*

It is indeed doubtful whether we should experience any improvement in vision if our eyes were sensitive to a wider range of wavelengths. We rely on reflected light and, as can be inferred from the last paragraph, radiation in the infrared and ultraviolet regions of the spectrum tends to be strongly absorbed, rather than being reflected by many of the materials that make up the objects around us.

Chapter 9
The chemical senses

In physiology, the olfactory and gustatory senses (smell and taste) are termed the chemical senses. They depend on chemical stimuli that are present either in food and drink, or in the air. In humans, these senses do not have the survival value of the other senses; but they add considerably to the quality of life. It was Marcel Proust (1871–1922) who said:

Fragrance is the most tenacious form of memory.

9.1 The sense of taste

When we enjoy a meal or a glass of wine, our chemical senses are working together to provide the variety of sensations that our brains interpret as 'flavour.' It is not just the '**tastebuds**' in our mouths that are active. They are supplemented by responses to odoriferous chemical compounds that are sufficiently volatile to float up into our nasal cavity and stimulate our sense of smell. If you have suffered a head cold and your nasal passages were blocked, you will probably have noticed that food tasted insipid; even apple and onion can taste alike.

If we try to separate out the elements of this complex process, we find that taste is the simplest part. It has long been recognized that there are four basic tastes: salt, sour, bitter and sweet. There are also other distinctive taste sensations that do not fall under these headings, like metallic, pungent, astringent and 'meaty' (for which the Japanese term **umami** is now used by food scientists).

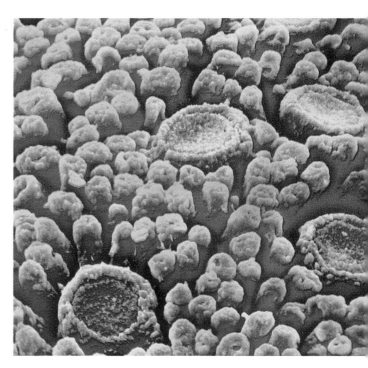

Figure 9.1
Electron micrograph of the surface of the human tongue showing the round papillae (pink) that contain the tastebuds (magnification × 150).

An adult's tongue is covered with about 9 000 tastebuds (Figure 9.1), each of which is sensitive to a particular taste; but they are not distributed evenly.

'The bitter lemon experiment' (Experiment 4.6) should convince you of this, so you might like to try it now.

Experiment 4.6 The bitter lemon experiment

In addition, some sensations like astringency and pungency seem to involve the whole of the inside of the mouth. This is why wine- or tea-tasters swill mouthfuls of liquid around in their mouths to appreciate the complete flavour.

After reading Book 3, you should be aware that tastebuds are the site of molecular receptors. The structure of the sweetness receptor was discussed there and a correlation drawn between the molecular structure of sweeteners like aspartame, cyclamate and saccharin.

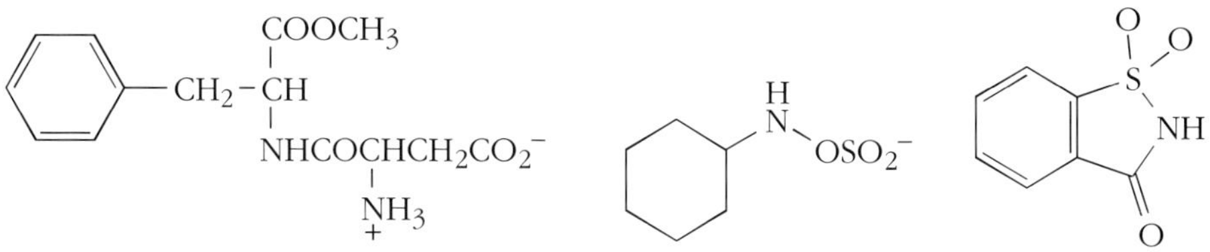

aspartame   cyclamate   saccharin

A similar correlation is not yet possible for bitterness. Quinine (see structure on following page), the antimalarial drug discussed earlier and which is also the bitter principle of bitter lemon, is one of the most bitter substances known. It is detectable in aqueous solution at a concentration of 0.000 05% by mass (compared with the sweetness of sucrose – at 0.5%, and the saltiness of sodium chloride at 0.25%). The humulones from hops, also complex organic compounds, provide the bitterness for bitter beer.

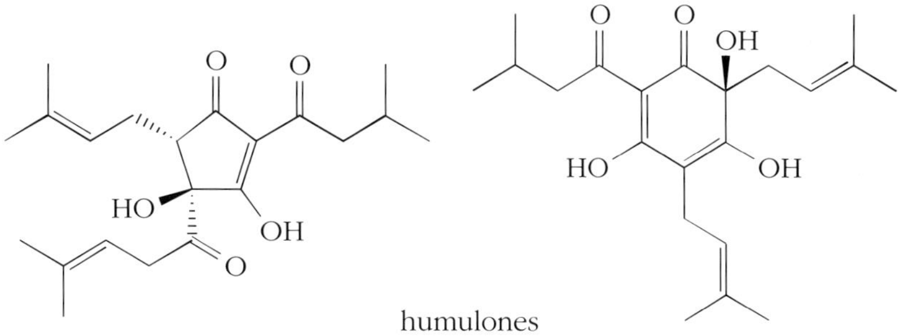

humulones

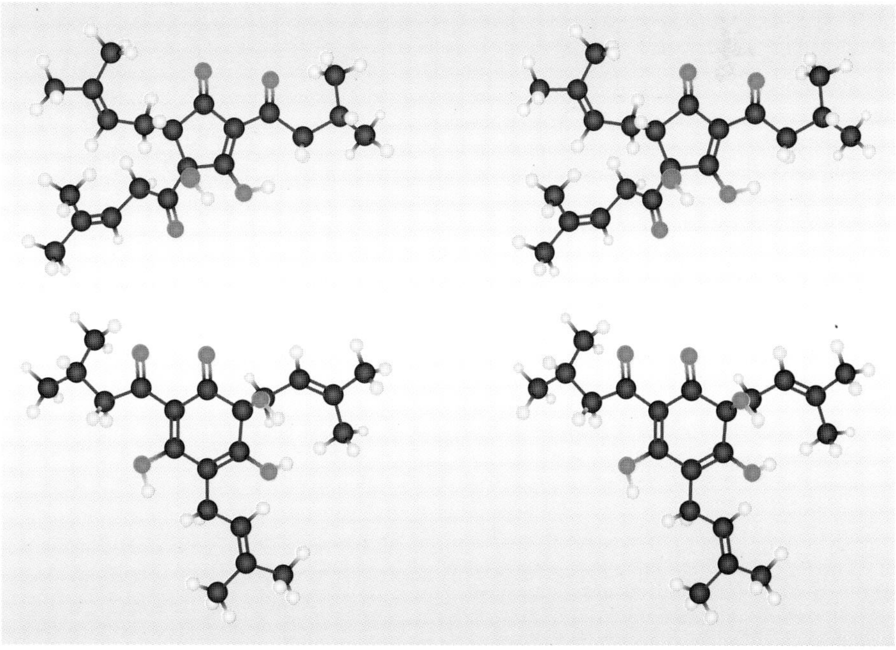

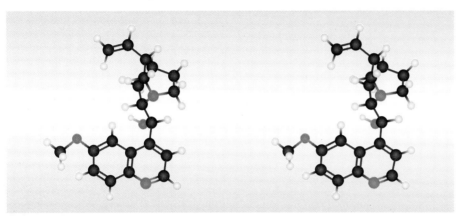

quinine

However, an aqueous solution of the simple inorganic compound magnesium sulfate ($MgSO_4$), the major constituent of Epsom salts, is also bitter, and some of the best beer is brewed in districts where there is a rather high concentration of magnesium in the water. In molecular terms, bitterness and sweetness are not very far apart, as is seen in the series below.

very sweet   slightly sweet   bitter

We naturally associate a sour taste with acids, of which vinegar, aqueous acetic (or ethanoic) acid is the most familiar. Indeed, many sour-tasting foods like fruit and the dairy products cheese and yoghurt contain acids whose names you may recognize.

citric acid   malic acid   lactic acid   tartaric acid
(most fruit)   (apples)   (cheese, yoghurt)   (grapes)

It might be thought that sourness is therefore associated with the characteristic feature of acids – the presence of H^+ ions in aqueous solution. Surprisingly, this seems to be incorrect. Hydrochloric acid diluted to the same H^+ ion concentration as vinegar does not taste sour, but salty. Sourness seems instead to be linked to the presence of carboxylic acid groups in the molecule. It has been suggested that the 'sour' receptors have negatively charged sites at their surface, and when the carboxylic acid transfers its H^+ to these sites this triggers the 'sour' response.

Pungency, or 'hotness', has long been a highly valued element of taste. Compounds extracted from three major spices are seen to have one common structural similarity, despite more obvious differences. All three have a benzene ring with two oxygen substituents in the same relationship to the attachment of a long chain. This may be the feature which generates the characteristic hotness that they all share.

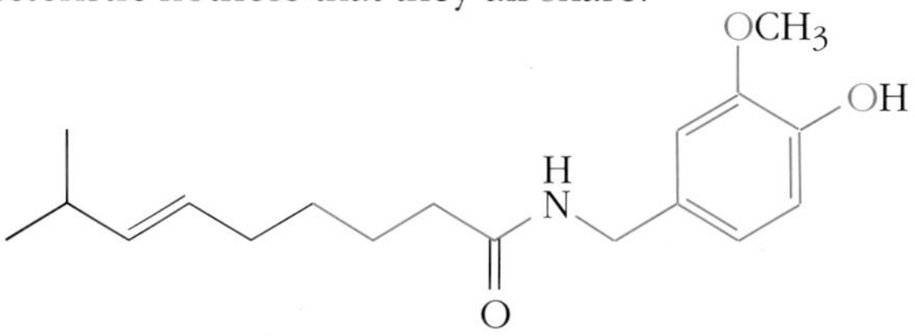

capsaicin (chilli)

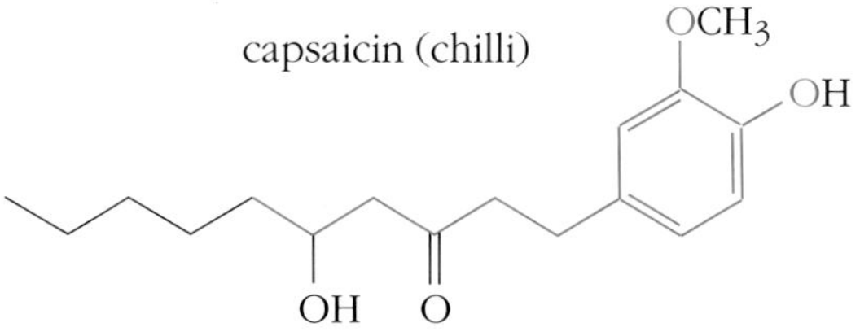

gingerol (ginger)

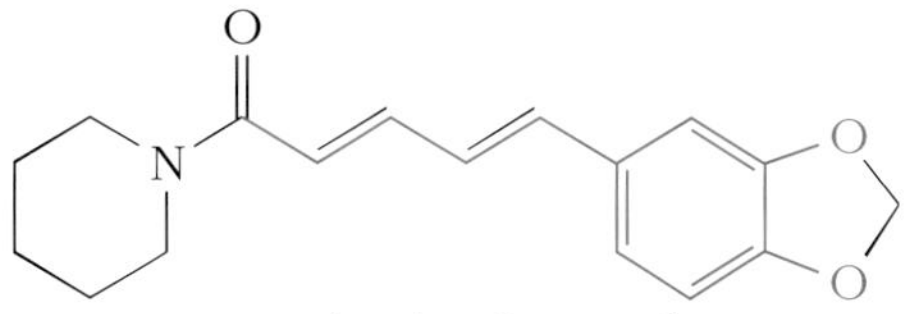

piperine (pepper)

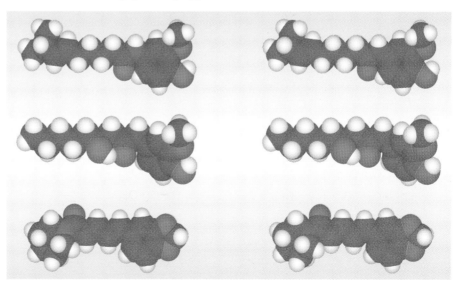

Question 18 The two compounds shown below have been recognized as the pungent principles of cabbage and watercress . Can you identify the common structural features of these molecules?

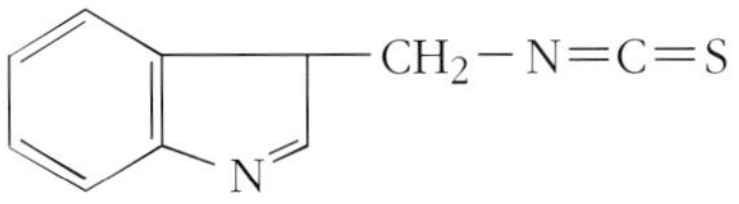

$$CH_2 - N = C = S$$

from cabbage

$$CH_2CH_2 - N = C = S$$

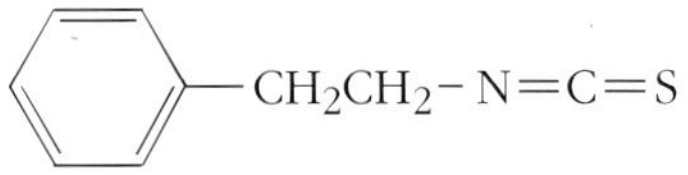

from watercress

Question 19 From the discussion in this Section, collect evidence supporting the hypothesis that the sensation of taste results from the interaction of a molecule with a receptor.

9.2 The sense of smell

A person with reliable colour vision has no difficulty distinguishing orange from yellow; similarly, a person with a good sense of smell can easily distinguish the scent of orange and of pineapple. It is curious to note that although there is a well-developed and quantitative theory to explain the different colours that our eyes see (and for that matter, the different sounds that our ears hear), surprisingly little is known about how and why substances smell as they do. There is no yardstick, corresponding to wavelength or intensity, frequency or loudness, to measure the nature or the strength of an odour. Nor is there a fully accepted theory to explain the amazing sensitivity and discriminatory power of the nose. Humans have a relatively poorly developed sense of smell compared with many other animals, especially insects. Nevertheless, most people would have no difficulty in detecting and accurately identifying some odours in quantities that would be at the detection limits of even the most sensitive of modern laboratory instruments.

Even describing the odour of a single chemical compound is difficult. The best that can be done is to make comparisons with familiar recognizable smells – earthy, fruity, floral, medicinal – always remembering that these in themselves may arise from a mixture of chemical compounds. Literally thousands of substances have characteristic fragrances. At Versailles in France, there is even a museum of smells – the *Osmothèque*. Finding a satisfactory method of classifying them has long provided a challenge.

Perfumers think of a complete perfume as a balanced sequence of 'notes'. This is shown in its extreme form in Piesse's 'gamut of odours' (Figure 9.2). He argued that:

> *If a perfumer desires to make a bouquet from primitive odours, he must take such odours as chord together; the perfume will then be harmonious.*

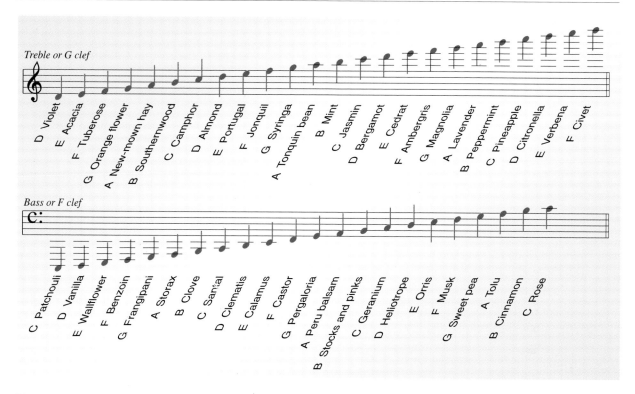

Figure 9.2
Piesse's 'gamut of odours'.

A less fanciful classification divides fragrances into top, middle and end (or basic) notes (Table 9.1). It is taken from the list of the doyen of British perfumery, W. A. Poucher, who spent four years assessing the principal odours of nearly 350 natural and synthetic perfume components.

Table 9.1 Some common chemicals used in perfumery.

Note	Source	Chemical, plus boiling temperature (or melting temperature in parentheses)
Top	galbanum (leafy, green)	undecanal (green) 117 °C
	lemongrass	citral (geranial 118–9 °C; neral 120 °C)
	citrus oils	limonene 178 °C
	peppermint	menthol (cool/minty) (43 °C)
	coriander	linalool 198 °C
	lavender	linalyl acetate 220 °C
	spearmint	carvone 230 °C
Middle	rose	nerol (rosy, orange blossom) 224–5 °C
		geraniol (floral) 230 °C
	lily	citronellol (rosy) 244 °C
	violet	butylcyclohexyl acetate (floral, woody) 232 °C
	jasmine	*cis*-jasmone, methyl dihydrojasmonate 118–9 °C
End	vanilla	vanillin (82–83 °C)
	musk	butyl nitrobenzenes (musk xylene) (114 °C)
	vetiver	vetivone (51 °C)

The critical feature seems to be volatility. The 'top notes' are the most volatile, and they are the immediately noticeable citrus and herb-like scents. The main effect of a perfume depends on the floral-scented 'middle notes', with the less volatile woody, musky 'end notes' providing a long-lasting base, which evaporates only slowly. Some of the molecular structures of perfume constituents listed in Table 9.1 are shown in Figure 9.3.

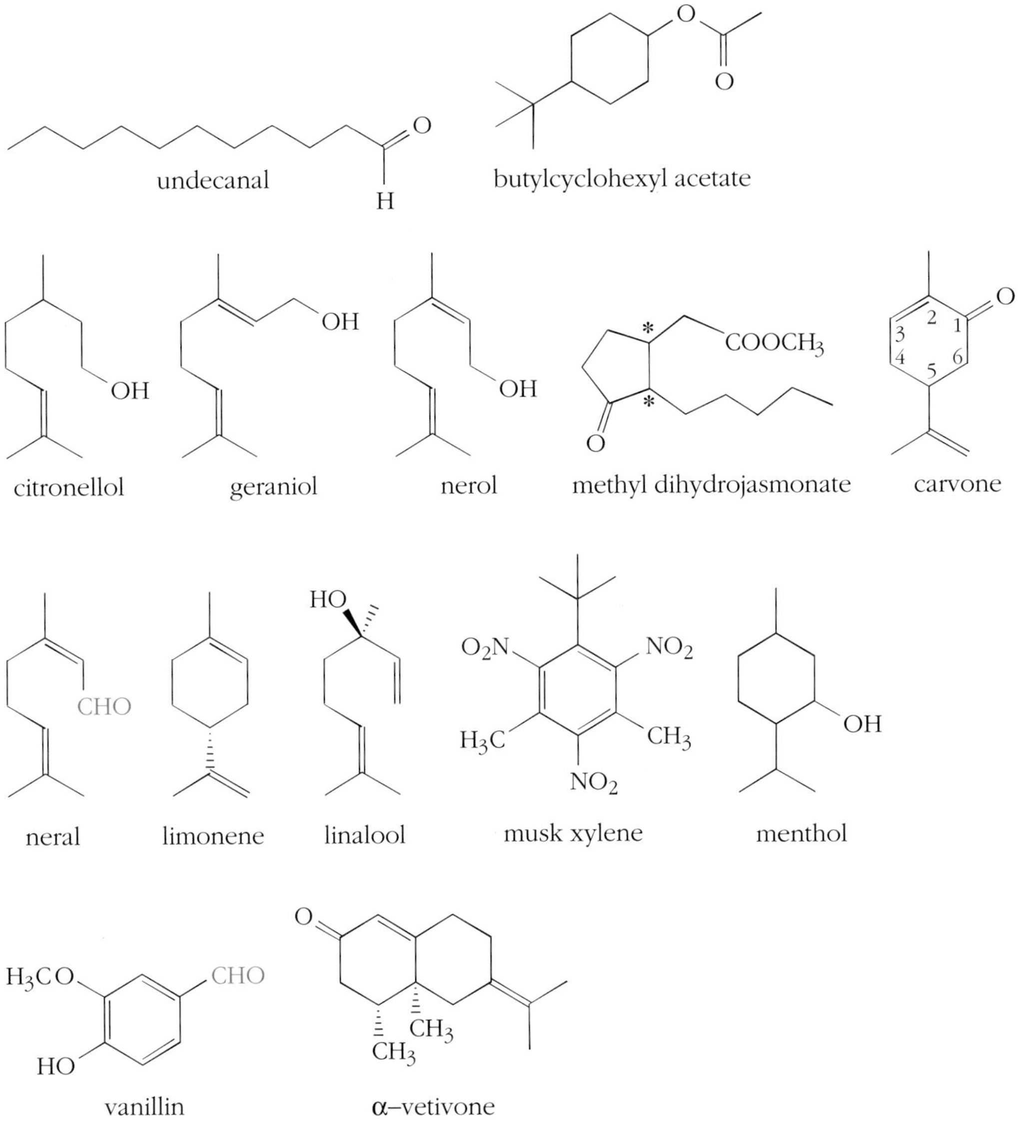

Figure 9.3
Molecular structures of some naturally occurring perfume constituents, and a synthetic musk. Butylcyclohexyl acetate and menthol both have **cyclohexane** rings as part of their structure. Note that this structure is not the same as the benzene ring that has been part of many of the dye molecules you encountered earlier in this part of Book 4. The numerical labelling of the carbon atoms in carvone relates to a discussion later in the text; similarly, the asterisks on the methyl dihydrojasmonate structure.

Box 9.1 Carbonyl groups – aldehydes

Neral and vanillin in Figure 9.3 contain a functional group that is new to you in this Book. This is the **aldehyde** group, abbreviated in structural diagrams to —CHO, but in its expanded form it is seen to be a carbonyl group flanked at one side (at least) by a hydrogen atom. The systematic names of molecules containing the aldehyde group have the suffix '**-al**'. Aldehydes, like ketones, esters and amides, can act as the receiving end of a hydrogen bond.

■ Why must an aldehyde group always be found at the end of a carbon chain, as in undecanal (Figure 9.3)?

■ Because one of the atoms attached to the carbonyl group is hydrogen, which can form only one bond, this effectively terminates a chain.

The aldehyde group occurs in molecules that are perfume constituents because it frequently contributes a sharpness, or pungency, to a fragrance. The aldehydes most commonly encountered in the home are probably acrolein, $CH_2{=}CH{-}CHO$, which has the characteristic smell of burnt fat on an overcooked joint of meat, and vanillin, which is a constituent of all food flavoured by vanilla (or vanilla essence).

■ Looking at the structures in Figure 9.3, which functional groups can you pick out?

■ As well as many carbon–carbon double bonds, you should have identified an aldehyde function in undecanal, vanillin and neral; the alcohol group in all the structures that end in '-ol' – nerol, menthol, geraniol, citronellol, linalool; the ester group in butylcyclohexyl acetate; ester and ketone in methyl dihydrojasmonate; and ketones in vetivone and carvone.

Question 20 The volatility of a compound is determined largely by its molecular mass (compounds of higher molecular mass tend to be less volatile) and by its ability to form hydrogen bonds (compounds that readily form hydrogen bonds tend to be less volatile). Use this information to account for the following observations:

(a) Aldehydes such as undecanal are useful as 'top notes' in perfumes, whereas alcohols such as geraniol are employed as 'middle notes'.

(b) 'End notes' like musk also help to 'fix' or retain the more volatile components of a perfume.

Question 21 In Book 2, you discovered that the polymers rubber and gutta percha were made up from the monomer unit from isoprene, C_5H_8. The C_5 carbon framework, neglecting the double bonds, is referred to as the **isoprene unit**. A great many perfume constituents are also made up from this same structural unit. Identify some of them in Figure 9.3. An example is shown for citronellol.

isoprene   isoprene unit   citronellol divided into isoprene units

These perfumers' classifications do little to encourage generalization. Some molecules with similar chemical structures have quite different smells, whereas other molecules with no obvious structural similarity have smells that are comparable. Nerol and geraniol (Figure 9.3) are *cis-* and *trans-*isomers, respectively; they only differ in the direction that the terminal —CH₂OH group points away from the double bond. Both have rose-like odours, but geraniol has a flowery fragrance and nerol a distinct overtone of freshly cut grass. The most surprising observation of all is that some pairs of molecules that are simply mirror images (stereoisomers) of each other have totally distinctive odours. One of the stereoisomers of carvone (Figure 9.3) smells of spearmint, but its mirror-image molecule smells of caraway.

- Recall why it is that carvone can exist in these two different (stereoisomeric) forms.

- Carvone can exist as object and mirror-image forms because it is chiral.

- Can you pick out the chiral centre in the carvone structure?

- It is the one numbered '5', in the structure shown in Figure 9.3.

Note that carbon atom '5' has four different groups attached to it. This is more clearly seen in the partial structure in the margin. Remember that if any carbon atom in a structural 'framework' has fewer than *four* bonds attached, we assume that the bonds not shown are bonds to hydrogen. A more detailed explanation of dealing with chirality in cyclic structures is given in Box 9.2 (opposite).

partial structure

The two carvone molecules have **(+) and (−) labels** to distinguish them. They are drawn below (Figure 9.5), showing the two different arrangements of the groups at the chiral centre.

(−)-carvone: spearmint   (+)-carvone: caraway

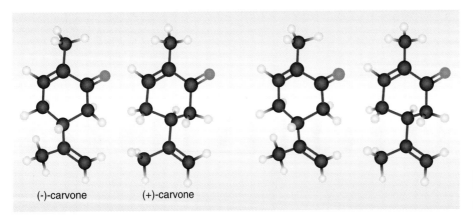

(-)-carvone   (+)-carvone

Figure 9.5
The two carvone stereoisomers.

■ From what you have read earlier in Book 3, can you recall what effect having a different arrangement of functional groups might have on the interaction between a molecule and a receptor?

■ Although the two molecules have a very similar shape, the arrangement of the functional groups will almost certainly result in *only one* of these molecules fitting into a specific receptor.

Box 9.2 Recognizing chirality in cyclic molecules

(a)    (b)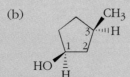

By looking at the two five-membered ring compounds (**cyclopentanes**) (a) and (b), it is possible to say that (b) is chiral but (a) is not. Recall that, using the convention introduced in Book 3, a solid wedge represents a group sticking up above the plane of the paper (i.e. *above* the ring) and a broken wedge represents a group down below the plane of the paper (i.e. *below* the ring). The rule used to determine whether a carbon centre in a ring system is chiral or not, is the same one we have used previously – it is chiral if it has four different groups attached. The skill lies in deciding if this is so.

In structure (a), two of the groups on the ring carbon atom labelled '1' (usually referred to as C-1) are clearly different, i.e. methyl (CH_3) and hydrogen (H). What about the other two?

□ Go round the ring clockwise and write down the formula for each carbon atom you pass until you get back to C-1. Remember that each angle with no other group attached represents a $-CH_2-$ group.

■ Carbon atoms C-2, C-3, C-4 and C-5 should give you the formula $-CH_2-CH_2-CH_2-CH_2-$. This is therefore one of the 'groups' attached to C-1.

□ Now go round the ring once more, but this time anticlockwise and note the formula of the other 'group' attached to C-1.

■ Carbon atoms C-5, C-4, C-3 and C-2 again give the formula $-CH_2-CH_2-CH_2-CH_2-$ identical with that obtained previously.

As these two groups are the same, C-1 cannot be a chiral centre.

Now look at structure (b). Once again the two groups methyl (CH_3) and hydrogen (H) on C-3 are clearly different.

□ What are the formulas of the other two 'groups' attached that you get by going clockwise and anticlockwise round the ring back to C-3?

■ Going clockwise the 'group' is $-CH_2-CHOH-CH_2-CH_2-$, but going anticlockwise it is $-CH_2-CH_2-CHOH-CH_2-$. These are definitely different 'groups' because you need to pass two $-CH_2-$ groups going anticlockwise before you reach the carbon atom with the hydroxyl group attached, but in the reverse direction you pass only one.

If you carry out the same procedure from C-1, you will discover that C-1 is also a chiral centre. The molecule represented by structure (b) is therefore chiral and can exist as the two mirror-image isomers shown in Figure 9.4.

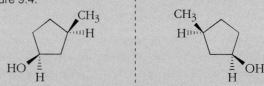

Figure 9.4
The two mirror-image isomers of structure (b).

Question 22 Which of the cyclic molecules below have chiral centres? Locate them on the structural diagrams (a) and (b).

(a) [structure with O, CH₃, H]   (b) [structure with CH₃, CH₃, HO, H]

Activity 5 The isomers of methyl dihydrojasmonate

In this Activity, we are going to examine the question: 'How many isomers exist having the structural formula of methyl dihydrojasmonate (Figure 9.3)?' Note before we begin that methyl dihydrojasmonate has *two* chiral centres, marked with asterisks in Figure 9.3. We shall use the model kit to help us reach the answer.

First, make up *two* models of the five-membered carbon ring. Insert the carbonyl group using two flexible bonds, but there is no need to put hydrogen atoms on the ring. Then choose *two* differently coloured balls to represent the two attached side chains; e.g. red for the hydrocarbon chain —C_5H_{11} and blue for the ester chain —CH_2COOCH_3.

Fix a red ball to the *top side* of both rings on the black centre next to the carbonyl group moving clockwise (Figure 9.6).

■ How many ways can a blue ball now be attached to the next carbon centre round the ring?

■ You will have found that there are two ways; the ball can be attached to the top side (label this as structure I) or the bottom side (label this as structure II) of the five-carbon ring.

Figure 9.6
Model at the start of Activity 5.

Before going any further, draw representations of these two possibilities (I and II) on the first two unsubstituted rings in Figure 9.7, using R for the red ball and B for the blue ball. Use the wedge notation as in Box 9.2. Now make two more models of the 'blank' ring and put the blue ball in its correct location on the top side of both rings. There are again two possible ways to fit the red ball. Compare the two new models with the previous two. (Don't complete any more blank rings in Figure 9.7 yet.)

■ How many *new* compounds have you modelled?

■ Only one; the model with the red and blue

balls on the same side is identical with one of the first pair, the one you labelled I.

Give the label III to the model with red and blue balls on opposite sides of the ring.

■ What is the relationship between models II and III?

■ They are mirror images. You may have to turn the model III over and place it alongside II to appreciate this.

Using the first broken line in Figure 9.7 as a mirror plane, draw a representation of III on the next blank ring. Now see if you can discover any other possible structures. Again take a systematic approach and start with the red ball underneath the ring. Fit the blue ball in its two possible positions. Then with the blue ball under the ring fit the red ball into its two positions. Compare your four new models with your diagrams I, II and III.

■ Do you have any new model structures?

Figure 9.7
Blank rings for use in Activity 5.

■ Two of the models match with II and III, but the other two are identical and are *not* the same as I.

Label the new model IV and draw its representation in the next blank ring in Figure 9.7. Then using the second broken line as a mirror plane draw a mirror image of IV on the next blank ring. Make up this model.

■ What structure does it represent?

■ By turning it upside down, you will see it is identical with I. So label your last drawing I (as well as your first drawing).

A completed version of Figure 9.7 is given in the Comment on Activity 5.

As we approached the analysis systematically, we can be sure we have now exhausted all the possibilities. We are left with the conclusion that there are *four* possible isomers of methyl dihydrojasmonate. We have also shown that they constitute *two* mirror-image pairs.

The conclusion from Activity 5 is a very important result. As we have already seen, a molecule with 1 chiral centre gives two possible isomers; with two chiral centres, $2 \times 2 = 4$ isomers are possible – two pairs of mirror images. Each time the number of chiral centres increases by *one*, we have to multiply the previous total of isomers by *two*. So there are $2 \times 2 \times 2 = 8$ stereoisomers for a molecule with three chiral centres; $2 \times 2 \times 2 \times 2 = 16$ for a molecule with four; and so on … .

Box 9.3 The electrochemical NOSE

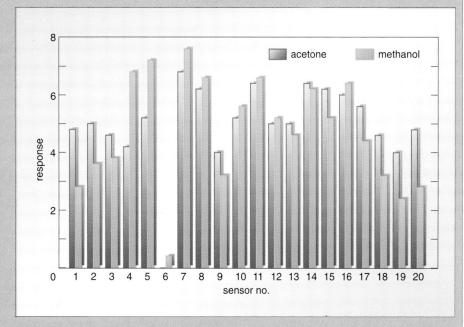

A trained human nose may be able to distinguish 100 000 odours, but it does have its limitations, particularly in recognizing individual components in a mixture. If an instrument could be designed capable of the accurate analysis of smells, it would have widespread application, and not just in the perfume, food and drink industries. The detection of gas leaks or the combustion products as early warning of fire are two obvious examples, but medical diagnosis and environmental monitoring are other exciting possibilities. For nearly 40 years, scientists have been tackling this challenge.

One ingenious device was made by coating an oscillating quartz crystal, like those used in watches, with antibodies. When exposed to a chemical that evoked a response in the antibody, the crystal oscillations were upset. This sensor was both sensitive and discriminating, being able for example to detect minute quantities of the pesticide parathion, but showing no reaction to the related insecticide malathion.

A breakthrough came in 1979 with the discovery of electrically conducting polymers which changed their conductivity when exposed to gaseous ammonia. Conductivity rapidly drops to normal when the gas is turned off. On making small structural changes in the polymer, a change in the sensitivity of the polymer to ammonia was observed; but even more significantly, with different volatile polar chemicals, each polymer showed a different response. An array of sensors based on these polymers, each a few micrometres thick and less than 1 mm square, could therefore give a 'fingerprint' (or rather a 'noseprint') of a particular compound (Figure 9.8). *(continued overleaf)*

Figure 9.8
Patterns produced by an array of conducting polymer sensors in response to acetone (propanone) and methanol.

Figure 9.9
George Dodd with the NOSE.

Based on this system, George Dodd (Figure 9.9) and the Neotronics Company have developed the *Neotronics Olfactory Sensory Equipment* (NOSE). This device, about as big as a television remote controller, contains just 12 sensors linked to a computer that processes their responses, like the brain processes the response from the thousands of sensors in the nose.

The NOSE can be standardized on a particular odour and then used to distinguish it from others that are similar. Figure 9.10 shows the response of the 'bouquet' of a white wine in comparison with champagne.

Figure 9.10
Response of the sensors of the NOSE (set up on champagne) to a white wine. Spikes outside the circle indicate a stronger response to white wine than champagne, and spikes inside the circle indicate a weaker response.

The Bass Brewery is also using this technology to check the aroma above fermenting beer for the molecule diacetyl, which gives beer an unpleasant buttery taste. Picking up this indication early could save a whole batch of nearly 350 000 pints from going to waste!

diacetyl

Before long, it may be possible to make early diagnosis of diseases like lung cancer this way, by comparing the breath of a sufferer with that of a healthy person.

9.3 Towards an explanation of the olfactory mechanism

Any theory to explain the sense of smell must first account for its high degree of sensitivity. Experiments in which highly sensitive microelectrodes are placed at the base and the tip of the antenna of a moth have shown that the impact of a *single* stimulating molecule on the antenna is sufficient to trigger an electrical response. Secondly, the theory must explain how the nose can handle such an enormous range of different scents, possibly as extensive as the range of colours perceived by our eyes.

The simple basis of the currently preferred theory was first postulated by the Roman poet Lucretius about 2 000 years ago. He speculated that inside the nose were minute pores of different sizes and shapes (we should now describe them as receptors). Every odoriferous substance gave off tiny but distinctive particles (molecules), and the odour was perceived when these particles entered the pores. Every particle that fitted a pore would give rise to a corresponding identifiable smell.

Lucretius' proposal seems to have been essentially correct. The **olfactory area** in the nose is a small region of the inner lining of the nasal cavity, only about 2 cm² in extent, and covered with approximately 5 million receptors (Figure 9.11). Humans have far fewer of these receptors than other mammals, which explains why our sense of smell is inferior to theirs.

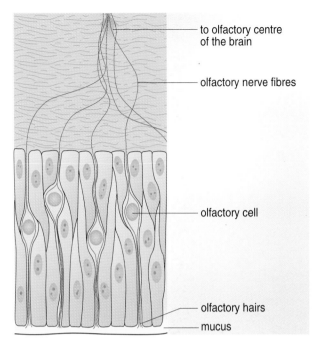

to olfactory centre
of the brain

olfactory nerve fibres

olfactory cell

olfactory hairs

mucus

Figure 9.11
Cross-section of the nasal
membrane.

In order to be detected in this system, a substance must obviously be volatile at normal temperatures. It must also be soluble both in water and non-aqueous liquids, even if only slightly, to penetrate first the watery film that covers the nasal cavity lining, and then the fatty layer that forms part of the surface membrane of the nerve cells, where the receptors are located. Nevertheless, interaction between a fragrance molecule and a receptor must be fairly weak, to account for the lack of persistence of the response unless a continuous supply of fragrance molecules is available.

In 1949, a Scottish chemist, R. W. Moncrieff, suggested that there might be only a few different types of receptor sites, each corresponding to a distinct **primary odour**; a 'lock and key' hypothesis. This proposal raises two fundamental questions: 'What are the primary odours?' and 'What are the shapes of the corresponding receptors?'.

An American chemist, John Amoore, tried to answer these questions by examining the structures of about 600 organic chemicals noted in the literature as having distinctive odours. He argued that a commonly noted smell was more likely to be 'primary' than one which occurred infrequently. For example, over 100 compounds were described as having a camphor-like odour, in comparison with only five or six with the smell of cedarwood. From his analysis, he selected *seven* primaries: camphor, musk, floral, peppermint, ether-like, pungent and putrid (Table 9.2).

Table 9.2 Primary odours.

Primary odour	Chemical example	Familiar substance
camphoraceous	camphor	mothballs
musky	angelica lactone	angelica root oil
floral	geraniol	roses
pepperminty	menthone	Kendal mint cake
ethereal	dichloroethene	dry-cleaning fluid
pungent	acetic acid	vinegar
putrid	hydrogen sulfide	bad eggs

To make his theory complete, Amoore also postulated that every other known smell could be made by mixing these seven primaries in the correct proportions. In this respect, the primary odours would be like the three primary colours of red, green and blue; or the four primary tastes of sweet, sour, salt and bitter.

If there are seven primary odours, there must be seven matching kinds of receptor. Working back from molecular models, it should then be possible to assign a distinctive size and shape to each receptor. When this was tried, all his camphoraceous molecules were roughly egg-shaped, with long and short

diameters of about 0.9 and 0.75 nm (Figure 9.12). It followed that the
receptor must have the shape of an oval bowl, about 0.4 nm deep. Many
camphoraceous molecules are rigid spheroids that inevitably fit into such a
bowl; others are slightly flexible and could easily shape themselves into it.

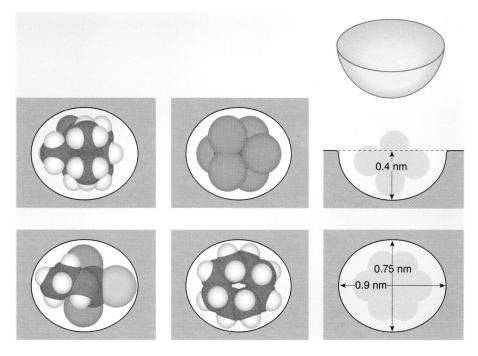

Figure 9.12
The camphoraceous
receptor, and some
molecules that fit.

Four of the remaining primary odours yielded to this approach (Figure
9.13). Only the pungent and putrid odours showed no common structural
pattern. For these, an alternative hypothesis would need to be proposed.

Figure 9.13
The shapes of other primary
odour molecule receptor
sites (after Amoore).

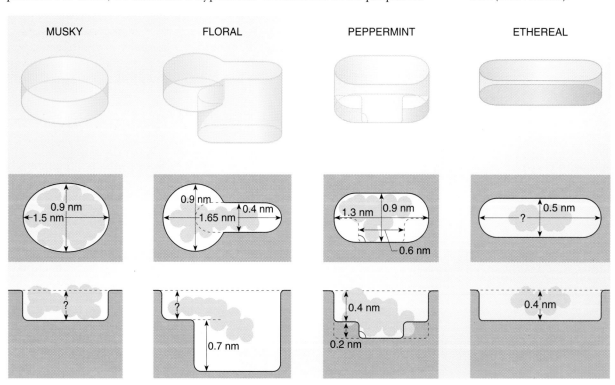

Question 23 Explain why the molecules pentylpyridine and diethyl ether (Figure 9.14) might be expected to fit, respectively, into the floral and ethereal receptors. You may find it helpful to make models of these two molecules.

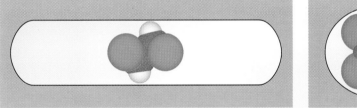

pentylpyridine   diethyl ether

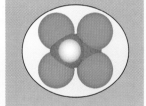

Figure 9.14
Pentylpyridine and diethyl ether.

If the receptor site has a shape and size corresponding to those of the primary odour molecule, the shapes of some molecules might allow them to fit into more than one receptor, although almost certainly to different extents. A more complex odour should then result, corresponding to the proportionate filling of the different sites (Figure 9.15).

Figure 9.15
The same molecule (tetrachloroethane, $CHCl_2-CHCl_2$) in different receptors.

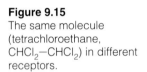

A second test was more challenging. Could a complex scent be synthesized by mixing primaries in the correct proportions? All chemicals yielding a cedarwood fragrance were found to have molecular shapes able to fit camphor, musk, peppermint and floral receptors. Amoore selected four definitive chemicals with these odours, and set out to make cedarwood. After 86 attempts with different blends, he managed to produce an odour indistinguishable from natural cedar oil to a panel of trained observers. A different blend of the same four primary odours reproduced the scent of sandalwood oil!

Amoore's was not the only set of primary receptors to be postulated. Another set is shown in Figure 9.16 (overleaf). Note that the number has increased as has the complexity of their shapes, but the basic principle remains the same.

Current research indicates that the dream of a simple unifying theory is not likely to be realized. Just as some people are partially colour blind, the phenomenon of partial odour blindness (called **anosmia**) is not uncommon. About 30 different types of anosmia have been identified, suggesting that there are at least 30 different types of receptor. Accumulating evidence has pushed this number up to 100 or more, and so research has moved on to investigate receptors for individual fragrances. A powerful new tool in this work is molecular modelling using a computer, as we shall see later in Part 2 of this Book.

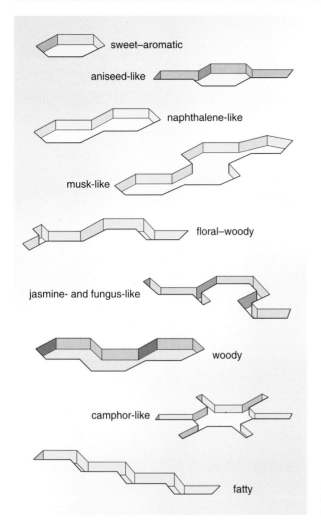

sweet–aromatic

aniseed-like

naphthalene-like

musk-like

floral–woody

jasmine- and fungus-like

woody

camphor-like

fatty

Figure 9.16
Another proposed set of
odour receptors.

Question 24 Benzaldehyde and methylbenzaldehyde both possess a
strong almond flavour, but isopropylbenzaldehyde does not. Use this
observation to speculate on the possible shape of an 'almond' receptor.

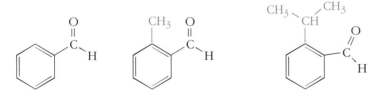

benzaldehyde   methylbenzaldehyde   isopropylbenzaldehyde

Activity 6 The sandalwood fragrance

Many compounds displaying the fragrance of sandalwood have been shown to require an —OH group on the first carbon, and a bulky group attached to a carbon atom six atoms away. *Convince yourself that compounds with the structure shown below follow that rule.*

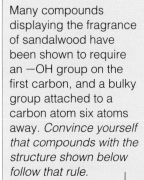

sandalwood trial molecule

The structure must also be able to lie flat, with the —OH group pointing down, to fit the proposed receptor (Figure 9.17). Look at the stereopictures of the four isomers shown (Figure 9.18), and decide which is the one most likely to have the strongest sandalwood note.

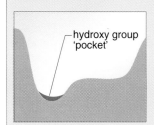

Figure 9.17
Cross-section of proposed sandalwood receptor.

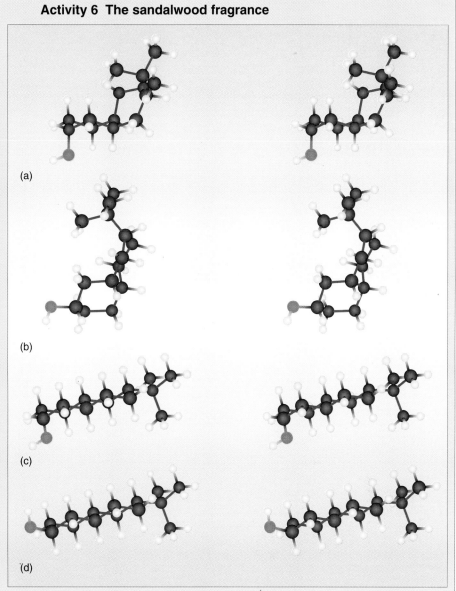

(a)

(b)

(c)

(d)

Figure 9.18
Models of molecules with possible sandalwood fragrance, on a slightly larger scale than Figure 9.17.

As can be seen, the stereochemical theory of odour is still far from complete. As a result, rival theories are not quite eliminated from the field. Principal among these is the idea that particular low frequency vibrations, generated by bending or stretching bonds within a molecule, are picked up by the receptors. It is certainly true that many perfume molecules absorb (and therefore *emit*) radiation in this part of the infrared spectrum. However, this theory runs into difficulties with mirror-image compounds that have different fragrances, because their absorption and emission of infrared radiation should be identical.

The most startling claims for this theory were made by a physicist, P. S. Callahan. Following up the observation by the distinguished entomologist, Henri Fabre, that a candle flame powerfully distracted male moths from mating, Callahan proposed that a strong molecular vibration in the sex attractant of the moth had the same wavelength as the infrared radiation (i.e. the radiant *heat*) coming from the candle flame. Attracted to the flame by the impact of this radiation on their receptors, the moths perish in a vain attempt to mate with the candle!

Summary of Chapter 9

In Chapter 9, you have seen how the sense of taste depends on the stimulation both of tastebuds in the mouth and olfactory receptors in the nasal cavity. There are four basic tastes – salt, sour, bitter, sweet – activated at different regions of the tongue; and some other taste sensations – metallic, pungent, astringent and meaty (umami) – less definitely located. A sour taste is linked to the presence of the carboxylic acid group in food molecules; the only other structure–taste correlation is with sweetness (Book 3).

A description of smells relies on familiar comparisons, and classification uses musical analogies. The chief determinant of top, middle and end notes is volatility. A specific odour response depends on the interaction of molecules of a volatile compound with a receptor. Matching geometry between molecule and receptor seems to be critical.

A molecule with two chiral centres gives rise to 2×2 stereoisomers; if there are three chiral centres, the number of stereoisomers is $2 \times 2 \times 2 = 8$.

Chapter 10
The perfume industry

Figure 10.1
The perfume counter.

The highest recommendation of a perfume is that when a female passes by, the fragrance which proceeds from her may possibly attract the attention of those even who till then are intent upon something else.
Pliny (d. 79 AD)

The perfume industry is a thriving modern enterprise, which in economic terms has more than doubled its worldwide cash turnover each decade since the 1960s. The natural response to the word 'perfume' is to conjure up an exotic liquid in a bottle of extravagant design (Figure 10.1).

The labour-intensive traditional processes used in obtaining the natural constituents have ensured that perfume like this has remained a luxury item (Figure 10.2).

Until the end of the 19th century, most European perfume strongly resembled natural floral fragrances. Only later did the idea arise of combining floral notes with fragrance ingredients from other categories to produce the fantasy perfumes of the 20th century. There was a particularly creative period up until about 1930, which saw the birth of such still-available perfumes as Shalimar (Guerlain), Chypre (Coty), and the worldwide, and all-time, best seller, Chanel No. 5, now (1995) almost 75 years old (Figure 10.3).

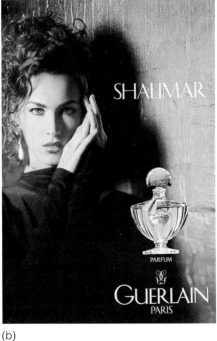

Figure 10.2
Jasmine flowers being picked near Grasse in Provence.

(a)

(b)

Figure 10.3
Advertisements from (a) *Vogue, c.* 1940 and (b) *Elle* 1994.

Today, the industry is much more concerned with providing perfume in large quantities for a wide range of everyday products. The range of toiletries and household products has increased dramatically and the demand for perfume ingredients is far in excess of the ability of traditional methods to supply the need. A higher specification is also required of fragrant materials that now need to show stability in a wider variety of environments and an absence of discoloration and dermatitic properties.

This is where chemistry comes to the aid of the manufacturer. Modern instrumental techniques can isolate and identify the chemical components of natural perfume materials; and modern synthetic methods can reproduce the chemicals of nature from scratch, or convert commonly available materials into more valuable perfume ingredients.

As a result, almost every toiletry and household cleaning and disinfecting product is scented, either to add interest to a normally odourless material or to mask a less acceptable natural smell. For example, not many people appreciate that unscented soap has quite an unattractive smell. Indeed, a pleasant and distinctive smell is recognized as a powerful promotional feature for many of these goods. So, although classical perfumes are still extravagantly expensive, sweet-smelling products have now become available for everyday use.

Box 10.1 Perfume in history

The earliest evidence for the use of perfumes and incense comes from Egyptian inscriptions and funerary objects dating back as far as 3500 BC. Perfume from the beautiful alabaster unguent (ointment) jars (Figure 10.4) found by Howard Carter in the tomb of Tutankhamen (1350 BC) was still 'elusively fragrant', and on analysis was found to consist mainly of animal fat mixed with some resins and balsam.

Incense had a practical as well as religious significance in that it masked the less pleasant smells associated with ritual sacrifice. The earliest

Figure 10.4
Unguent jar from the tomb of Tutankhamen.

Biblical record of spices and perfumes (*Genesis* 37: 25) suggests that the Israelites could have learned their perfumery from Egypt. Thereafter, there are numerous references to aromatic substances, of which the most familiar are myrrh and frankincense.

'Arabia' was an early production centre for perfumes, even supplying ancient Egypt, so it is not surprising to find references in the Koran. Musk was one of their most esteemed perfumes (*Sura*, 83). Shakespeare reminds us of the importance of the 'Arabian connection' when Lady Macbeth complains: 'All the perfumes of Arabia will not sweeten this little hand' (*Macbeth*, Act 5, Scene 1).

In the 10th century AD, Avicenna – an Arabian doctor – was the first person known to try to extract perfumes by distillation. He produced the first samples of otto (or attar) of roses, later to become an item of international trade. It was probably brought into Europe by the returning Crusaders.

The Greek, Theophrastus, in the 4th century BC, described perfumers' techniques in detail, including the extraction of perfumes from plant material with solvents, the use of fixatives and the need for low-temperature processing to avoid the loss of volatile substances.

Figure 10.5
Lavender growing in Provence.

Figure 10.6
Harvesting lavender in Norfolk.

Figure 10.7
Jasmine blossom.

10.1   Natural perfumes

The natural ingredients of perfumes have both plant and animal origins. The town of Grasse in Provence (Figures 10.2 and 10.5) became the premier centre of the natural flower perfume industry in the 18th century and, because of its ideal climate, maintained its position until recent times. Growing, harvesting and processing the plant material to produce the **essential oils** is very labour-intensive, and much of this activity now takes place in developing countries, superseding traditional European centres in France, Italy and Bulgaria. Only by extensive mechanization (and some astute marketing) has the Norfolk lavender industry survived in the UK (Figure 10.6). Interestingly, English lavender yields an essential oil with a different bouquet and composition from the lavender of Provence.

One of the major products of Grasse is jasmine; there are 6–8 million hand-picked flowers in a tonne of jasmine blossom (Figure 10.7).

After extraction with petroleum ether (a hydrocarbon solvent from the distillation of crude oil, boiling over the range 60–80 °C) and evaporating the solvent, only 2.7 kg of a waxy solid (jasmine **concrete**) is obtained. Treatment with warm alcohol then dissolves out 1.4 kg of jasmine oil (or **absolute**), leaving the wax behind. It is not surprising that each kilogram is valued at up to £5000 (in 1995).

■ Look back at the structures of perfume molecules in Figure 9.4. Why do you think they will be extracted into a solvent like petroleum ether, which is mainly the saturated hydrocarbon heptane, C_7H_{16}.

■ The molecules show a variety of functional groups – aldehyde, ketone, ester – often in large complex hydrocarbon skeletons; only occasionally is a single alcohol group present. These molecules will therefore not be very polar, and, using the 'like dissolves like' rule, they should dissolve in the non-polar hydrocarbon solvent.

The traditional extracting 'solvent' for jasmine flowers is animal fat, a process called *enfleurage*. The spent blossoms are replaced with fresh blossoms every 24 hours. The reason for this time delay is that the perfume molecules are only gradually generated from a more complex chemical substance produced by the plant. Even after the flowers are picked, enzymes continue to break down this precursor, generating more of the fragrant oil.

In recent years, extraction has been carried out with liquefied butane gas (the liquid in camping gas cylinders!) in pressurized equipment. The products, called *Butaflors*, retain the full freshness of the flower perfume in all its delicacy. Liquid carbon dioxide, sometimes used in decaffeinating coffee beans too, has also been tried.

◻ What do you think might be among the disadvantages, and advantages, of using liquefied butane gas as an extracting solvent?

◼ Liquid butane is both very volatile and very flammable. All the equipment used must be able to withstand pressure, and every precaution must be taken against accidental leakage that could result in fire or explosion. However, because it will evaporate at low temperature, rather than needing to be distilled, delicate fragrance components will not decompose through heating.

◻ How might some of these problems be overcome if liquid carbon dioxide is used instead?

◼ Liquid carbon dioxide is non-flammable, and need not be recycled, as it can be allowed to evaporate into the atmosphere.

Otto of roses is even more valuable than jasmine absolute. To produce one kilogram of this essential oil, with a value of about £10 000, approximately 200 million rose petals must first be boiled up in water. The vapour that distils is condensed to give a layer of rose oil floating on rose water. This is another example of the process of **steam distillation** that, as you may recall from Book 3, was used for the purification of carbolic oil (Figure 10.8). Some water-soluble chemicals may also be extracted from the rose water, but even when this extract is added to the insoluble oil the total yield represents only 0.03% by mass of the starting material.

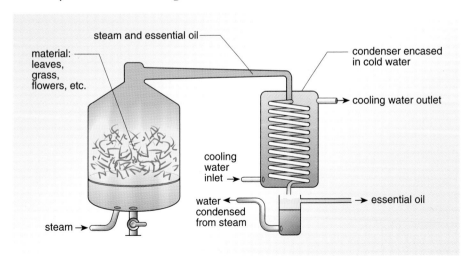

Figure 10.8
The process of steam distillation. As steam passes through the plant material, a mixed vapour of essential oil and steam is driven into the coiled condenser. The vapour condenses to liquid which separates into two layers. The lower water layer is recycled to the steam generator, and the essential oil is tapped off the top.

(a)

(b)

Figure 10.9
(a) Civet cat. (b) Musk ox.

Question 25 The yield of mimosa concrete from mimosa blossoms is 0.30–0.55% by mass, and of mimosa absolute from mimosa concrete is 40–50% by mass. Starting with 1 tonne (1 000 kg) of blossom, what is the maximum yield that the perfume manufacturer could hope to extract?

These two methods, solvent extraction and steam distillation, are commonly used to obtain a whole range of chemical mixtures not only from flower petals, but also from the seeds (e.g. bitter almonds), leaves (lavender), bark (cinnamon), fruits (citrus), stems or roots (angelica) of plants. Essential oils of cloves, mimosa, rosemary, patchouli, sandalwood, vetiver and many others, are obtained like this, and are the stock-in-trade of the industry.

Question 26 From which part of the plant would you expect the following perfumes to be extracted: carnation, lime, cedar, rosemary, ginger?

The traditional animal products used in perfumery are obtained from the scent glands of the Ethiopian civet cat (Figure 10.9) (civet), the Himalayan musk deer and musk ox (musk), and the beaver (castor). A secretion of the sperm whale, ambergris, has also been used.

Some of these materials add characteristic odours to a perfume, but their main action is as **fixatives**, slowing down the evaporation of the more volatile components, and maintaining the balance of the perfume for longer. Since the glands beneath the tail of an adult musk deer yield at most 50 g of musk, it is not surprising that these natural products command high prices. The fragrant substances of these secretions are based on unusually large rings of carbon atoms (Figure 10.10).

Figure 10.10
Models of the muscone (a), civetone (b), cyclopentadecanone (c) and cyclohexadecenone (d) molecules.

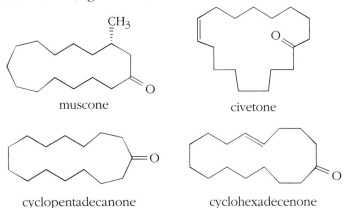

muscone

civetone

cyclopentadecanone

cyclohexadecenone

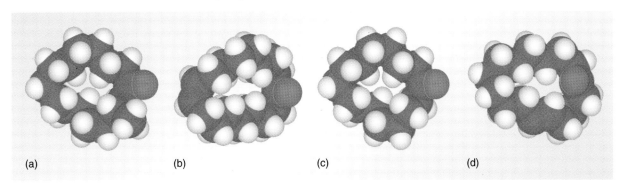

(a) (b) (c) (d)

The two actual chemical compounds of musk and civet (muscone and civetone) are both difficult to make in the laboratory, so the more easily accessible cyclopentadecanone and cyclohexadecenone (with similar characteristics) are produced instead. Today, for sociopolitical and ecological, as well as economic, reasons, these animal products have been almost entirely replaced by their synthetic equivalents.

However, this is not true of the plant extracts. Although the natural oils may have principal components (e.g., citronellol (40–60%), geraniol (Figure 9.3) and 2-phenylethanol ($C_6H_5CH_2CH_2OH$) are the chief ingredients of otto of roses), they are usually such complex mixtures that it is impossible to reproduce their fragrance exactly using only synthetic chemicals. The complexity of jasmine absolute can be shown by gas–liquid chromatography (glc – see Box 10.2 below). Figure 10.11 shows a chart, the **chromatogram**, on which the more than 200 components of jasmine absolute are registered. Each 'spike' on the chromatogram indicates the presence of a separate chemical component in the mixture.

Increasingly, high performance liquid chromatography (hplc) is being used for these analyses. Since hplc is carried out at room temperature, the more delicate components of the mixture that might otherwise decompose on vaporization survive intact.

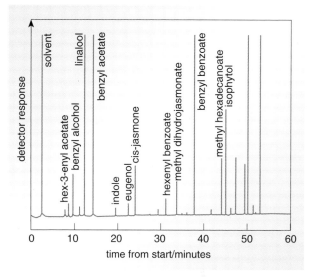

Figure 10.11
Gas–liquid chromatogram of jasmine absolute. Major components, i.e. those giving the tallest 'spikes' that have been identified, are labelled.

Box 10.2 Gas–liquid chromatography and high performance liquid chromatography

If we have a complex mixture, such as might be obtained as a plant extract or clinical sample, it is often important to be able to separate and identify individual components. The best way to do this will probably be to use **chromatography**. This can claim to be a British invention since it was first applied to the separation of chemical mixtures by J. M. Synge. His shared 1952 Nobel Prize for Chemistry was commemorated in 1977 by the issue of a UK postage stamp (Figure 10.12).

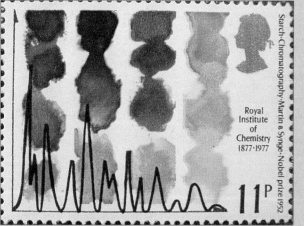

Figure 10.12
Postage stamp commemorating J. M. Synge's award of the Nobel Prize for Chemistry in 1952.

The principles behind chromatography are straightforward. Differences in the chemical structures and functional groups of components of a mixture will determine how strongly the molecules of each compound will interact with their environment. In particular, each component will have a different tendency to be absorbed onto the surface of a solid or to dissolve in a liquid. These often small differences can be exploited in a range of powerful chromatographic techniques.

In **high performance liquid chromatography** (**hplc**), a small sample of a liquid mixture (or a concentrated solution if the sample is solid) is injected into a stream of liquid flowing under pressure through a packed stainless steel column (Figure 10.13). The usual packing is very small (10^{-6} m diameter), uniform, porous silica particles. The molecules of each compound in the mixture are absorbed to a different extent on the surface and in the pores of the silica particles. This means they are held for different times – weakly held molecules passing through quickly, and more strongly held molecules at a slower rate. At the exit from the column, the passage of each component is detected and recorded. The technique of **gas–liquid chromatography** (**glc**) is similar. The mixture is rapidly vaporized and swept in a stream of gas through a long, coiled column, mounted in an oven (Figure 10.14). The column is packed with tiny solid particles each coated with a high boiling liquid – an oil or grease. The fineness of the particles ensures the gas comes into contact with a very large surface area of liquid, resulting in efficient transfer of molecules between the liquid and the gas. Components of the mixture dissolve in the liquid coating to

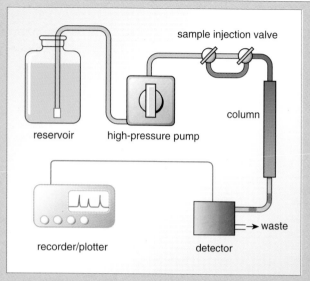

Figure 10.13
Block diagram for hplc equipment.

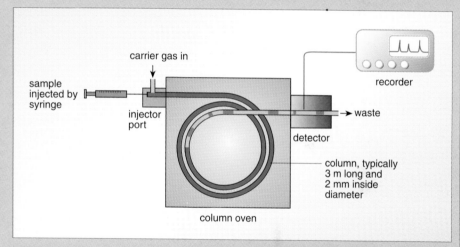

Figure 10.14
Block diagram of glc equipment.

different extents according to the strength of their molecular interactions, and so are held in solution for different periods of time before returning to the gas stream. Once again, the separate components are detected as they leave the column.

Both detection systems give a signal that is related to the quantity of each compound present. This allows the proportion of each component of the mixture to be determined. If the conditions (i.e. flow rate and temperature) remain the same, the time taken from injection to detection for an individual compound will not change from sample to sample.

Question 27 One way of confirming the presence of a known compound in a mixture is to take a second sample and add a little authentic material to it. A second chromatogram is then run. What result might you expect to see?

10.2   Synthetic perfumes

Despite the most careful processing, there are still many desirable fragrances that cannot be captured as components of an essential oil. These include lily of the valley, lilac, honeysuckle, violet and clover. This serious gap in the 'spectrum' of fragrances available to the perfumer has led to continuous research and development activity, not in the field but in the laboratory!

Box 10.3   Vanillin, and the birth of the synthetic perfume industry

In 1874, W. Haarman discovered a process for synthesizing vanillin (Figure 9.3), the chief flavour constituent of vanilla. On the strength of this discovery, he set up a factory in Holzminden, Germany, for its manufacture. It was a laborious process requiring the sap of nearly a thousand freshly felled conifers and 1 700 working hours to produce 1 kg of vanillin!

It will not surprise you to learn that, although it was cheaper than the natural extract, gram for gram it was still more expensive than gold!

Vanillin has a simple chemical structure but,

as more complex fragrant compounds were isolated and their structures identified, their synthesis has been attempted, too. Normally, other readily available natural products are used as starting

materials. For example, citral, a major constituent of the relatively cheap lemon grass oil, can be converted into ionone, the much scarcer fragrant principle of violets.

i, $CH_3COCH_3/Ba(OH)_2$
ii, H_2SO_4

citral   ionone

From the 1930s, in parallel with the search for medicinal drugs, an enormous number of randomly modified natural fragrance compounds were tested for their olfactory or **organoleptic** properties. The success rate of this activity was spectacularly low, but one product from 1955 which is still used is Freesiol, a lily of the valley fragrance. Its synthesis from citronellal, a component of geranium and citronella oils, is shown:

i, oxidation
ii, $- CO_2$

citronellal   hydroxycitronellal   Freesiol

- How many chiral centres are there in citronellal and Freesiol?

- In citronellal, there is only one – the one with the methyl and —CH_2CHO groups attached. In Freesiol, there are no carbon centres attached to four different groups so although citronellal (and hydroxycitronellal) are chiral compounds, Freesiol is not. We shall see that this makes its manufacture very much easier, and therefore cheaper, than a chiral fragrance.

In the so-called classical period up to 1945, a great many naturally occurring organoleptic chemical compounds were separated, identified and synthesized in marketable quantities. A second period, up to the mid-1970s, saw a frenzy of not always well-directed experimentation, where the failure rate far exceeded the success rate. However, many basic components, such as geraniol, citronellol and citral, previously isolated from natural extracts, were now manufactured at a lower price, a more consistent quality, and without the need to rely on the vagaries of supply. Some of the most successful synthetic substances were obviously derivative from pre-war discoveries (Table 10.1).

Table 10.1 The development of synthetic fragrance chemicals.

Fragrances	Pre-1945	Post-1945
lily of the valley	hydroxycitronellal	Lyral
cedar	cedrol	acetylcedrene
musk	cyclopentadecanolide	Tibetogen

10.2.1 Synthetic menthol

Menthol (Figure 9.3) is another molecule that can exist in different stereoisomeric forms. Although all the stereoisomers of menthol have a characteristic minty fragrance, only one of them provides that additional cool, refreshing sensation. Fortunately, as this is the one with the highest commercial value, it is also the one present in the highest proportion in peppermint oil extracted from mint (*Mentha piperita*). Thousands of tonnes of mint oil are produced each year for use in cigarettes, cosmetics, sweets, toothpaste, chewing gum and medicines.

> **Question 28** How many chiral centres are there in menthol? How many stereoisomers having this structure are therefore possible? How many pairs of mirror images would you therefore expect to exist?

As well as peppermint, an important source of natural mint oil was *Mentha arvensis* (cornmint), cultivated most successfully in Brazil. Unfortunately, it was a product of the notorious 'slash and burn' policy, and each new cornmint plantation on reclaimed forest land only lasted 5 to 7 years before the soil became exhausted. Clearly, this is environmentally unacceptable. A synthetic route to menthol was urgently required. The chosen starting material was the antiseptic, thymol, that you encountered in Book 3. The synthetic step is easy: hydrogenation of thymol readily produces menthol.

thymol $\xrightarrow{3H_2/catalyst}$ menthol

▨   Why therefore should this product give rise to difficulties for the perfume manufacturer?

▮   As we saw in Question 28, the simple structure of menthol represents *eight* different stereoisomers; only one of these has commercial value.

The approximate distribution of the various mirror-image pairs of isomers from the hydrogenation plant is shown below:

Table 10.2 Menthols from the hydrogenation of thymol.

	Menthol	Neomenthol	Isomenthol	Neoisomenthol
approximate distribution	59%	28%	12%	1%
boiling temperature/°C	217	211	219	215

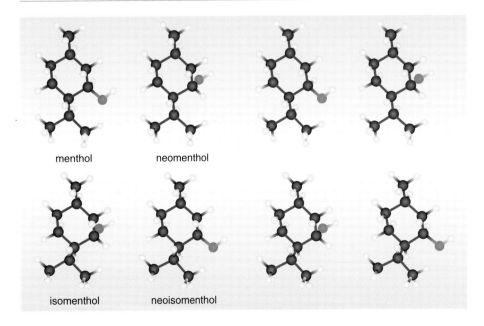

menthol   neomenthol

isomenthol   neoisomenthol

Each *member* of a mirror-image pair has identical physical and chemical properties, but each *pair* also has properties, like their boiling temperatures, that differ from all the others. Although these boiling temperatures are very close together, the pair of menthol isomers can be separated by careful distillation from the neomenthol, isomenthol and neoisomenthol pairs, giving menthol of 99% purity. Unfortunately, the synthetic processes used here tend to give equal amounts of both the mirror images, so only *half* the 59% of purified product is the desirable, cool, minty menthol. The question now becomes: 'How do we separate the valuable half from the half that is not required?'

The solution is a clever one and was first carried out as long ago as 1858 by the biologist, Louis Pasteur. How this can be done is shown through the Activity that follows.

Activity 7 Separating mirror-image pairs

Using the model kit, begin by making up two models that are *mirror images* of each other, consisting of black centres with white, red, yellow and blue balls attached. Now make up two new models that are *identical,* with black centres and white, green, silver and purple balls attached (Figure 10.15a).

If these were molecules, each pair would have identical physical properties, like melting temperature and boiling temperature.

Now 'react' each one of your mirror-image pair of molecules with one of the identical pair by taking away the two white balls (one with its bond still attached) and joining the models with the remaining bond (Figure 10.15b). Examine the two joined models; you will need to rotate the groups about the bond joining them to do this thoroughly.

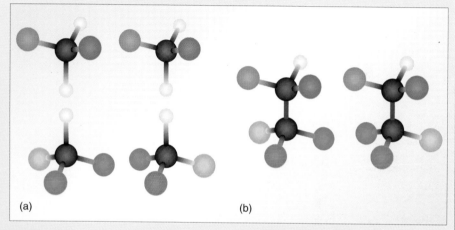

(a)   (b)

Figure 10.15
'Ball-and-stick' models of mirror-image isomers: (a) before separation; (b) after 'reaction'.

■ Are they identical?

■ No. Since only one of the two components making up each of the two new molecules was the same to start with, you would not expect them to be identical now that they have been joined together.

■ Are they mirror images then?

■ No. However you rotate the groups, you cannot get a mirror-image relationship at both black centres.

The truth is that by reacting a pair of mirror images with just one of a possible pair of mirror images, we can produce a pair of new molecules that are distinctly different. If we were to label the mirror-image pair (+) and (−), and the single reagent (+), the two new molecules could be labelled (+)–(+) and (−)–(+). The two new compounds will have sufficiently different physical properties to allow their separation by distillation or crystallization.

By carrying out the process described in Activity 7, it is possible to convert the two menthol mirror images into two esters that can be separated by crystallization. Each of the esters is then hydrolyzed separately, making it finally possible to obtain pure samples of each mirror-image compound.

'But what about the other isomers arising from the hydrogenation of thymol?' you might be wondering. 'Menthol was only 59% to start with, so our total yield at best will be less than 30% overall!' Fortunately, it is possible by further chemical treatment to recycle all the unwanted isomers and produce a new mixture with the same high proportion of the menthol component as after the first hydrogenation. As a result, in continuous production, more than 90% of the starting material, thymol, can be converted into the commercially valuable menthol isomer.

10.2.2 Current activity

We are now in a third period of more methodical research, directed at high impact, or trace aroma, chemicals. Comparison with the development of medicinal chemistry is striking and reflects the greater control that can now be exercised over both analysis and synthesis. Detailed analysis of natural oils has shown that many of them contain very small amounts of materials with intense fragrances. An example is shown in the gas–liquid chromatographic analysis of peppermint oil shown in Figure 10.16.

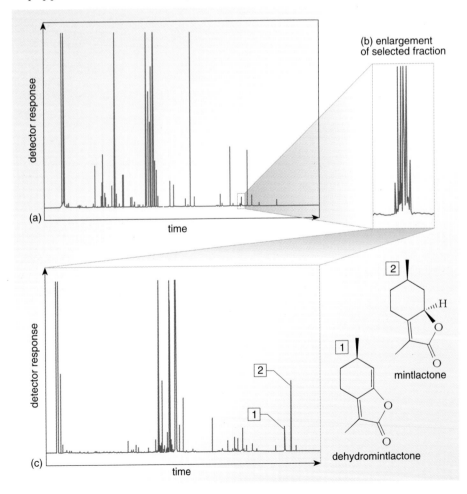

Figure 10.16
Gas–liquid chromatogram of: (a) whole peppermint oil; (b) enlargement of a selected fraction; (c) fraction selected in (b) rechromatographed under different conditions.

From the original trace (a), the small fraction of components (b) was collected and analysed a second time under different conditions. Tiny quantities of two intensely organoleptic materials were isolated, even though they were present in too small a proportion to be visible in the original chromatogram. These two compounds, named mintlactone and dehydromintlactone (i.e. mintlactone from which two hydrogen atoms have been removed), were identified and synthesized for testing. Valuable materials that would have been impossible to *extract* from the natural mint oil in sufficient quantity for use were thus made available to the perfume blender.

Figure 10.17
Cost and production levels (in 1995) for natural and synthetic jasmine products.

The ultimate quest in the search for synthetic routes to natural organoleptic molecules is to harness micro-organisms to carry out the chemical conversion of readily available materials into more valuable compounds. Interestingly, Haarman and Reimer GmbH have had some success with this biotechnological production of vanillin – the compound with which they launched the synthetic perfume industry 120 years ago.

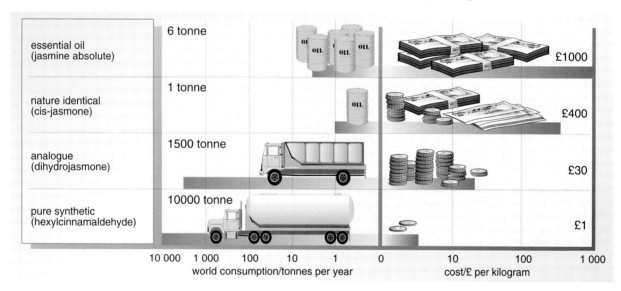

The 'histogram' in Figure 10.17 encapsulates the activities of the perfume industry. A small quantity of jasmine oil is still extracted by traditional methods but its cost is prohibitive. Two of the major constituents of jasmine oil (Figure 10.11), *cis*-jasmone and methyl (dihydro)jasmonate, are principally responsible for its fragrance. These compounds can be made quite easily in the laboratory, and although they lack the subtlety of the natural oil, the cost per kilogram of such **nature-identical** synthetics is very much lower.

cis-jasmone   methyl jasmonate

It is even easier, and therefore even cheaper, to prepare the compounds dihydrojasmone and methyl dihydrojasmonate. These materials are not present in the essential oil, but have very similar odours. Such synthetic chemicals used as substitutes for the natural ingredients are called **analogues**.

dihydrojasmone   methyl dihydrojasmonate   hexylcinnamaldehyde

Lastly, the perfumer is sometimes able to use quite unrelated chemicals to reproduce a particular scent. Hexylcinnamaldehyde has a jasmine-like fragrance, but it has not yet been identified in nature. It can be obtained very cheaply from a by-product of the petrochemical industry.

After the components have been extracted or synthesized, it is the job of the blender to produce an acceptable perfume. It is not just the natural perfumes that are complex chemical mixtures. Table 10.3 shows a typical list of ingredients of a perfume which might be used in an aftershave, or similar cosmetic product. If the constituents of the perfume bases are included in the count, then even a relatively cheap perfume like this could contain several thousand different chemical compounds.

Getting the fragrance right is not, however, the only concern of the commercial perfumer. The perfume has to be stable in the presence of the other chemical components of the product. If it were to cause discoloration, or to change from a pleasant to an unpleasant odour on standing, it could cause an economic as well as an aesthetic disaster. Disinfectants, fabric conditioners and antiperspirants are usually acid; aftershaves and shampoos are about neutral; and soaps and household cleaners are alkaline. Bleaches have oxidizing properties as well; and there are probably fewer than 30 perfume chemicals that are stable when both acid and oxidizing components are present together. A sound knowledge of the chemistry of the perfume constituents is therefore essential before suggesting a perfume for trial in a new product.

The perfume industry is still buoyant, and, although it stretches back thousands of years, it is encouraging to be able to finish this Section with a quotation from Ernest Beaux, the perfumer who created Chanel No. 5:

> *One has to rely on chemists to find new aroma chemicals, creating new, original notes. In perfumery, the future lies primarily in the hands of the chemists.*

As you move on to study Part 2 of this Book, I hope you will come to appreciate that it is not just in perfumery that the chemist has an important role in determining the future.

Table 10.3 The formulation of a typical perfume which might be used as an aftershave or similar cosmetic product.

Category	Ingredient	% by mass	Category	Ingredient	% by mass
1	aldehyde C9 10% in benzyl alcohol	0.6	4	labdanum absolute	0.6
1	aldehyde C10 10% in benzyl alcohol	1.2	2	lixetone	3.6
1	aldehyde C11 10% in benzyl alcohol	0.8	1	methyl dihydrojasmonate	5.9
1	aldehyde C12 10% in benzyl alcohol	1.4	1	methyl ionone alpha iso	5.6
3	amber base	1.8	3	moss base	2.0
1	amyl salicylate	0.9	2	mousse de chene absolute decolorée	2.3
4	angelica seed	0.8	1	musk ketone	2.8
4	basil comores	1.4	4	neroli Italian	0.8
2	benzoin Siam hyper absolute	2.8	4	orange Italian	1.1
1	benzyl salicylate	1.1	4	patchouli	2.2
2	bergamot (bergapten free)	7.5	3	peach base	1.0
2	cedar English	2.3	3	pomeransol base	0.5
2	clove bud rectified	1.9	2	rose absolute artificial	2.8
4	civet absolute 10% in dipropylene glycol	0.5	1	rosewood	3.8
1	1-coumarin	0.9	4	sage clary	1.4
1	cyclopentadecanolide 10% in diethyl phthalate	1.9	2	sandalone	3.8
3	dianthine CN	1.2	2	styrax hyperessence	2.3
4	geranium Bourdon	0.7	1	tonalid	1.9
1	heliotropin	0.9	3	tuberose base	3.0
1	hydroxycitronellal	2.0	1	vanillin 10% in benzyl benzoate	1.1
1	eugenol	1.0	2	vetyvenol	5.6
2	jasmin sous product	3.8	2	vetyvenol acetate	2.8
4	lavender revesle	0.6	4	ylang extra	3.1
				TOTAL	**100**

Notes for Table 10.3

The four categories are as follows:

1 'Single' chemicals, such as amyl salicylate, most of which are synthetic in origin.

2 Complex mixtures, some of which are made available as 'specialities' to other perfumers. Typically, these mixtures contain about 50 different chemical compounds.

3 Perfume bases which are 'miniperfumes' of a particular odour type. A perfume base is likely to contain about 50 different chemical compounds.

4 Natural products such as essential oils. Such products are likely to be made up of about 200 different chemical compounds.

5 The data for '% by mass' are only correct to two significant figures, and hence do not add up to exactly 100%.

Summary of Chapter 10

In Chapter 10, you have seen how the extraction of perfumes has its roots in antiquity. Most perfumes are now used in household goods and toiletries, rather than as exotic fragrances. Perfume components have to be stable in preparations as well as have acceptable fragrances.

Essential oils are extracted from plants using non-polar solvents like hydrocarbons, animal fat and liquid carbon dioxide. Alternatively, they may be steam distilled. They are complex mixtures, present as tiny percentages of the raw material, and are very expensive because of labour-intensive production methods. Animal products civet, musk and ambergris have largely been replaced by synthetic materials. Valuable fragrances can be obtained synthetically by modifying chemicals from readily obtainable plant extracts. Nature-identical, analogue and unrelated fragrances may be synthesized in the laboratory for use by the perfumer. Synthetic perfume components benefit from more consistent quality, lower price and guaranteed supply.

Single isomers of a mirror-image pair can be obtained by reacting both with another chiral compound; separating the products, which will now have different physical properties; and then regenerating each isomer.

Objectives for Part 1 of Book 4

When you have completed Book 4 Part 1, you should be able to:

1   Describe how reflected or transmitted colour results from the absorption of certain wavelengths from white light, using the principle of subtractive colour generation.

2   Relate the photon energy of a particular radiation to its wavelength, and perform calculations using this relationship.

3   Outline the operation and uses of a spectrophotometer, and the equipment used for high performance liquid chromatography (hplc) and gas–liquid chromatography (glc).

4   Describe why only light having specific wavelengths can be absorbed by a material.

5   Describe electronic structure in terms of a 'ladder of energy levels', and describe promotion and ionization using this model.

6   Describe the generation of light by the emission process.

7   Recognize in given sets of molecular structures:

(a) the natural colouring materials chlorophyll, carotene, alizarin, indigo, and the flower colours of the benzopyran family;

(b) the different types of molecules that form fibres;

(c) direct, azoic, vat and disperse dyes; and

(d) organoleptic compounds constituted from isoprene units.

8   Outline developments in the dye and perfume industries.

9   Describe how flower colours change according to whether plant sap is acid, alkaline or neutral.

10   Given the structure of a synthetic product, identify components within that structure that are derived from the starting materials.

11   Describe the characteristic shape of a dye molecule.

12   Using a diagram, indicate the variety of intermolecular forces between fibre molecules and between fibre and dye molecules.

13   Recognize the structural characteristics of a dye that make it suitable for application to a particular fibre.

14   Describe the principles behind the application of azoic and vat dyes to fibres.

15   Describe the action of a mordant.

16   Use the principles of subtractive colour generation (through energy absorption and electron promotion) to describe how colour arises:

    (a) from individual metallic ions in a crystal or a glass;

    (b) by charge transfer between ions of different metals, or ions of the same metal with different charges; and

    (c) from molecules.

17   Given the absorption spectrum of a dye, estimate its hue, colour intensity (pure, tint or shade), and appearance (bright or subdued).

18   Identify within a molecular structure different types of polyene chromogen and auxochromes.

19   Suggest why increased conjugation is likely to result in colour in compounds.

20   Show how the trichromacy theory is used:

    (a) to describe colour vision and colour blindness;

    (b) to work out perceived colours when coloured light is (i) reflected from coloured surfaces; (ii) viewed through colour filters; or (iii) when coloured pigments are mixed;

    (c) in the practical applications of colour photography, colour printing, and colour television.

21   Name the additive and subtractive primary colours, and show how they are:

    (a) related to each other; and

    (b) generated from white light.

22   Recall the basic taste sensations and their location on the tongue.

23   From a series of molecules known to stimulate taste or odour receptors, pick out common structural features that could be responsible for their activity.

24   Provide evidence to support a receptor hypothesis for the molecular stimulation of the chemical senses.

25   Outline the basis of fragrance classifications.

26   With or without the help of molecular models:

    (a) identify chiral centres in a structural formula;

    (b) draw all the stereoisomers of a molecule having up to two chiral centres.

27   Outline a theory for fragrance receptors based on molecular shapes, give examples of its successes, and recognize its limitations.

28   Distinguish between essential oils, and individual natural or synthetic organoleptic compounds.

29   Outline the methods for obtaining essential oils from plant material.

30   Describe the synthesis of nature-identical menthol from thymol.

31   Describe a general technique for separating mirror-image isomers.

Comments on Activities

Activity 1

The outstanding feature is surely the 'flatness' of both models. Dye molecules can be thought of as having the shape of a slip of paper; that is, having length and breadth, but very little thickness. The majority of them also have quite large structures with most of the constituent atoms lying in the same plane. The dye molecules can enter only the amorphous regions of the polymer system. Although flat, they still have too much bulk to penetrate the small interpolymer spaces in the crystalline regions of the fibre.

Activities 2 and 3

The comments for these Activities are in the text.

Activity 4

	Viewed through red filter	Viewed through blue filter
red	red	black
green	black	green
violet (blue)	black	blue
yellow	orange	green
cyan	black	blue
magenta	red	purple

All colours with a red component (yellow, red, magenta) will be visible through the red filter, and all those with a blue component (cyan, violet (blue), magenta) will be visible through the blue filter. Our eyes are particularly sensitive to yellow which is near to the maximum overlap of red and green cone stimulation (Figure 7.4) and probably accounts for the persistence of yellow (as orange and green respectively) through the red and blue filters.

Activity 5

A completed version of Figure 9.7 is given below:

I II III IV I

Activity 6

You should have found that the model for compound (c) matches the criterion best (Figure A1). It has the bulky butyl group sticking out in the same plane as the rings and the —OH group pointing down, as specified. None of the other molecules fits the receptor very well. Notice how the way in which the rings are joined together makes a big difference to how long or how flat the molecule will be.

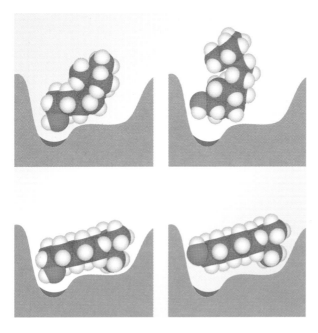

Figure A1
The fit of 'sandalwood' molecules in the proposed receptor. Fragrances for the molecules are: (a) weak, woody with some aspects of sandalwood; (b) weak, pine needles, leather-like:
(c) strong sandalwood, with a musky note: (d) weak, woody.

Answers to Questions

Question 1 The complementary colour to orange is blue, so oranges will absorb light having wavelengths in the blue region of the spectrum, i.e. 435–480 nm. It is the mixing of light of wavelengths 400–435 nm and 480–700 nm that generates the orange colour. Blood is red, and will absorb wavelengths corresponding to the green–blue colour, cyan (480–490 nm). Blue jeans will absorb wavelengths corresponding to orange (595–605 nm).

Question 2 In spectrum (a), absorption takes place from the visible region between 350 nm and 600 nm. Most of the yellow and green and much of the blue is absorbed, so the dye will be red. In (b), absorption is at higher wavelengths, between 450 nm and 650 nm. Green, yellow and much of the red is now absorbed, so the predominant colour will be blue. These are in fact the spectra of the dyes used to colour red and blue litmus paper, respectively.

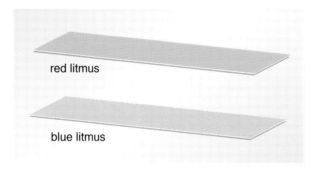

red litmus

blue litmus

Question 3 Using the equation $E = hc/\lambda$, the energy gap for the absorption of red light ($\lambda = 700$ nm) is given by:

$$E = \frac{(6.63 \times 10^{-34}\,\text{J s}) \times (3.00 \times 10^{8}\,\text{m s}^{-1})}{700 \times 10^{-9}\,\text{m}} = 2.84 \times 10^{-19}\,\text{J}$$

To convert to joules per mole, we must multiply by the value of Avogadro's constant:

$$(2.84 \times 10^{-19}\,\text{J}) \times (6.02 \times 10^{23}\,\text{mol}^{-1}) = 1.71 \times 10^{5}\,\text{J mol}^{-1}$$

$$= 171\,\text{kJ mol}^{-1}$$

Question 4 In order for us to perceive radiation, it must have wavelengths between 400 nm (violet) and 700 nm (red). Light with these wavelengths will be emitted if the gaps between rungs on the energy ladder fall in the range 299–171 kJ mol^{-1}. Figure 2.18 shows that the rungs of the energy ladder rapidly get closer together as we move away from the bottom rung. As a result, when electrons cascade down the higher steps (Figure 2.19), photons of lower energy are emitted and the 'light' emitted is invisible to our eyes.

Question 5 The high voltage electrical discharge provides the energy to ionize the krypton atoms. Electrons will recombine with the ions and cascade down to the lower excited levels. From there they will finally drop into the lowest energy level, emitting light as they do so.

If the energy given out when *one mole* of electrons crosses the gap is 204 kJ mol⁻¹, then each electron emits a photon with an energy of:

$(2.04 \times 10^5$ kJ mol⁻¹$)/(6.02 \times 10^{23}$ mol⁻¹$) = 3.39 \times 10^{-19}$ J (i.e. joules *per electron*)

To find the wavelength of the light corresponding to this energy, we use the equation: $E = hc/\lambda$, or transposing, $\lambda = hc/E$

$$\lambda = \frac{(6.63 \times 10^{-34} \text{ J s}) \times (3.00 \times 10^8 \text{ m s}^{-1})}{(3.39 \times 10^{-19} \text{ J})}$$

$$= 5.87 \times 10^{-7} \text{ m}$$

$$= 587 \text{ nm}$$

This wavelength lies in the yellow region of the spectrum, close to the sodium line. Similarly, 215 kJ mol⁻¹ corresponds to a wavelength of 557 nm in the green region. The colour of the display will therefore be a yellow–green.

Question 6 To obtain the red compound, one H and a plus charge must be added. As H^+ is present in aqueous acidic solutions (like sap!), flowers with acidic sap will be *red*. Similarly, the blue compound has lost one H and gained a minus charge. The OH^- ion is present in alkaline sap and will abstract H^+ from the violet compound according to the equation: $H^+ + OH^- = H_2O$. So, if the sap is *alkaline* the flowers will be blue. This plant dye shows the same colour changes as litmus paper.

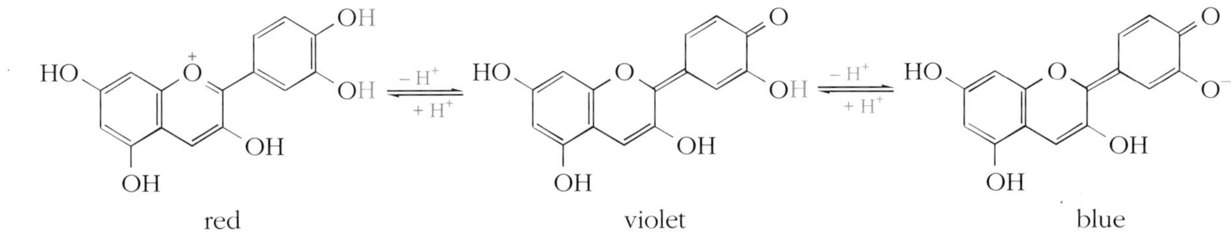

red   violet   blue

Question 7 The advantages arose because synthetic indigo was a purer product. It was of uniform composition, so accurate concentrations could be measured, and the colour produced could be made consistent between one batch and the next. It also resulted in a brighter colour. Natural indigo always contained residual plant material which meant it gave a more drab shade.

Question 8 The structural elements of the three molecules of aniline that occur in the structure of magenta are outlined in Figure A2. It is interesting to note that an *extra* carbon atom is required as well. In fact, the original magenta could only have been formed because aniline contaminated with toluidine was used. Now that the structure of magenta is known, aniline and toluidine are used in a 2 : 1 ratio in the manufacturing process.

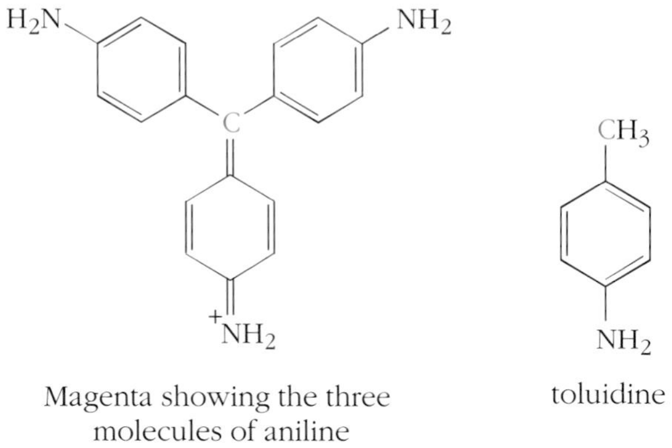

Magenta showing the three molecules of aniline

toluidine

Figure A2
Magenta, showing how three molecules of aniline could be incorporated into the structure of the molecule. The extra carbon atom comes from a molecule of toluidine.

Question 9 See Table A1.

Table A1

(a) Fibre type	Suitable dyes
cellulosic (cotton, viscose)	direct, mordant, azoic, vat
protein (wool, silk)	direct, azoic, mordant
acetate	azoic, disperse, pigment
polyamide (nylon)	disperse, mordant
acrylic	azoic, disperse, pigment
polyester	azoic, disperse, pigment

(b) Dye	Type of interaction
direct	H-bonds, ionic, London
azoic	London, H-bonds
vat	London
disperse	London
mordant	London, ionic, lake formation
pigment	no interactions

Question 10 Charge transfer must be possible between the dipositive Fe^{2+} and tripositive Fe^{3+} ions in the crystal structure of Prussian blue. To give the deep blue colour, the energy of transfer must correspond to wavelengths in the visible spectrum (170–300 kJ mol^{-1}) that give the complementary colour, orange; i.e. around 600 nm, equivalent to about 200 kJ mol^{-1}.

Question 11 When the mixture of borax and the metallic compound is heated in the flame, metal cations are dispersed in the melt. The bead cools rapidly, and forms a borate glass. The electronic energy levels of the metal cation, and therefore the colours of the beads, are again determined by the surrounding oxygen atoms. Again, as in the blast furnace, a flame has both oxidizing and reducing zones. A bead containing metals that can have differently charged cations will therefore show varying colours when heated in different parts of the flame.

Question 12 The order is: CN (6 nm difference); COOH (7); Br, SO_3H, $COCH_3$ (11); CH_3 (15); NO_2 (20); CH_3O (28); OH (32); NH_2 (69); and $(C_2H_5)_2N$ (97) in increasing order of effectiveness.

Question 13 The chromogens are shown in Figure A3. Within both the series, the nitrogen functional group can also be included.

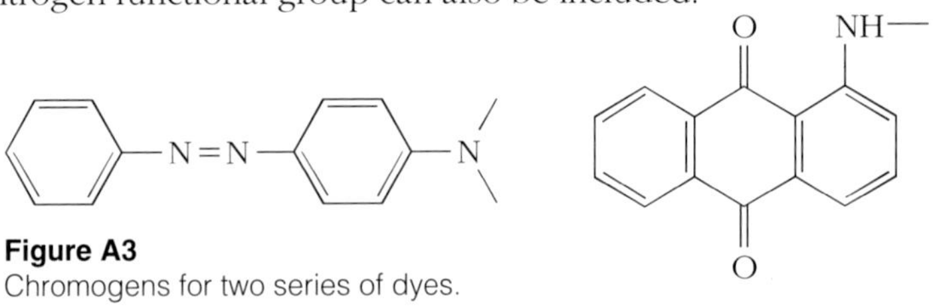

Figure A3
Chromogens for two series of dyes.

The four dyes on the left of Figure 6.3 are azo dyes, but because they lack the solubilizing sulfonic acid groups they would probably be prepared *in situ* as azoic (or 'ice colours'), or introduced directly as disperse dyes. The four dyes on the left have structures similar to alizarin and so could probably be mordanted. However, they also have the typically small molecules of the disperse dyes. Both azoic and disperse dyes would be ideal for dyeing acetate fibres.

Question 14 Dalton was unable to distinguish red from blue, but could distinguish red from green. He must therefore have been lacking blue cones – a very rare form of colour blindness.

Question 15 (a) Magenta light includes the wavelengths corresponding to red and blue. When blue light falls on blue squares, it will be reflected. Yellow squares will absorb blue, and normally reflect red and green. As magenta contains no green, only the red will be reflected, giving the appearance of a red and blue chequered surface.

(b) A red filter will only pass red light. The yellow squares would be able to reflect the red and green components of white light but as there is no green component in the filtered light they will appear red. A blue square will only reflect blue light and absorb red and green. Therefore, all the light reflected from a blue square will be absorbed by the red filter, and the square will appear black. This will give an overall red and black chequered pattern.

You can check this analysis by looking at blue and yellow sections of your spinning discs through your red gelatine filter.

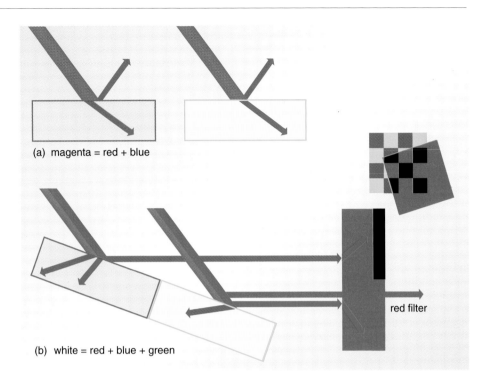

Figure A4
(a) Reflection of magenta light from blue and yellow squares. (b) View of yellow and blue squares through red filter.

(a) magenta = red + blue

(b) white = red + blue + green

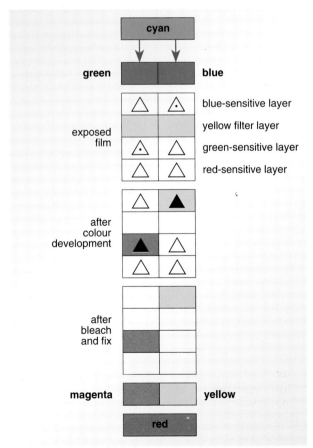

Question 16 Cyan light can be treated as a mixture of blue and green. It will therefore affect the blue-sensitive layer (black dot in triangle) and then the green component will pass through the yellow filter (as yellow will not absorb green, only blue). The green component then activates the green-sensitive layer (another black dot) where it is absorbed; and no light passes through to the final red-sensitive layer. On development, this activated area will produce a patch of red (the colour complementary to cyan) from a mixture of yellow and magenta dyes (complementary to blue and green respectively) in two of the layers.

Figure A5
Reaction of colour-negative film to cyan light.

Question 17 Both dyes contain a common chromogen (Y). The magenta dye has only one additional group (CH_3) which will not affect the light absorption very much. However, it does also have a nitrogen atom in the left-hand ring. The cyan dye has the auxochromic group (X) which will extend the conjugation and allow further delocalization of the electrons. As a result, the energy gap will be reduced and the wavelength of absorbed light increased. Consulting Table 2.1 shows that magenta results when green (λ = 530 nm) is absorbed. To generate cyan, red light with a longer wavelength (λ = 650 nm) must be absorbed, which is what the theory led us to expect.

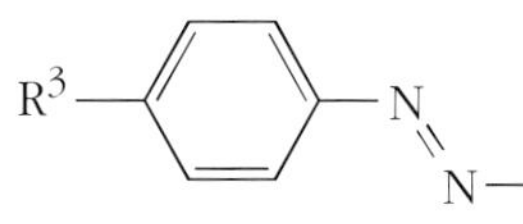

auxochromic group X 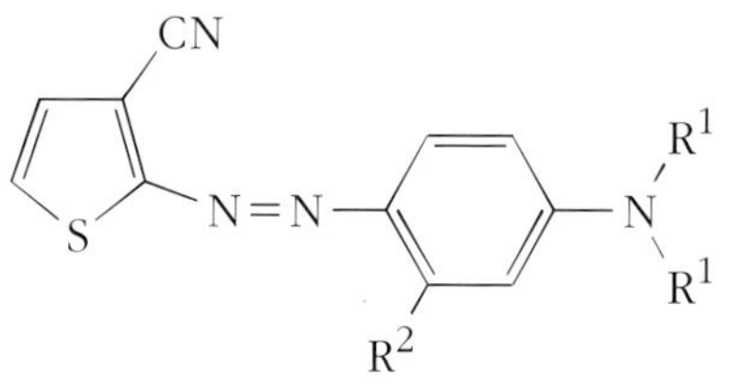   chromogen Y

Question 18 The obvious common feature is the $-N{=}C{=}S$ group, called *isothiocyanate*; in both examples it is attached to a $-CH_2-$ group. However, more careful inspection reveals that the compounds actually have in common the extended structure shown in Figure A6.

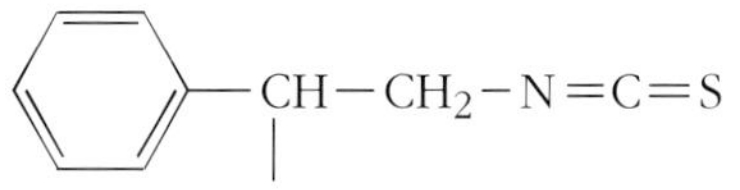

common structural element

Figure A6
Common structural element.

Question 19 You might have suggested some of the following:

1   The sensation of taste is experienced at particular sites.

2   Different parts of the mouth respond to different tastes.

3   Very small quantities of a material can trigger the sensation of taste.

4   Molecules with similar structural features generate similar taste sensations.

Question 20 (a) Aldehyde molecules are not hydrogen-bonded together, but only held together by weak dipole–dipole and London forces; so if they have similar molecular masses they will be more volatile than alcohols, which readily form hydrogen bonds.

(b) Musks are compounds with relatively large molecular masses and they also have oxygen- and nitrogen-containing groups that will form hydrogen bonds, particularly with alcohols. The former feature will reduce their own volatility, and the latter feature will reduce the overall volatility of the mixture.

Question 21 As well as citronellol; carvone, geraniol, limonene, linalool, menthol, neral and nerol are all derived from *two* isoprene units. Vetivone looks as though it might have been formed from *three* isoprene units but is in fact one carbon atom short (see Figure A7).

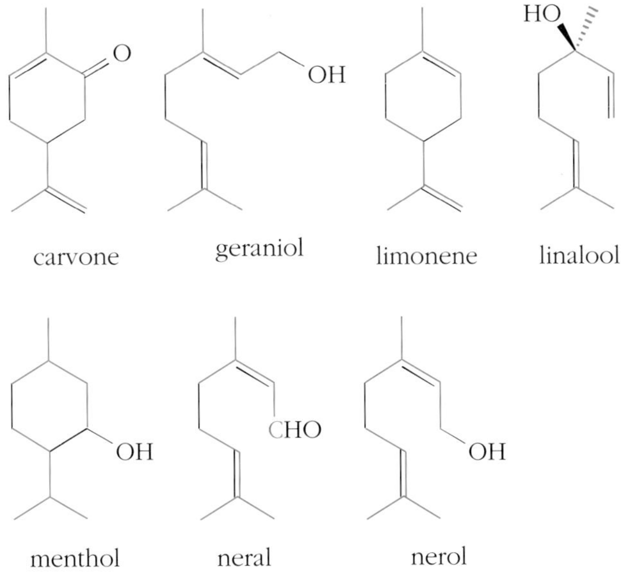

carvone   geraniol   limonene   linalool

menthol   neral   nerol

Figure A7
Contribution of isoprene units to the molecules of fragrant compounds.

Question 22

(a) 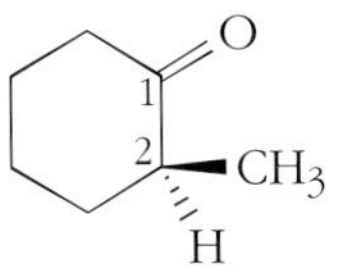   (b)

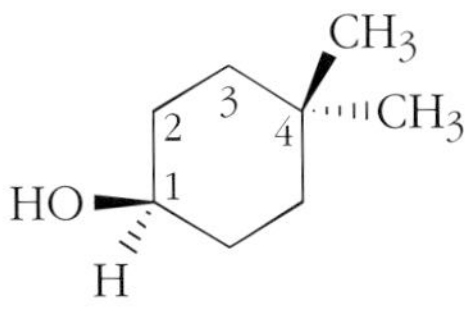

Molecule (a) does have a chiral centre at C-2. This time we do not have to count all the way round the ring because going clockwise we first arrive at a $-CH_2-$ (C-3), but going anticlockwise we reach a C=O (C-1). Carbon atom C-2 therefore has four different groups attached and is chiral.

Molecule (b), however, has no chiral centres. Carbon atom C-4 clearly has two identical methyl groups (CH_3) attached, but C-1 is slightly trickier. Whether we go clockwise or anticlockwise round the ring back to C-1, we encounter the same sequence of groups, i.e.
$-CH_2-CH_2-C(CH_3)_2-CH_2-CH_2-$.

Structure (b) therefore represents a non-chiral molecule.

Question 23 Pentylpyridine has the form of a flat disc with a tail, which fits
the keyhole shape of the floral receptor; diethyl ether, in its extended zig-zag
conformation, fits into the trench-like ethereal receptor. The space-filling
models of the molecules shown with the shapes of the receptors (Figure A8)
make this clearer.

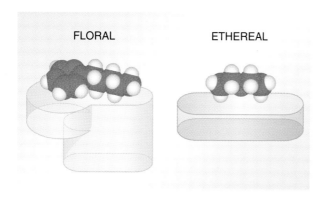

Figure A8
Space-filling models and
receptors.

Question 24 A receptor responsible for the almond flavour must be of such
a size and shape that it can accommodate both benzaldehyde and
methylbenzaldehyde. However, the added bulk of the side chain of
isopropylbenzaldehyde must preclude it from fitting these receptors. The flat
figure of eight-shaped receptor (Figure A9) is a possible suggestion.

Figure A9
Possible shape for the
'almond' receptor.

Question 25 The maximum yield of mimosa concrete is 0.55%, and the
maximum yield of mimosa absolute is 50%. Therefore the maximum yield
overall is:

50% of 0.55% of 1 000 kg, i.e. $50/100 \times 0.55/100 \times 1\,000$ kg = 2.75 kg tonne^{-1}

Question 26 Carnation (flowers); cedar (wood, or possibly bark); rosemary
(flowers and leaves); ginger (roots, or more accurately the rhizomes of the
ginger plant). There are two lime fragrances – one obtained from the blossom
of the lime (linden) tree and the other from the peel of the citrus fruit.

Question 27 All the component 'spikes' of the original mixture will still be
present, but if the suspected compound is a component, one of the spikes
will be much increased in size. Figure A10 shows the result of adding the
drug theobromine to an extract of tea which confirms that it is one of the
minor components.

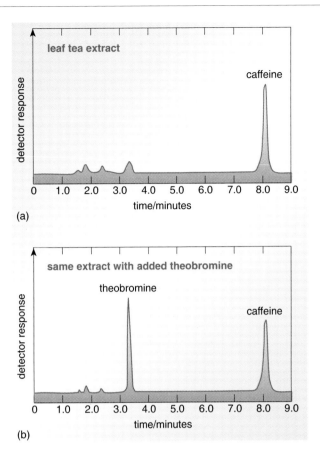

Figure A10
Chromatograms of tea extract before (a) and after (b) the addition of theobromine.

Question 28 There are *three* chiral centres in menthol so there will be $2 \times 2 \times 2 = 8$ stereoisomers. With eight isomers, you might have guessed (correctly) that there will be four pairs of mirror images. They are drawn below, labelled, just for information, with the names given to each mirror-image pair.

menthol   neomenthol

isomenthol   neoisomenthol

Acknowledgements

Grateful acknowledgement is made to the following sources for permission to reproduce material in this part of Book 4:

Figure 1.2 (advert): Hitachi Sales (UK) Ltd; *(aircraft):* COI; *(operating theatre):* Commanding Officer, HMS *Victory*; *Figure 1.3* Kunsthistorisches Museum, Vienna; *Figures 1.5, 1.6, 5.10 and 10.4* Ancient Art and Architecture Collection; *Figures 1.7 and 3.1* The National Gallery, London; *Figure 1.8* The Louvre; *Figure 1.9* Photo © 1994 Museum of Modern Art, New York. © ADAGP, Paris and DACS, London, 1995; *Figure 2.1* Science Museum, London; *Figure 2.2* The Royal Society; *Figure 2.8* Pharmacia LKB Biochrom Ltd; *Figure 2.16* Deutsches Museum, Munich; *Figures 2.20 and 3.8* GeoScience Features Picture Library; *Figures 3.2a,c and 3.10* Heather Angel/Biofotos; *Figure 3.2b* Planet Earth Pictures; *Figure 3.4* Dr J. Burgess/Science Photo Library; *Figure 3.6* Godfrey Argent Ltd.; *Figures 3.7, 10.5, 10.7 and 10.9* Ardea Ltd., London; *Figure 3.9* British Museum; *Figure 3.12* © A. N. Gagg, Birmingham; *Figures 3.13a and 3.15a,b* paintings by Gretel Dalby-Quenet in J. and M. Cannon, *Dye Plants and Dyeing*, The Herbert Press; *Figure 3.13c* courtesy Curator of the Colour Museum, Society of Dyers and Colorists; *Figure 3.14* The Royal Collection © Her Majesty The Queen; *Figure 3.16* courtesy of Zeneca Specialities; *Figure 3.18* courtesy of the Kirkpatrick Family and Zeneca Specialities; *Figure 3.20* National Portrait Gallery; *Figure 4.11* BASF; *Figures 5.1, 5.4 and 5.6* Natural History Museum, London; *Figure 5.9* S. Halliday and L. Lushington; *Figure 7.5* Mansell Collection; *Figure 7.11* courtesy Kodak Ltd; *Figure 7.16* *Macmillan Family Encyclopedia*, V. 19, Macmillan 1980; *Figure 9.1* Omikron/Science Photo Library; *Figure 9.8* Charlotte Winn; *Figure 10.3* Advertising Archives and Guerlain, Paris; *Figure 10.6* Norfolk Lavender Ltd.

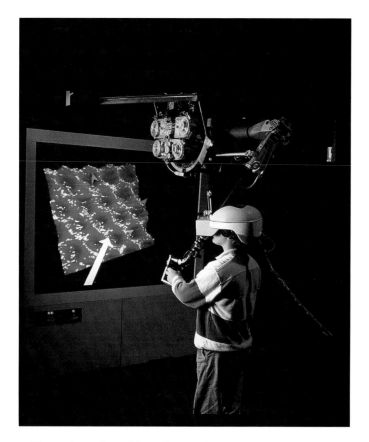

The surface of graphite at the atomic scale examined using a
scanning tunnelling microscope, a head-mounted display, and a
force feedback arm.

PART 2 TOMORROW'S CHEMISTRY

Prepared for the Course Team by David Roberts

Contents

Chapter 1
Our chemical tomorrow

If you were to ask people what they regarded as the most exciting scientific developments of recent years, it is highly likely that many would talk about progress in our knowledge of the cosmos brought about by space probes or by the observations now possible with the Hubble telescope. Or they might mention the advances in our understanding of genetics that lie behind the human genome project, the massive international programme to determine the complete genetic code for human beings. But it would probably come as something of a surprise if you told them that some of the most useful and fascinating scientific advances in the past decade have been brought about not by astronomers or molecular biologists but by chemists. You, of course, having now studied this Course, know better!

In this, the final segment of the Course, we are going to explore the frontiers of chemistry. Our exploration will take in a selection of exciting and important chemically based innovations, some of which result from advances in traditional areas of chemistry whereas others involve new fields of knowledge. We shall also attempt a degree of crystal-ball gazing to try to predict some of the advances that are likely over the next decade or so (from a 1995 viewpoint!). You may think that this is a foolhardy thing to do: certainly we shall make no attempt to predict any completely new areas of chemistry that might develop.

- What major problem areas can you think of that are likely to be amenable to a solution based, in part at least, on the application of chemical expertise?

- There are many that you might have thought of, including perhaps the conquest of disease; the provision of adequate food; the development of effective methods of reducing present and minimizing future pollution; and the need for renewable sources of energy on a large scale. Chemistry will also continue to play a major role in the areas of communications and information technology which have so revolutionized our lives in the last quarter of the 20th century.

It is true that molecular science has been involved in all these areas for many years, but there remains much still to be done. For this Part of Book 4 we have selected four major topic areas that are especially active at present, and which we think are likely to be of particular importance in the future. Even if our predictions turn out to be completely wrong, we think these areas are of intrinsic interest and will at the very least serve to reinforce many of the concepts and ideas that you have met earlier in the Course. Furthermore, the exercise of applying these ideas to unsolved problems will, we hope, show that the science of chemistry, far from being outdated, is increasingly likely to provide the key to solving many of the problems facing humanity over the coming decades.

The four topic areas we have chosen are: the application of computers to design novel molecular structures; the custom design of new materials; the development of renewable energy sources suitable for large-scale use; and finally nanotechnology, the ultimate in miniaturization techniques, which enables individual atoms and molecules to be seen and manipulated.

The first topic area relates to the use of computers in chemistry. The recent giant strides in the processing power of computers have led to the development of computer graphics systems that enable virtually any molecular assembly to be constructed, and manipulated, on screen. The ways in which molecules interact play a vital role in the action of drugs in the treatment of disease, in the strengths of polymers, and in the behaviour of different types of catalyst: the ability to model these interactions enables new molecules to be designed for use as more effective drugs, stronger polymers, or better catalysts (Figure 1.1).

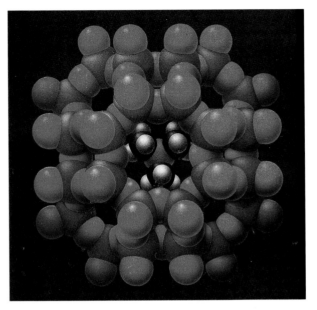

Figure 1.1
Computer-drawn molecular model of a zeolite used as a catalyst in the production of dimethylamine, an important chemical building block for producing dyes, fibres and pharmaceutical products. Zeolites are porous solids with large cavities connected by molecule-sized channels (see Book 2 Part 2). The model shows a molecule of trimethylamine, an unwanted by-product, which fits the channel so tightly that it is unable to escape.

The second topic area is the design of new materials. One of the most obvious impacts that molecular science has had on everyday life over the past fifty years has been in the development of manufactured materials, both to replace traditional ones and for new applications. Although the changes apparent in our own lifetimes have been great enough, and one might think there is now much less scope for further improvement, the pace of research and development into new materials has not slackened. Indeed, with our increased understanding of the relationship between molecular structure and macroscopic properties, the development of tools such as computer-based molecular modelling, and progress in new methods of manufacturing, the pace has hotted up.

◻   From your own experience, can you think of examples where new materials are currently being used to replace more traditional ones?

◼   One example is in the construction of motor vehicles; another is in surgery for such uses as hip replacements, artificial limbs and artificial skin; a third is in the development of new aircraft, with ever more powerful engines.

Changes in the methods and materials used in car manufacture have arisen, in part, as a response by the automotive industry to the environmental and safety concerns of society. The medical applications of new materials have enabled many people to lead more normal lives than otherwise would have been possible. The development of new aircraft relies more than ever on the discovery of new alloys and new ceramics (Figure 1.2). These are just a few of the many ways in which new materials increasingly affect our lives.

The third topic area to be considered is the need for renewable energy sources, particularly for transport use. In the medium term, the internal combustion engine is likely to be the main means of powering motor vehicles, but most of the energy sources used today are finite. This problem has many different facets and we shall concentrate on a few selected ones.

Figure 1.2
A cube of the porous glass ceramic material used to make the heat-shielding tiles attached to the underside of the US space shuttle. The material is such an effective insulator (it contains 93% air) that, though the centre is still glowing, the cube can be held just moments after being removed from an oven at a temperature of 1200 °C. Any future hypersonic aircraft would almost certainly require the use of an insulator material such as this.

Figure 1.3
The 2 MW photovoltaic power plant near the closed Rancho Seco nuclear power station in Sacramento, California.

■ Which aspects of this problem do you think are most suited to the application of chemical ideas?

■ There are several, but the three we shall examine are the large-scale use of fuels from renewable sources, solar-generated electricity, and the development of better batteries.

As an energy source, the Sun is for practical purposes limitless. However, despite much research, a widely applicable and economic way to use solar energy still remains to be discovered. One way is to use nature's own method of storing the Sun's energy, namely photosynthesis, but living off income rather than capital as at present with our dependence on fossil fuels. We shall look at various fuels that can be obtained from plants on a renewable basis. Another possibility that looks increasingly realistic is the generation of electricity using photovoltaic solar cells (Figure 1.3).

Once generated, electricity needs to be stored in a convenient, practical and efficient way. Electricity is a peculiarly difficult commodity to stockpile: it can be stored only by temporary conversion into some other form of energy, for example chemical energy. One way of achieving this is to use electric power to convert water into hydrogen gas for use as a fuel, and another is storage using batteries. The major reason that the development of electrically powered vehicles has been held back is the adverse power-to-weight ratio of existing batteries. Consequently, the development of new types of battery is being hotly pursued.

Finally, we shall look at new methods of manipulating matter on the very small scale, down to the atomic and molecular level. Research workers all over the world are creating new materials made of particles in the nanometre size range, so-called nanomaterials. Chemically, the atoms or molecules of a substance, such as gold or water, are identical whether there is just one or one mole. The properties of a single atom or molecule, however, are very different from the familiar properties of matter in bulk. Nanomaterials, made of particles containing a few dozen or a few hundred atoms, are in between the two extremes and display quite unexpected properties: for example, ceramics that are transparent and behave like chewing gum, liquids that are magnetic, and materials containing iron particles that can have their conductivity vary over 14 orders of magnitude at will, simply by altering the proportions, have all been made.

At the level of fundamental scientific research, scientists are now able to achieve the ultimate dream of chemists for centuries, the manipulation of individual atoms and molecules. One of the most exciting developments has been the invention of the scanning tunnelling microscope and its cousin, the atomic force microscope. With these instruments, it is now possible to 'see', and indeed manipulate, individual atoms and molecules (Figure 1.4). Although still at an early stage, these new techniques have already had a significant impact on our understanding of events at the molecular level. Looking to the future, they seem certain to give rise to new methods of information storage and retrieval and to revolutionize catalyst development and manufacture, to take just two examples.

As we indicated at the beginning of this chapter, in choosing these four main topics, we have selected areas that we think are likely to be of particular importance in the future. Professor George Whitesides of the Chemistry Department at Harvard University in Boston, Massachusetts, came to similar conclusions when he wrote an article in 1990 entitled 'What will chemistry do in the next twenty years?' In it he identified two major driving forces that are likely to shape tomorrow's chemistry:

> *Chemistry advances on two feet: one is utility, one curiosity. A prediction of its future path can only be a guess, based on its past progress and its present position. The most interesting and important directions to come – those that represent radical departures from the present – I cannot predict. What I can identify are societal concerns that seem certain to require solutions that are (at least in part) technical, and scientific ideas that seem equally certain to drive basic research for at least some time.*
>
> *(G. Whitesides, Angewandte Chemie Int. Ed. Engl., 1990, vol. 29, p. 1209.)*

In trying to predict the future directions of a subject so active that it currently produces a million new compounds and around three-quarters of a million publications each year, we can do no better.

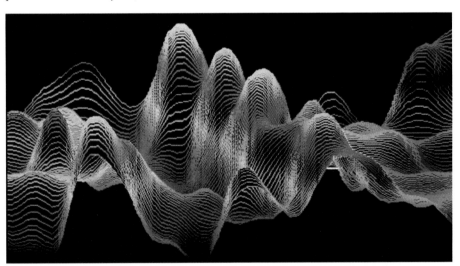

Figure 1.4
False-colour image of part of a DNA molecule produced by a scanning tunnelling microscope (STM). This image shows a section of a double-stranded DNA molecule, with the coils of the helix appearing as the row of orange-yellow peaks in the centre of the image. The average distance between each peak is 3.5 nanometres.

Chapter 2
Drug design by computer

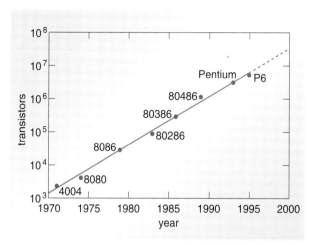

2.1 Computers and molecular graphics

There is no doubt that, like so many areas of our lives, chemistry has been profoundly affected by the advent of powerful desktop computers. With microprocessors now being an integral part of everyday life, at least in the developed world, from washing machines to automobiles, from supermarkets to libraries, it is easy to forget that these systems have been commonplace only since about the mid-1970s. The widespread incorporation of computer 'chips' has been possible through the continued increase in their processing power, allied with and resulting from their continued miniaturization (Figure 2.1).

Figure 2.1
The growth in the number of transistors per microchip for the Intel family of microprocessors. (Note that the vertical scale is logarithmic.) These microprocessors have powered the majority of personal computer systems since the early 1980s. From the very first microprocessor, the 4004 with some 2 300 transistors (1971), through to the P6 with 5.5 million transistors (1995), the number of transistors has approximately doubled every two years. There has been a corresponding increase in the number of calculations per second that can be handled from 60 000 (4004) to 300 million (P6).

There have been corresponding developments in the more specialist mid-range scientific computers known as workstations: at the time of writing (1995), individual microprocessors used in workstations are capable of more than 10^9 instructions per second. Similar developments have given rise to immensely powerful supercomputers which can process several calculations simultaneously. Such systems are called 'parallel' computers and have several individual microprocessors connected together (Figure 2.2). With the development of 'massively parallel' computers in which the number of microprocessors linked together is limited only by the cost, it is now only a matter of time before the much discussed 'teraflop' computer capable of 10^{12} calculations per second becomes a reality.

Figure 2.2
A Cray T90 parallel supercomputer. The most powerful T90 containing 32 individual processors linked together is capable of up to 60 billion (6×10^{10}) calculations per second.

This massive increase in processing power has enabled the development of computer graphics systems capable of drawing complex pictures so quickly that movements of three-dimensional objects can be carried out in real time: in other words, animation of complex objects is possible at a rate too fast for the eye to perceive the individual pictures (or frames), and the impression gained is of continuous motion.

These developments have given chemists a powerful new tool. As you have learnt, one of the most powerful methods in science is that of modelling.

■ How would you describe the process of modelling in science?

■ Modelling involves the creation of a simplified representation of the system under study that can explain known observations and then be extended to predict the behaviour of the system (and analogous systems) under a variety of other conditions. The model may be mathematical, descriptive or physical.

In chemistry, molecular model kits of the type used in the Course have for many years been essential aids both for teaching purposes and for visualizing the shapes of molecules in research. One of the great discoveries of the 20th century, that of the structure of DNA and the genetic code (Book 1), was made by James Watson and Francis Crick using just such a physical model (Figure 2.3a). But generally, while useful for small molecules, physical models become of more limited use as the molecular system of interest gets larger. The effect of gravity means that such models can be manipulated in only a limited fashion, and they are prone to falling apart! With the advent of molecular graphics packages, scientists have been released from all such limitations: these create mathematical models of molecular systems, which are presented on a computer screen in a graphical form that mimics the physical model kits used for so many years (Figure 2.3b).

(a)

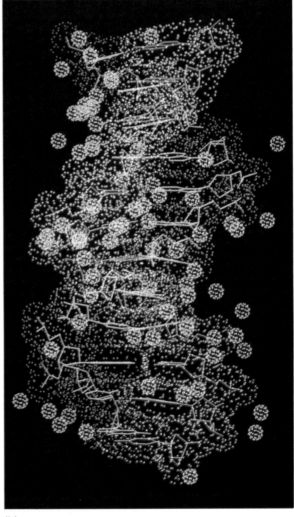

Figure 2.3
(a) James Watson and Francis Crick with the model of DNA that they built in the early 1950s; (b) computer graphics image of DNA (the green circles show where water molecules are likely to bind on the outside of the DNA molecule).

(b)

An immediate further advantage is that the same molecule can be represented in different ways with a simple keyboard command: each representation has its own advantages and disadvantages, and so it is very useful to be able to switch from one to another at will. Take the amino acid methionine as an example, with the structural formula shown in Figure 2.4a. The simplest type is the framework model (Figure 2.4b); this allows the interiors of complex models to be examined more readily but gives a misleading impression of the size of the molecule. Sometimes, with this representation, the hydrogen atoms are left out altogether to simplify the model even further (for example Figure 2.17 in Book 3 Part 1). At the other extreme is the space-filling representation (Figure 2.4d); this gives a good idea of molecular size, but it is not easy to examine the interior of larger molecules. In between is the ball-and-stick representation (Figure 2.4c), which is a compromise between the other two. (The model of DNA shown in Figure 2.3b is another type of compromise, in which the framework model is overlaid with a 'dotted' version of the space-filling representation.) You have become familiar during the Course with these different ways of representing molecules.

Figure 2.4
The amino acid methionine shown in four different ways: (a) structural formula; (b) framework representation; (c) ball-and-stick representation; (d) space-filling representation.

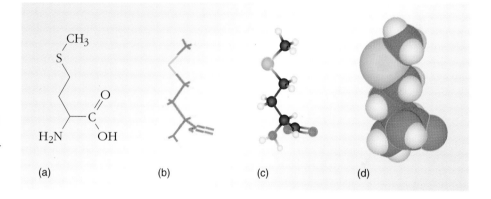

(a)   (b)   (c)   (d)

Another limitation of physical models is the fact that, as the molecule of interest increases in size, it generally becomes more and more flexible. This is a result of the free rotation about all the single bonds in the model. It is not obvious which particular arrangement, or **conformation**, is the one adopted by the molecule in reality. Most molecular graphics systems, by using one of a number of theoretical models, can calculate the conformation that has the lowest energy. The forces between molecules as they interact can also be calculated. For example, the preferred way in which a molecule 'docks' into a receptor molecule can be predicted.

It is also possible, by calculating the energies of different conformations or different arrangements of groups of molecules, to find out how molecular systems change with time (Figure 2.5, overleaf). This gives greater insight into the general behaviour of the molecule or molecules of interest, and can reveal the best molecular structure for a particular application.

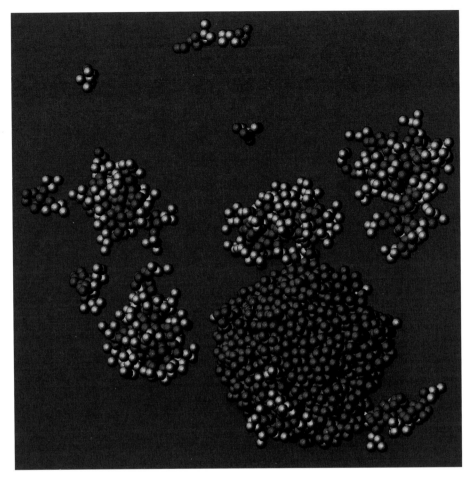

Figure 2.5
Molecular modelling study of the process of oil being solubilized by a solution of a surfactant. The simulation was carried out on a supercomputer and involved 852 oil molecules, 501 surfactant molecules and 25 096 water molecules. The solubilization process was followed for a set time, and a total of over 1.6 million 'snapshot' images of the system like this one were calculated. This is the instantaneous configuration at step number 836 000. The molecules are drawn in a simplified representation: oil molecules are coloured green, and surfactant molecules are drawn in yellow (headgroup) and red (tails). The water molecules are not shown.

Thus it is not surprising that the power of computer-based molecular graphics has found wide application: from devising chemical sensors to the search for alternative sweeteners, from the creation of designer polymers to understanding the mode of action of zeolite catalysts. Perhaps the most far-reaching is the search for new drugs. These may be to cure diseases for which there are currently no suitable medicines, or they may be better drugs to replace ones that have undesirable side-effects, or, in the case of antibiotics, to which various bacteria have developed resistance. In the next Section we shall describe how molecular graphics has been used in the search for drugs to combat influenza.

> **Question 1** What advantages does computer-based molecular modelling have over the use of physical models? Can you think of any disadvantages?

> **Question 2** Why do you think computer-based molecular modelling has become routinely used by chemists only since the late 1980s?

Video 2 'Modelling Molecules' is linked to the material described in the remainder of Chapter 2. This two-part video should preferably be watched before you read the text.

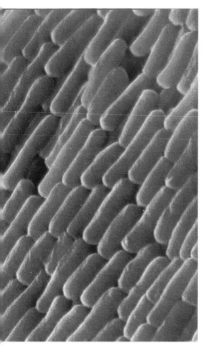

Figure 2.6
False-colour image of the large rod-shaped bacteria *Bacillus anthracis*, causative agent of anthrax in farm animals (magnification ×9 000). The disease is transmitted to humans by contact with infected animal hair, hides or excrement. The bacilli attack either the lungs, causing pneumonia, or the skin, producing severe ulceration. In the body the bacteria appear singly or in pairs, but when cultured they grow in long chains as seen here. This image was obtained using an electron microscope and is called an electron micrograph. The principle of operation of electron microscopes is described in Box 2.1 (see later).

2.2 The influenza virus

Many of the diseases from which humans suffer are caused by micro-organisms, notably bacteria and viruses. Bacteria are single-celled organisms with all the necessary biological apparatus to enable them to reproduce (including both deoxyribonucleic acid, DNA (Book 3 Part 2) and the related molecule ribonucleic acid, RNA) (Figure 2.6).

◼ What are two main features always present in biological cells?

◼ All cells have a membrane and a nucleus. The membrane essentially holds the cell together, and the nucleus contains the DNA residues that carry the information essential for replication.

In the presence of suitable nutrients, bacteria can reproduce at a phenomenal rate: a colony of bacteria grown overnight from a single cell can contain as many as 10^8 cells by the next morning! Fortunately, there are a large number of medicines that can be taken, notably various antibiotics, which specifically combat many disease-causing bacteria (Book 3 Part 2 Chapter 7).

Viruses are very different from bacteria. They are smaller (typically 20–200 nm in diameter compared with 500–5000 nm for bacteria) and consist of a core of nucleic acid (either DNA or RNA, but no virus is yet known that contains both) protected by a coat of protein (Figure 2.7). They do not carry out any biochemical reactions, such as synthesizing proteins or metabolizing nutrients to provide energy. Most crucially, although the nucleic acid contains the information necessary for reproduction, they are unable to multiply by themselves. Instead, the virus needs first to infect a living, susceptible host cell. It then takes over or 'hijacks' the host's 'chemical workshop', and the host cell makes copies of the virus according to the instructions provided by the original virus. Because viruses do not engage in metabolic processes of their own, they are not susceptible to antibiotics or indeed to many other types of drug. In most cases, all that can be done to treat virus-caused diseases is to alleviate the symptoms and allow the body's own immune system to deal with the infection in due course.

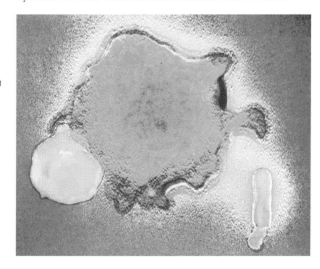

Figure 2.7
False-colour electron micrograph of a single virus particle of the measles virus (magnification ×80 000). The virus's lipid and protein envelope (orange) has been ruptured and the genetic material (yellow) is emerging at lower left. The genetic material is in fact a long thin filament, coiled up into an almost spherical ball. The filament consists of a single strand of RNA wrapped in a protein coat.

Interest in viruses has greatly increased in recent years because of the implication of the human immunodeficiency virus (HIV) in the development of acquired immunodeficiency syndrome (AIDS). The huge publicity generated by AIDS has had the effect of relegating other viruses to relative obscurity as though they are no longer a problem and the diseases they cause can be effectively combated. Yet there is one extremely well-known disease caused by a virus that has no effective drug to cure it, and which as recently as 1975 (before AIDS hit the headlines) was described as 'the last great plague'. That disease is influenza, more commonly known simply as 'the flu'.

Influenza has been present for much of recorded history. One of the earliest epidemics occurred in Greece and was reported by Hippocrates in 412 BC. The name 'influenza' was introduced by the Italians during an outbreak in 1504 in the belief that it was caused by the influence ('influenza' in Italian) of the stars, though later writers make reference to 'influenza di freddo' (influence of the cold). It has been known since the 1930s that influenza is caused by a virus. Giving rise to an elevated temperature and muscular aches and pains, flu tends to be regarded more as a nuisance than a life-threatening disease. Yet each winter many older people and small children are killed by flu, and in years when there is an epidemic, many thousands die. In the 1918–19 epidemic, flu was responsible for more deaths in a short time than any other cause, some 20 million or more world-wide.

As with other viral diseases, there is neither a cure nor even a very effective treatment currently available for flu. Even the best anti-flu drug, amantadine, is only effective against a limited number of strains of the virus. One of the reasons why flu is particularly difficult to treat is that new strains are constantly appearing. When only a minor variation occurs, then the incidence of flu is relatively low because most of the population has antibodies from a previous outbreak, such as in 1993 in the UK (Figure 2.8). If a more substantial change has occurred, then an epidemic can result. The appearance of a completely new strain can cause a severe and widespread epidemic, which is given the name pandemic. The pandemics this century were in 1918, 1957 (Asian flu) and 1968 (Hong Kong flu).

Figure 2.8
The path of the *Beijing A* strain of the flu virus responsible for the 1993 outbreak in the UK from its source in China in 1989. There are three main types of influenza: A, B, and C. C is generally mild but both A and B can cause widespread epidemics. The full title of the 1993 UK strain is *A/Beijing/32/92*, which identifies its type, place of origin, virus structure and year it appeared.

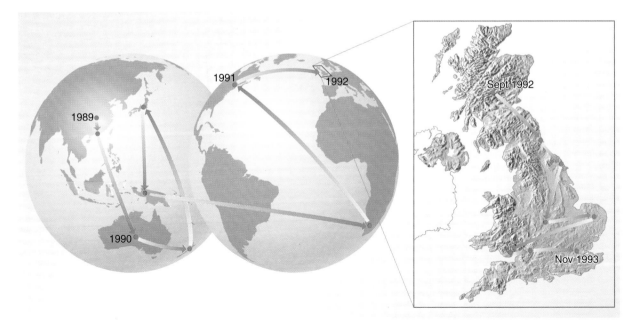

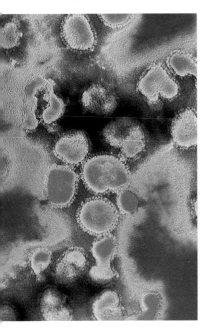

Figure 2.9
False-colour electron micrograph of influenza viruses (magnification × 80 000). Each virus contains a core of ribonucleic acid (RNA, orange), surrounded by a spiked protein envelope (green dots). The spikes can change structure to create a new strain such as this *Beijing* strain which spread as an epidemic in 1993.

Vaccination against flu can be carried out and is partially effective. However, the vaccine is made to counter previous strains of flu. By its very nature, the next strain is unknown, so vaccines are always one step behind. The search for drugs that cure or at least provide effective treatment has been proceeding for many years, mainly by the trial-and-error method of screening possible candidates. Though this approach has been remarkably successful at discovering drugs to treat other diseases, little progress in finding a cure for flu has been made.

The flu virus is roughly spherical in shape (Figure 2.9) and contains a core of RNA within a shell of proteins and lipids (Figure 2.10). The whole virus is covered by hundreds of spikes. There are two kinds of spike, each type being made of a particular protein. One type of spike, made of a protein called haemagglutinin (Figure 2.10), has a vital role in the first stages of infection, the penetration of host cells. Each haemagglutinin spike has a number of clefts at its end. These clefts are receptor sites for attachment of the virus to the surface of the host cell. They recognize a particular molecular feature, a molecule called sialic acid, which is attached to the surface of susceptible cells within the body (Figure 2.11 and structure 2.1), such as those within the respiratory tract.

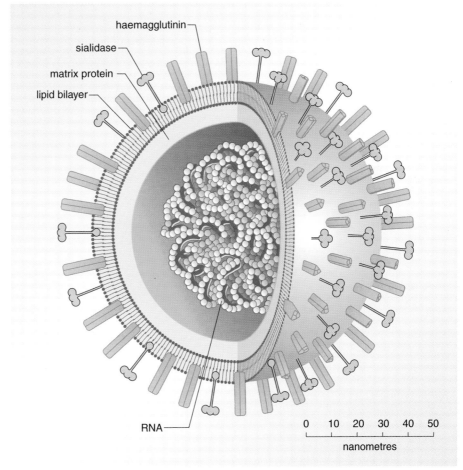

Figure 2.10
Schematic diagram of an influenza virus.

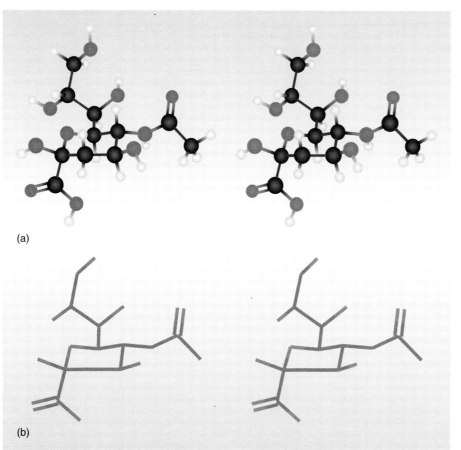

2.1 sialic acid

(a)

(b)

Figure 2.11
Stereoscopic models of the sialic acid molecule, which is chemically bound to the surface of susceptible cells and which fits the receptor site in the haemagglutinin spike: (a) ball-and-stick representation; (b) skeletal representation (a framework representation that does not show the hydrogen atoms).

The second type of spike is made of a protein called sialidase, which is an enzyme (Figure 2.10).

▨   What in general is the function of an enzyme?

◼   Enzymes are proteins that catalyse reactions. Enzymes are usually quite specific as to the substances that they transform (Book 3 Part 1).

The specific role of sialidase seems to be to help the newly formed viruses to escape from the host cell. They are then able to move on and infect other cells. As part of this process, sialidase cleaves off sialic acid molecules (hence the name 'sialidase'). As with the haemagglutinin spikes, the sialidase spikes also have clefts. However, these differ in that they are not receptor sites but are the active sites of the enzyme into which the bound sialic acid fits during the cleavage process.

The structure of the operative part of the sialidase active site seems to remain constant across the various influenza strains. What varies is the amino acid residues that surround the active site (Figure 2.12). It is for this reason that natural antibodies or vaccines are only partially successful: they work by recognizing the outer surface of the protein rather than the inner region of the active site and so do not recognize the modified viral surface. Any effective anti-influenza drug must take account of this fact.

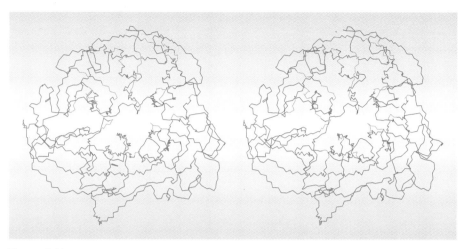

Figure 2.12
Stereoscopic skeletal model of sialidase from the influenza virus *A/Tokyo/3/67* strain. Just the backbone atoms are shown for clarity. The active site is the deep cavity at the centre of the model. The residues shown in orange are those associated with the active site which are conserved in all known strains; those shown in red are conserved but located remote from the active site; the rest shown in blue are subject to variation. Note that the inner regions of the active site are largely conserved whereas it is surrounded by variable residues. Antibodies or vaccines interact with the protein surface rather than the inner regions of the active site.

> **Question 3** Why is it particularly difficult to find a drug to treat influenza successfully?

2.3 A possible cure for flu

In the search for effective anti-influenza drugs, some researchers have concentrated on the initial infecting action of haemagglutinin. Other groups have focused their attention on sialidase.

▪ Given that sialidase is an enzyme, what type of compound should be sought that might act to prevent infection from spreading?

■ A compound that blocks the action of sialidase, that is a kind of molecular 'plug' that could occupy the active site of the enzyme in preference to the sialic acid group. Once the enzyme is plugged, then the newly formed viruses would be prevented from escaping from the host cell and spreading to other cells.

A compound that inhibits or blocks the action of an enzyme is called, not surprisingly, an **inhibitor**. Sialidase inhibitors have been sought for many years but without much success. In attempting to design an inhibitor, an obvious starting point is with the structure of sialic acid.

▪ Why do you think the sialic acid structure is a good place to start?

■ Because sialic acid is the natural substrate, it is known to bind to the active site of the enzyme. A sialidase inhibitor would also need to bind to the active site, so using the sialic acid structure as a starting point should increase the chances of discovering a molecule that binds strongly.

One such synthetic derivative of sialic acid, called Neu5Ac2en (pronounced 'new-five-ack-two-enn') (Figure 2.13 and structure **2.2**) was reported in 1969. It is essentially a molecule of sialic acid that has lost a molecule of water to give a double bond adjacent to the carboxylic acid group. Neu5Ac2en was shown to inhibit the action of influenza sialidase. Unfortunately, it does so only weakly, so large doses would be required if it were to be used as a drug. Even more worryingly, Neu5Ac2en was not very specific. Other sialidase enzymes occur in bacteria and in mammals, and Neu5Ac2en was shown to inhibit the action of these sialidases to a similar extent to that found with influenza sialidase. Finally, Neu5Ac2en was found to act as an inhibitor only *in vitro*, in other words in the test-tube, and not *in vivo*, that is in living systems.

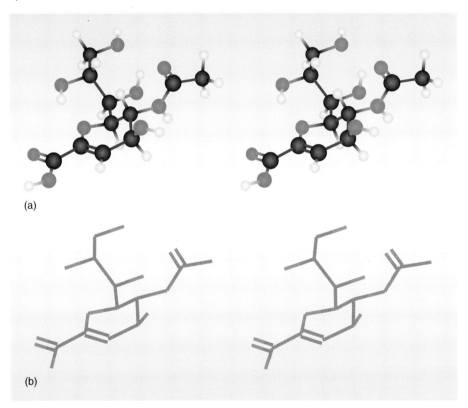

(a)

(b)

Figure 2.13
Stereoscopic models of the sialic acid derivative, Neu5Ac2en: (a) ball-and-stick representation; (b) skeletal representation.

2.2 Neu5Ac2en

Many analogues of Neu5Ac2en were synthesized over the years using the trial-and-error method, but none was a significantly more effective inhibitor, and none was shown to be effective *in vivo*. Clearly, an entirely different approach was needed. This was made possible when a research group at the CSIRO Division of Protein Chemistry at Victoria in Australia managed in the early 1980s to determine the detailed molecular structure of influenza sialidase (Figure 2.14) using the technique called X-ray crystallography (Box 2.1).

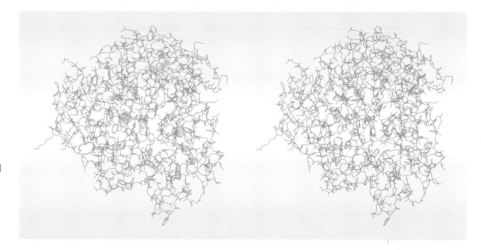

Figure 2.14
Stereoscopic skeletal model of the structure of sialidase from flu virus type *A/Tokyo/3/67*. The cavity that forms the active site can be seen clearly at the upper centre.

Box 2.1 Visualizing the structures of molecules

The smallest objects that can be distinguished with the naked eye are about 0.1 mm across. To see smaller objects, a microscope has to be used. Ordinary microscopes can magnify up to around 500 times: this means that they can be used to see a typical bacterium (about 2 µm across) but not a large virus (about 100 nm across). It turns out that, in order to 'interact' with a light wave, an object has to be no smaller than about half the wavelength of light. This sets a limit of about 250 nm for even the best optical microscope.

It is possible to see even smaller objects than this by using, not light, but electrons. You

may recall from Book 1 that electrons behave sometimes as if they are particles and sometimes as if they are waves. Their wave-like properties are used in the electron microscope. Instead of lenses, the electrons are focused using magnetic fields. Because the wavelength of electrons depends on their energy, very short wavelength electrons can be generated using high energies. Electron microscopes are often used to look at bacteria (Figure 2.6) and are essential to be able to see viruses (Figures 2.7 and 2.9). The practical limit on the size of objects that can be distinguished using an electron microscope is about 100 pm. This is just about enough to resolve

individual atoms, but in practice it is not a useful technique for determining the structure of individual molecules because the high energies involved damage the materials being examined.

If, instead of electrons, X-rays are used, then it is possible to obtain information about the structures of individual molecules. Unfortunately, there are no substances that can be used to make lenses for X-rays, and X-rays are not affected by magnetic fields, so an indirect method has to be used. This depends on the fact that objects of a similar size to the wavelength of radiation used can diffract that radiation. (The process of diffraction is a type of scattering.) If X-rays with

wavelengths similar to the covalent bonding distances between atoms in molecules are used, the X-rays are diffracted by the individual atoms. That is why this technique is sometimes called **X-ray diffraction.**

In order to be able to make use of this technique, it is necessary for the molecules to be arranged in a regular pattern, as they are in a single crystal. Hence the alternative name for the technique is **X-ray crystallography.** Fortunately, the crystals do not have to be large. Protein crystals used for structure determination are typically less than a millimetre across. *(continued overleaf)*

However, growing single crystals of such large molecules is no easy task, and sometimes necessitates tens or even hundreds of trial crystallizations.

The X-rays are scattered by the electrons associated with each atom in the molecule. The regular arrangement of the molecules in the crystal, and hence of the atoms within each molecule, means that the scattered X-rays reinforce one another in particular directions around the crystal producing a characteristic diffraction pattern (Figure 2.15).

In a typical X-ray crystallography experiment, a single crystal is mounted in an X-ray diffractometer, a computer-controlled instrument that can orientate the crystal at many different angles with respect to the X-ray beam. The positions and relative intensities of the reflections are related to the positions of the   . atoms within the molecule. Systematic measurement and computer analysis of these data make it possible to 'solve the structure' and work out these atomic positions. The data give rise to an electron density map, the contours of which define the positions of the various atoms, which can be displayed on a computer screen (Figure 2.16 top). However, this is not the end of the story.

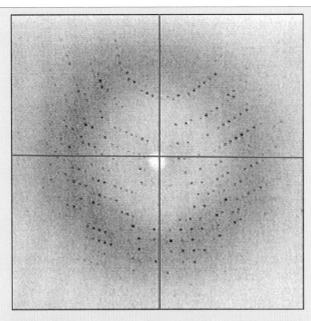

Figure 2.15
X-ray diffraction pattern from a protein crystal.

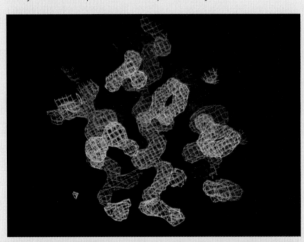

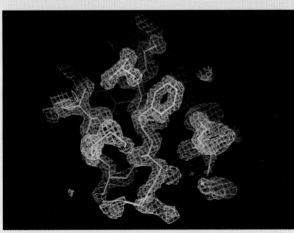

First, hydrogen atoms, because they have only one electron, do not scatter X-rays very effectively and so are not usually 'seen' in the resulting electron density map. Second, for biological molecules in which most of the atoms have very similar numbers of electrons, namely carbon, nitrogen and oxygen, it is not obvious which atoms are which. Separate experiments are carried out to determine the sequence of amino acid residues in the protein. This means that a computer model of the protein molecule can be constructed and fitted to the electron density map (Figure 2.16 bottom). By reprocessing the data to give the best fit to the computer-generated model, a much better molecular structure can then be determined.

Figure 2.16
Electron density map of part of a protein (top); the electron density map with a computer-generated model fitted (bottom).

In addition to determining the structure of the enzyme itself, the Australian scientists took a crystal of sialidase and 'soaked in' sialic acid by immersing the crystal in a solution of the acid. Some of the sialic acid molecules migrated to the active site. By determining the structure of the enzyme again, but this time with the substrate in place, the researchers were able to find out how the sialic acid was disposed in the active site (Figure 2.17). By soaking in Neu5Ac2en they were similarly able to determine the structure of sialidase with the inhibitor in place. They found that the way in which the inhibitor occupied the active site was very similar to the way in which sialic acid was bound.

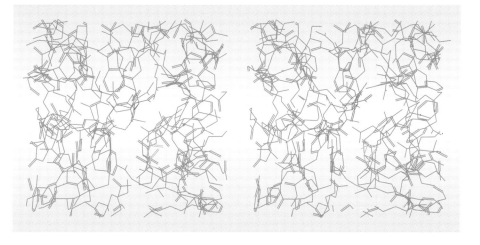

Figure 2.17
Stereoscopic skeletal model showing sialic acid bound to the active site of sialidase. The two coloured residues are the ones that were crucial in the search for a better inhibitor (see below): glutamic acid residue 119 is coloured orange and glutamic acid residue 227 is coloured red.

With this information available, it was possible to examine in more detail the pocket in which the sialic acid or the inhibitor resides. This is precisely what a group of scientists at Monash University's Victoria College of Pharmacy did, in collaboration with the group at CSIRO Victoria, and with the additional involvement of scientists in the UK from the pharmaceutical company Glaxo. The aim was to see first if there was additional space to accommodate possible different molecular groupings that could be attached to the Neu5Ac2en template, and second what amino acid residues were adjacent to these positions with which such new groups might be able to interact.

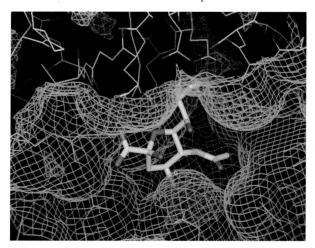

Careful examination of the active site cavity with sialic acid bound in place revealed that there was indeed space for fitting other groups (Figure 2.18). The next question was how to decide which additional groups would be most suitable. As an aid to this process, they used a computer program called GRID, which had been developed at Oxford University in the mid-1980s.

Figure 2.18
Structure of the sialidase active site with sialic acid bound, showing the region of the pocket with space for fitting an appropriate extra group. The blue 'net' delineates the accessible surface of the sialidase molecule. The additional space is underneath and slightly to the right of the sialic acid molecule.

The GRID method involves calculating the interactions between a 'probe' group (such as an amino group or a carboxylic acid group) and atoms and groups in the protein. The method gets its name from the fact that the calculations are carried out for each of a regular array of points (a three-dimensional 'grid') encompassing the protein molecule. Using the GRID method it is possible to discover those locations on the surface of the protein where there is a net attraction for a particular group. Such a location is called a 'hot spot' and signifies a potentially favourable binding site for a molecule containing that particular group.

The interactions are treated as being made up of a sum of the individual contributions from the various forces that the probe group can experience. The first contribution takes account of what occurs where atoms of the probe come very close to an atom of the protein. When this happens the two atoms experience a repulsion, which can become very large as the centres of the atoms approach one another.

The second contribution results from the universal attraction between atoms and molecules due to London forces (Book 1).

The next contribution comes from the attraction or repulsion experienced between charged and/or polar groups. Carboxylic acid groups (COOH) often lose an H^+ ion to form a carboxylate ion (COO^-), which is negatively charged; amino groups (NH_2) often gain an H^+ ion to form an NH_3^+ group, which is positively charged (Book 3). Interactions between such groups give rise to a net electrical attraction or repulsion. In addition, molecules containing polar bonds, such as C—O or C—Cl, have permanent electric dipoles (Book 1). This also gives rise to a net electrical attraction or repulsion when two dipoles come close to one another.

The final contribution takes account of the possibility of hydrogen bond formation between O—H or N—H bonds of the probe and groups such as C=O at the surface of the protein, or vice versa.

The Monash group first tested the GRID program by using a carboxylic acid probe to investigate the sialidase active site. Sure enough, a 'hot spot' was duly found precisely where the carboxylic acid group of sialic acid or Neu5Ac2en sits when it binds to the enzyme.

Careful inspection of a model of the active site enabled the Monash group to spot a nearby glutamic acid residue (Glu-119) (Figure 2.17) close to one particular hydroxyl (OH) group on the inhibitor Neu5Ac2en. Glutamic acid (Figure 2.19) has a free carboxylic acid group attached, which could strongly attract an amino (NH_2) group, particularly if it was protonated to form an NH_3^+ group. When a fresh GRID calculation was carried out, this time using an amino probe, a hot spot appeared exactly where one was expected. The presence of other amino hot spots from the GRID results, together with further visual inspection, revealed an additional glutamic acid residue (Glu-227) (Figure 2.17) potentially within reach.

These results provided the vital clue the Australian chemists needed. They designed and synthesized two new compounds, amino-Neu5Ac2en (Figure 2.20 and structure **2.3**) and guanidino-Neu5Ac2en (Figure 2.21 and structure **2.4**), in which an OH group of the original inhibitor (Figure 2.13) was replaced by either an amino group or a guanidino group (Figure 2.22), which is effectively a bigger group with *two* amino groups at its end. The excellent match between guanidino-Neu5Ac2en and the GRID calculated hot spots can be seen in Figure 2.23.

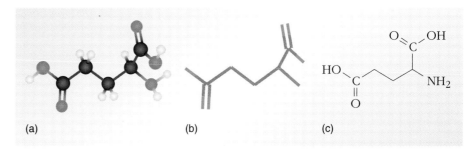

Figure 2.19
Glutamic acid: (a) ball-and-stick representation;
(b) skeletal representation;
(c) structural formula.

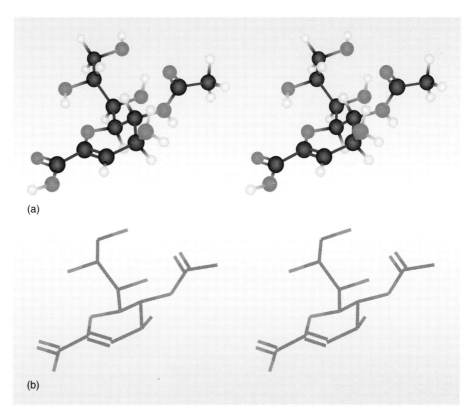

Figure 2.20
Stereoscopic models of amino-Neu5Ac2en: (a) ball-and-stick representation;
(b) skeletal representation.

2.3 amino-Neu5Ac2en

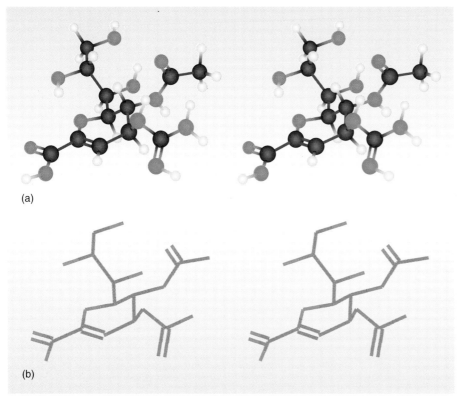

(a)

2.4 guanidino -Neu5Ac2en

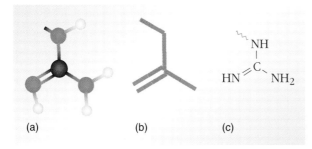

(b)

Figure 2.21
Stereoscopic models of guanidino-Neu5Ac2en: (a) ball-and-stick representation; (b) skeletal representation.

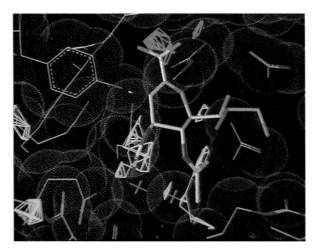

(a)   (b)   (c)

Figure 2.22
Guanidino group: (a) ball-and-stick representation; (b) skeletal representation; (c) structural formula.

Figure 2.23
GRID results for sialic acid active site. The dotted blue spheres and pale skeletal structures are parts of the sialidase structure. The red shape shows the carboxylic acid hot spot lying exactly where the carboxylic acid group of guanidino-Neu5Ac2en inhibitor is located; the various blue shapes are amino hotspots, two of which match up with the location of the ends of the guanidino group.

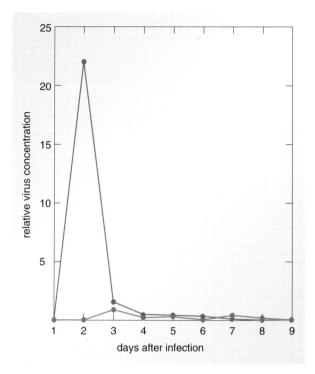

Figure 2.24
Results of the application of the guanidino compound to ferrets infected with the flu virus. The red line denotes the group that received therapeutic doses of the trial compound; the blue line denotes the control group which were treated with just distilled water.

In vitro tests of the amino compound revealed it to bind some 20 times more strongly than Neu5Ac2en itself, and the guanidino compound was bound at least 5000 times more strongly. Furthermore, the two compounds seemed to be much more selective for influenza virus sialidase than was Neu5Ac2en, and to bind much more weakly to other types of sialidase.

These initial results alone provided vindication for the approach taken, namely basing the design of a new inhibitor on detailed knowledge of the active site of the enzyme. But even more encouragingly, subsequent tests showed the two compounds to be active *in vivo* as well. The guanidino compound in particular showed dramatic inhibition of viral replication, both in tissue cultures (cells grown in a dish on the laboratory bench), and in ferrets infected with influenza virus (Figure 2.24).

There are two points to note about the way in which these compounds were discovered. First, the information obtained from the computer modelling and the GRID program was not of itself sufficient to design the new inhibitors; in other words, experience of the field together with some chemical intuition was still required to know where in the active site to look and what functional groups to use to make a viable molecular structure. There was also still a need for the skills necessary to make the compounds once the desired molecular structures had been specified. The second point is that both the modelling process and the calculation of the GRID data are only approximations. There was no certainty that the new compounds would necessarily turn out to be better inhibitors in practice. What the method does is greatly to increase the likelihood of success compared with the traditional trial-and-error approach.

Demonstration of the impressive activity against influenza virus displayed by the guanidino compound is not adequate evidence to be certain that this will prove to be the long-sought treatment for flu. It is only the first step in a long process of testing necessary before any new drug is made available for general use. Unforeseen side-effects may be discovered or it may be unacceptably toxic, for example. However, these initial results were sufficiently promising for Glaxo to put out a press release about the new compounds:

Computer designs powerful flu drug

Powerful new drugs for treating flu may soon be available, scientists from Australia and from Glaxo Group Research announce today.

They have used computers to design two compounds that inhibit the growth of the flu virus in test-tubes and in animals. Trials on human patients have not yet begun. ...

*Tested against the flu virus in tissue cultures and in experiments with
mice and ferrets, the compound known as GR 121167X [the guanidino
compound] proved the most potent inhibitor of flu virus yet discovered. It
is 1000 times as effective as the existing flu drug, amantadine.*

*Glaxo said yesterday that the next step would be to set up a trial in which
the compounds were tested for toxicity on volunteers. Then the drug could
be tested in flu patients in a full-scale clinical trial.*

(The Times Business Section, 4 June 1993)

This story of the discovery of new inhibitors for influenza virus sialidase is but
one example of the application of computer-based molecular modelling in the
design of novel biologically active compounds. In addition to the use of the
modelling program, it also involved the use of other software in processing the
X-ray diffraction data and in calculating the GRID data. It serves to show how
the application of computers in chemistry is transforming the way in which the
development of new drugs is carried out. Such is the power of these methods
that pharmaceutical companies world-wide are investing heavily in the
currently available technology. But there are developments on the horizon that
may dramatically affect the way in which drug design takes place in the future.
Just what these advances are we shall examine briefly in the next Section.

Question 4 Explain why a sialidase inhibitor would be expected to act as
a drug against influenza.

Question 5 In Book 3 Part 2 you saw how the drug captopril was
designed as an inhibitor to compete with the natural substrate for
angiotensin-converting enzyme (ACE) in the absence of any direct
structural information about the ACE active site. Describe the steps
required if you were to attempt to design an improved ACE inhibitor
using the approach adopted in the design of guanidino-Neu5Ac2en as a
potential drug against influenza.

Question 6 If the procedure discussed in Question 5 were followed,
what do you think the chances would be of designing a drug significantly
better than captopril?

2.4 The future

Workstations used for computer-based modelling can be thought of as
involving two main components: the processor, which carries out all the
necessary calculations, and the interface between the computer and the
operator. In the future, progress can be expected in both increased processing
power of computers and in an improved interface. There is every sign that the
steady increase in processor power seen over the past decade or more (Section
2.1) is likely to continue. More open to speculation is the interface that
computer modellers will be using a decade from now. Perhaps the most
obvious area to begin with is the way the images are displayed.

Currently, most modelling is done using a workstation with a large-screen
monitor (50 cm or larger). Many of them are also equipped with special
spectacles that allow images to be viewed in three dimensions (3D). As you
know from Book 1 and your own use of the Course 3D viewer, we perceive

Figure 2.25
'Crystal-eyes' liquid crystal spectacles for 3D viewing. At the instant the picture was taken, the left lens was darkened and the right lens was clear. You will learn about liquid crystals and some of their uses in Section 3.2.

Figure 2.26
Double image produced on a computer modelling screen for 3D viewing.

Figure 2.27
A virtual reality system.

objects as being three-dimensional because the left eye and the right eye see two slightly different views. The brain then fuses these to produce the 3D perception.

The special spectacles used for modelling, called by the trade-name Crystal-eyes™, have liquid crystal eyepieces that can be switched between dark and clear positions. This is done alternately, with first the left eye being made dark while the right eye is clear, and vice versa (Figure 2.25). This switching process is synchronized with the image on the screen by means of an infrared beam. So, the left eye image is shown when the left eyepiece of the spectacles is clear, and the right eye image is shown when the right eyepiece is clear. This is done rapidly enough that, because of the eye's persistence of vision, the brain fuses the two images as though they were viewed simultaneously. Without the glasses, a double image is seen on the screen (Figure 2.26).

Another possibility being investigated is to adapt some of the techniques employed in state-of-the-art computer games, and in particular the method known as **virtual reality**. In principle, this would give the user the impression of being in the same space as the molecules. In the usual set-up, the virtual reality system consists of a headset with two small colour video screens embedded inside. The headset cuts you off from your surroundings, and the miniature screens provide a stereoscopic image of the virtual world to which the software transports you (Figure 2.27). A joystick or three-dimensional 'mouse' provides the means of interacting with the images, allowing you to control the direction both of viewing and of motion.

Prototype virtual reality molecular modelling systems have been developed at the University of York Chemistry Department and at the Computer Sciences Department of the University of North Carolina in the USA (Figure 2.28). One of the limitations of present head-mounted displays is the low resolution of the small liquid crystal screens currently available. Other headsets use cathode-ray tubes like miniature TV sets, which have higher resolution, but these are much more expensive. Another problem is the need for more detailed models. Constructing a virtual world of complex molecules such as proteins 40 times a second using ball-and-stick models is at the limit of current technology.

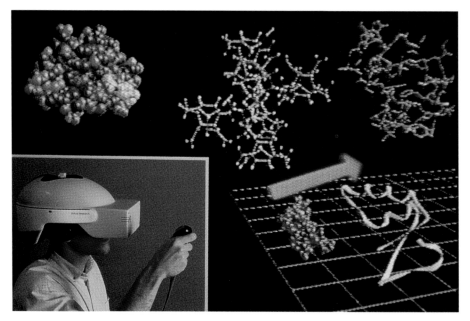

Figure 2.28
Virtual reality molecular modelling system at the University of North Carolina. Wearing the head-mounted display and using a three-dimensional 'mouse', the user is able to 'fly through' a virtual world of large molecules. Moving their head allows the user to survey the scene. The user 'flies' by pressing a button on the 'mouse'. The arrow shows the direction of flight; the speed of flight is controlled by how far the hand is extended from the body.

The example of the development of possible anti-flu drugs described in the previous Section illustrated the use of computer-based molecular modelling in the design of an enzyme inhibitor. In that process, an indirect method was used to fit the trial inhibitor molecules into the model enzyme, with the aid of the GRID software. But suppose it were possible to grab hold of a candidate molecule and actually insert it into the active site. If the forces encountered during this process could be experienced by the operator, it should then be much more straightforward to find out the optimum relative orientation of the potential inhibitor and the enzyme.

This might seem an impossible dream, but attempts to design systems that provide such **force feedback** have been going on for many years. Such a system has been in use at the Computer Sciences Department of the University of North Carolina in the US for some years. The system has a so-called servo-manipulator called the Argonne 'arm' (Argonne Remote Manipulator) (Figure 2.29). In the molecular modelling system, the arm is linked to the parts of the program that generate movement of the docking molecule and of the protein, and the modelling software calculates the forces between the two. Use of the servo device enables the whole view (drug molecule and protein together) to be manipulated, or the drug molecule to be moved while the protein remains fixed. As the drug molecule approaches the receptor site, the operator experiences directly, through his or her hand and arm, the forces between the molecules, whether attractive or repulsive.

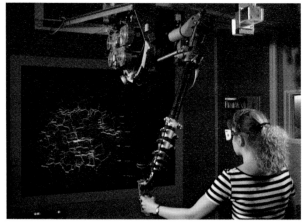

Figure 2.29
The Argonne arm in use for docking studies. This was originally built as the master station of a remote manipulator for use at Argonne National Laboratories in Illinois for the manipulation of radioactive materials without danger to the operator. Instead of using a monitor, the image is projected on to the back of a translucent screen. However, it is still possible to link in liquid crystal spectacles, which allow the operator to see the protein, drug, and docking process in 3D on the large screen.

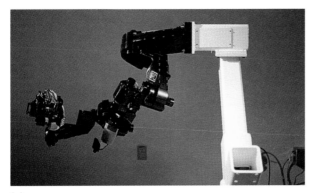

(a)

(b)

Figure 2.30
(a) The Sarcos arm;
(b) modelling studies using
the Sarcos arm system
equipped with 'Crystal-eyes'
liquid crystal spectacles.

Although the Argonne arm has provided much insight into the requirements for a force feedback system, it is based on 1960s technology and has a number of shortcomings. It requires the operator to be standing up rather than sitting in a more comfortable position. Its positioning is accurate to only about one centimetre, and its use involves fairly large movements. Finally, it can feedback only a relatively small force and it is relatively slow to respond.

Most of these defects are not present in a more modern manipulator called the Sarcos arm (Figure 2.30a). Rather than relying on electrically driven servo-mechanical motors, it is driven by very high-pressure hydraulics. It is used by the operator while seated (Figure 2.30b). It is much more precise in its positioning, to within a millimetre, and works in a smaller volume. It can respond much more quickly to changes, and it can deliver a much stronger feedback force. Development using this arm is still in its early stages.

Both the Argonne arm and the Sarcos arm are extremely expensive, costing hundreds of thousands of dollars each, so they are unlikely to find widespread use elsewhere. However, there are a number of groups both in academic institutions and in industry that are carrying out research and development activities to try to produce an affordable force feedback device. Because force feedback is also of interest to the computer games industry, the chances of an affordable device becoming available within the next 5-10 years are fairly high.

All these developments individually offer enhancements to the tools currently available for molecular modelling. What is likely to happen over the next few years is that these tools will be further developed and refined, and they will be interfaced with one another as scientists work towards the ultimate in molecular modelling systems. Whether that will involve virtual reality-type headsets or large-screen technology remains to be seen.

Whatever the precise form of future developments, the use of molecular modelling by computer will undoubtedly play an increasingly important role in new drug development. As our understanding grows, the need to screen hundreds of different substances for desired activity should lessen dramatically. This should lead to the design of novel drugs effective against hitherto intractable conditions, as well as a marked decrease in the time needed to bring new drugs to the market.

Question 7 Which would you regard as being the more useful development for molecular modelling: a viable force feedback device or a head-mounted display with high resolution screens for use with a virtual reality modelling system?

Summary of Chapter 2

The advent of ever-faster computers has enabled the development of computer graphics systems capable of drawing complex objects at a rate so fast that the impression is gained of continuous motion. These developments have given chemists a powerful new tool, computer-based molecular modelling.

Computer models of molecules have several advantages over physical models: they do not fall apart even when large molecules are represented; different types of model can be produced by a simple command; and the energies of molecules in different situations can be calculated. Computer-based molecular graphics has found many applications, but perhaps the most far-reaching is the search for new drugs.

Many of the diseases from which humans suffer are caused by micro-organisms, notably bacteria and viruses. Bacteria are single-celled organisms with all the necessary biological apparatus to enable them to reproduce. Viruses are different: they are smaller, they do not carry out any biochemical reactions themselves, and most crucially, they are unable to multiply by themselves.

One extremely well-known viral disease is influenza. As with many other viral diseases, there is currently no cure for flu. The flu virus is roughly spherical, and covered by hundreds of spikes made of two different kinds of protein, haemagglutinin and sialidase. In the search for effective anti-influenza drugs, some researchers have concentrated on the initial infecting action of haemagglutinin. Other groups have focused their attention on sialidase.

Using the technique of X-ray crystallography, a group at Victoria in Australia determined the molecular structure of sialidase, by itself and with the substrate sialic acid bound to the active site. They also determined the structure of the enzyme with the weak inhibitor Neu5Ac2en bound in place.

With this information, a group at Monash University was able to design better inhibitors, based on the Neu5Ac2en template, which had an additional group (amino in one case and guanidino in another) that assisted the binding process. The use of the software GRID, which locates 'hot spots' on the surface of the protein where particular groups might bind, was crucial to the design process.

Tests of the two new compounds indicated that they were much more effective inhibitors (particularly the guanidino compound) than the parent Neu5Ac2en. The two compounds are currently undergoing trials for use as a drug to combat flu.

The design process was not simply a mechanical activity. Experience of the field together with some chemical intuition was still required, together with the skills necessary to make the compounds. Also, there was no certainty that the new compounds would necessarily be better inhibitors. However, the method does greatly increase the likelihood of success compared with the traditional trial-and-error approach.

Molecular modelling in the future is likely to be made more powerful and easier to carry out by advances in processing power and improvements to the user–computer interface. Most workstations already have special 'active' glasses that allow molecules to be perceived in 3D. Likely changes to the interface include the application of virtual reality methods and force feedback techniques.

Chapter 3
Materials to order

3.1 The materials revolution

The vital role of materials as an enabling factor for future technological developments is now widely recognized. As you have already seen in Book 2 Part 1, this recognition of the importance of materials to society is not new. Throughout history, humans have appreciated the worth of materials:

> *Of course materials of one kind or another have been vitally important throughout human history. Do we not talk of the Stone Age, the Bronze Age, and the Iron Age, implying that a material was the defining technology of an era? Likewise historians have argued that the invention of hydraulic cement by the Romans played an important part in the growth of the Roman Empire... Indeed, the Industrial Revolution itself was based on new ways of processing the materials coal, iron and steel. Since then, progress in the more efficient use of the 'traditional' manufacturing metals, iron and steel, has continued...*
>
> *(T. Forester ed.,* The Materials Revolution, *MIT Press, Cambridge, Massachusetts, 1988, p. 6)*

Figure 3.1
The wide range of materials available from a metals and materials supplier:
(a) metals and alloys;
(b) polymers; (c) ceramics;
(d) composites.

What *has* changed in recent times is the range of materials that are now available (Figure 3.1). As a consequence, the field of materials science has become much broader, encompassing scientists of many different disciplines. Furthermore, the role of chemistry is becoming ever more crucial.

(a)

(b)

(c)

(d)

Yesterday materials makers were mainly metallurgists. Today they must also be chemists, ceramists, engineers, and physicists. In their labs you often see them staring at the wall; follow their gaze and you see a copy of the periodic table, that cryptic tabulation of the elements they so cleverly manipulate.

(T. Y. Canby, Advanced Materials—Reshaping Our Lives, *National Geographic, Vol. 176, No. 6, December 1989, p.752)*

The development of such materials provides a powerful reminder that chemistry is a profoundly creative subject. Because the range of materials available is now so wide, we can look at only a small selection. We have chosen examples that we think are representative, and are likely to be of increasing importance in the near future. The materials we have selected are liquid crystals, two contrasting types of polymer, and ceramics.

3.2 Liquid crystals

One of the more obvious changes to have occurred during the past decade or two is the widespread appearance of **liquid crystal displays** (LCDs). LCDs are evident in such disparate applications as electronic calculators, clocks, car instrument panels, petrol pumps, and airport and rail station information boards (Figure 3.2).

- What other examples can you identify of the commercial uses of liquid crystal displays?

- Almost any device that needs to display information is likely to have a liquid crystal display. Examples you may have thought of are digital watches, photocopier displays, FAX machines and mobile paging devices.

(a)

Perhaps the application of LCDs with the biggest impact, and the one with greatest future potential, is their use in computer displays (Figure 3.3a), and for pocket TVs and video cameras (Figure 3.3b).

What are **liquid crystals**? And what features cause molecules to behave as liquid crystals?

- What are the properties that distinguish the liquid state from the crystalline state?

- You may recall from Book 1 that liquids have a fixed volume but take up the shape of the container in which they are placed; they also flow. At the molecular level, there is little order and molecules can move around freely. In contrast, crystals have a very ordered structure, and have both a fixed volume and a fixed shape. At the molecular level, the atoms, ions or molecules do not change their positions in the lattice.

(b)

Figure 3.2
(a) Range of devices with liquid crystal displays: kitchen scales, calculator, video controller, mobile telephone, and travel clock; (b) the display board at Paddington Station, London.

(a)

(b)

Figure 3.3
(a) Laptop computer with LCD screen; (b) video camera with LCD viewfinder.

Figure 3.4
Schematic illustration of (a) crystal, (b) liquid crystal and (c) liquid phases. The cylinders symbolize individual molecules.

As you might expect from the name, liquid crystals have properties that are intermediate between true liquids and solid crystals. Liquid crystals have a degree of **orientational order**, and sometimes even some **positional order** (Figure 3.4). By orientational order we mean that molecules orient themselves relative to adjacent molecules in a regular, rather than a random, fashion; by positional order we mean that molecules are constrained to a particular position and cannot move about freely. Movement of the molecules that make up a liquid crystal does occur, however, and there is much less orientational order than in a solid crystal, which has high degrees of both positional and orientational order.

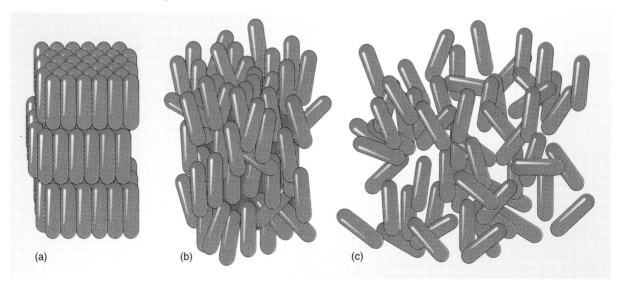

(a)   (b)   (c)

Is it possible to say whether a liquid crystal is more like a liquid or more like a crystal? The answer is yes.

▨   The loss of order on converting a crystal into a liquid is associated with an enthalpy change. Can you recall from Book 2 Part 2 what this enthalpy change is called?

■   The enthalpy of fusion, or melting.

The size of the enthalpy change associated with a transition from one state to another is a useful indication of how different the two states are. The conversion of a crystal into a liquid crystal and of a liquid crystal into a liquid both have associated enthalpies. For the liquid crystal material cholesteryl myristate (Figure 3.5), for example, the enthalpy change involved in changing from the crystal into the liquid crystal is 272 J g^{-1}, and only 29 J g^{-1} are needed to convert the liquid crystal into the liquid. It is apparent that most of the order present in the crystal is lost when the liquid crystal is formed, and the small enthalpy change required to convert the liquid crystal into the true liquid indicates that the degree of order present in the liquid crystal is relatively small. Clearly, for cholesteryl myristate, the liquid crystal is more 'liquid-like' than 'crystal-like'. This is generally the case with liquid crystals.

Figure 3.5
Cholesteryl myristate:
(a) space-filling model;
(b) structural formula.

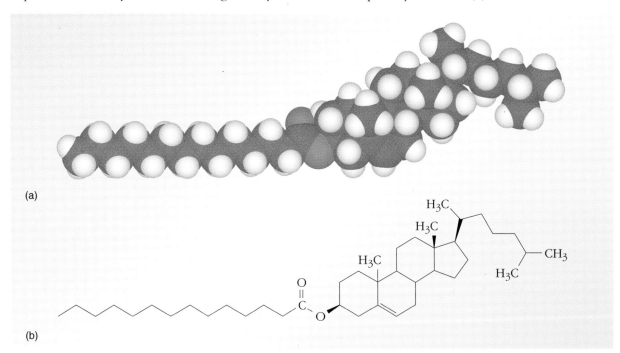

(a)

(b)

What types of material give rise to liquid crystals? It has been found that many such materials have three features in common:

●   the molecules are much longer than they are wide (liquid crystals are also formed by disc-shaped molecules but we shall not be considering these);

●   the molecules have a rigid part, usually in the middle;

●   there are groups at one end or both ends that are long and fairly flexible.

In addition, the presence of a polar group at one end seems to enhance liquid crystal formation. Some examples are shown in Figure 3.6.

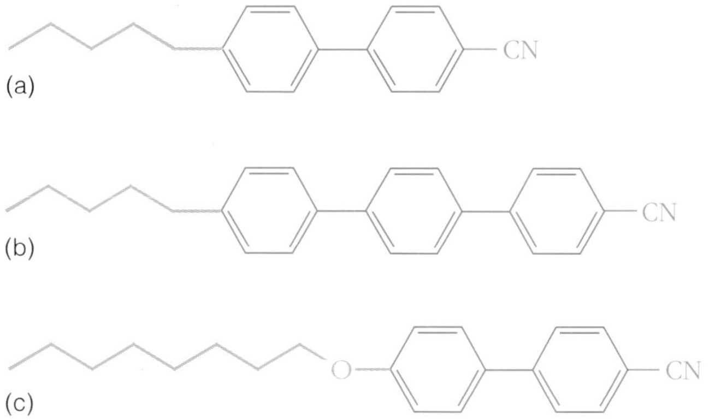

Figure 3.6
Some examples of liquid crystal materials used in current LCDs: (a) 4-cyano-4′-pentylbiphenyl; (b) 4-cyano-4′-pentylterphenyl; (c) 4-cyano-4′ octoxybiphenyl. The rigid part is highlighted in red, the flexible group in green, and the polar cyano group in blue.

Liquid crystals can form a number of different types of phase. Perhaps the most common is the **nematic phase**, as formed by biphenyl compounds, such as those shown in Figure 3.6. In nematic liquid crystals (Figure 3.7), the molecules tend *on average* to have a preferred orientation along a particular direction. This direction is called the **director**.

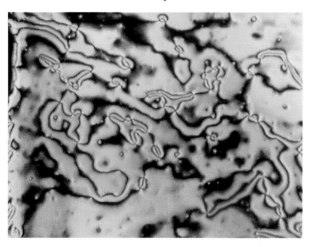

Figure 3.7
Nematic liquid crystal seen under a microscope through crossed polarizers (see text).

Liquid crystals have the property of rotating **polarized light**. Polarized light is light in which the waves vibrate in only one direction at right angles to the direction of travel, whereas ordinary light vibrates in all directions (Figure 3.8a). Polarizers have the effect of transmitting only light vibrating in a particular direction (Figure 3.8a), and so if a second polarizer is oriented with its polarization axis at right angles to the first, the polarized light is unable to pass through. If a liquid crystal is placed between the crossed polarizers, the polarized light is rotated, and so is no longer at right angles to the second polarizer. Consequently, some of the light is able to pass through the second polarizer (Figure 3.8b). Because the director direction is not constant through the liquid crystal sample, when white light is used the effect is to produce coloured images (e.g. Figure 3.7). Viewing liquid crystals, or any other materials such as thin sections of rock or other crystals (e.g. Book 1 Figure 8.10), through crossed polarizers enables features to be seen that are invisible with ordinary light.

Liquid crystals that are chiral also form a nematic phase called **chiral nematic**. In these phases, the direction of preferred orientation changes from one molecule to the next and the orientation of the director rotates through the sample (Figure 3.9). The effect is to form a helix, rather like the thread on a bolt. The material cholesteryl myristate referred to earlier forms this type of liquid crystal structure (Figure 3.10).

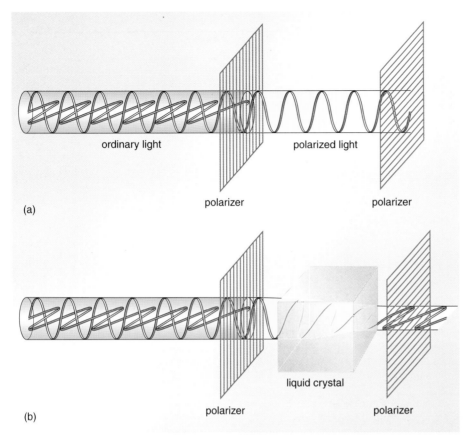

(a)

(b)

Figure 3.8
(a) Ordinary light passing though a polarizer emerges as polarized light which vibrates in only one direction at right angles to the direction of travel; on meeting a second polarizer oriented at right angles to the first, the polarized light is unable to pass through, and the effect observed from the other side is of blackness. (b) If a liquid crystal is introduced between the polarizers in (a), the polarized light is rotated through an angle that depends on the nature and amount of the material; the light beam is then able, at least partially, to pass through the second polarizer and can be observed from the other side.

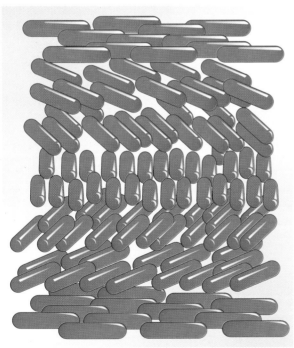

Figure 3.9
Schematic illustration of molecules in a chiral nematic liquid crystal.

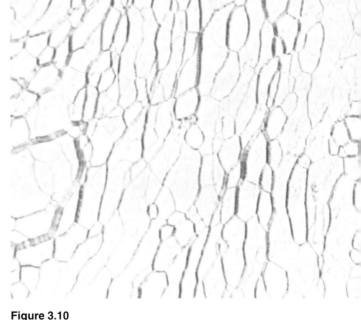

Figure 3.10
Chiral nematic liquid crystal seen under a microscope through crossed polarizers.

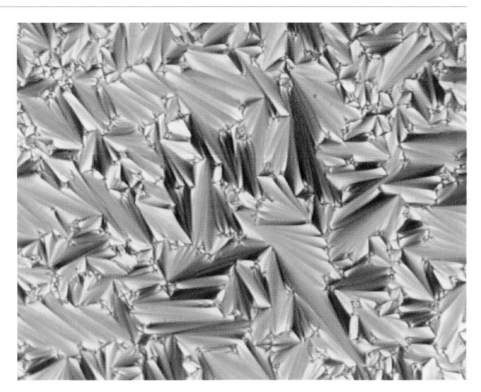

Figure 3.11
Smectic liquid crystal seen under a microscope through crossed polarizers.

A substance may form either a nematic or a chiral nematic phase but not both. In both these phases, there is a degree of orientational order but essentially no positional order. However, some materials also form a third type of structure called a **smectic phase**, in which, in addition to the orientational order, there is also some positional order (Figure 3.11). The smectic phase, if present, is always the initial type of liquid crystal to be formed; further heating then gives rise to the nematic phase if present, followed by the true liquid. The substance 4-cyano-4'-octoxybiphenyl (Figure 3.6c) shows this behaviour: at 54.5 °C the solid crystals change to a smectic liquid crystal; at 67 °C this changes to the nematic phase; then finally, at 80 °C, the nematic melts to the true liquid.

The most common type of display for laptop computers is based on nematic liquid crystals (Box 3.1). The fact that such displays require relatively low amounts of electric power to operate, that they are both light and slim, and that they give off no radiation of the type emitted by conventional desktop displays using TV-type cathode-ray tubes (CRT) all make them eminently suitable for this particular application. Indeed, it is widely predicted that because of their inherent advantages, LCDs will displace CRT displays for desktop computers and TVs in the not too distant future. Some of the earlier types of display do suffer from a relatively low degree of contrast, and passive colour LCDs (Box 3.1) can appear rather dull. However, newer displays including thin film transistor (TFT) displays (the type shown in Figure 3.3a) have excellent performance, though they are currently expensive to manufacture (Box 3.1).

Box 3.1 Liquid crystal displays

The heart of a liquid crystal display (LCD) is a layer of liquid crystal material sandwiched between two glass plates (Figure 3.12). The glass plates are coated on one side with a polymer that is then 'stroked' in one direction to produce microscopic grooves in the polymer; the two plates are then orientated so that the grooves are at 90 degrees to one another. The liquid crystal molecules prefer to align themselves with the grooves, but at the same time try to remain aligned with one another. The result is that the molecules twist to form a spiral, hence the name **twisted nematic** for this kind of display.

Long, thin transparent electrodes are attached to the reverse side of the glass plates, which enable a small voltage to be applied at different points on the screen (Figure 3.12). For a typical monochrome screen there are 640 vertical electrodes and 480 horizontal ones. This gives a grid of 640 × 480 individual dots (called pixels), a total of 307 200 dots; a colour screen requires three dots (one each of red, green and blue) for each pixel of the monochrome screen, so it has three times as many individual pixels, that is 921 600. The colours are produced using appropriate colour filters (Figures 3.12 and 3.13).

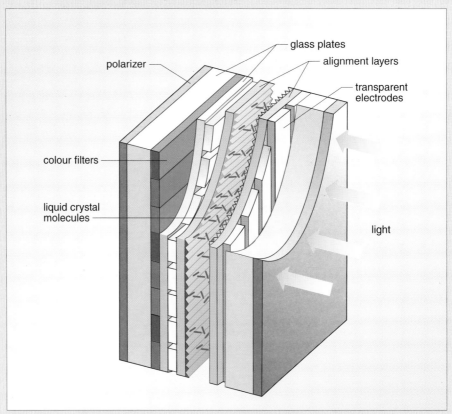

Figure 3.12
Cross-section of a twisted nematic liquid crystal display.

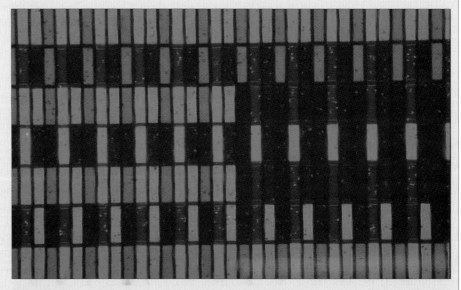

Figure 3.13
Enlarged view of a liquid crystal display showing the arrangement of the red, green and blue coloured pixels.

Providing the outer layers of the multi-layer sandwich are two polarizers set with their axes also at right angles (Figure 3.12). Polarized light produced by the first polarizer is then twisted through 90° as it passes through the liquid crystal and so is able to pass through the second polarizer. The effect is then a bright appearance to the display. However, if a small voltage is applied to particular areas of the liquid crystal, say in the shape of an alphabetic character, the molecules in these areas are forced to line up perpendicular to the plates. Now the polarized light is not rotated and it cannot therefore pass through the second polarizer. The effect is of dark character on a light background. If only one or two of the coloured pixels that make up a group of three are switched then the effect is of a coloured character.

Screens that operate as described above are called passive displays. For technical reasons to do with the way in which each individual dot is switched on and off, leakage of the electric charge tends to occur and adjacent pixels interfere with one another. Also switching is rather slow. These disadvantages are removed in active displays, in which each pixel consists of a minute individual transistor laid out on a silicon wafer; switching these on or off does not affect adjacent pixels and so the display is brighter and sharper. Also, because transistors can be switched more quickly, they have faster response times. Because the whole panel is laid out on a single piece of silicon, and even one faulty pixel shows up clearly, the rejection rate is very high. This makes active matrix displays (also known as thin film transistor or TFT displays) very much more expensive. Despite this, their advantages often outweigh the extra cost. For example, in 1994, the New York Stock Exchange was able to double the number of displays in the limited space available on the trading floor by replacing all the traditional monitors by TFT displays.

Another application of liquid crystals is in thermometry. You may well be familiar with the convenient strip thermometers used for taking someone's temperature by placing the thermometer on the forehead (Figure 3.14). The colour changes according to the temperature and reveals the appropriate number. Other liquid crystals are even more sensitive to temperature, and using them it is possible to monitor temperature visually over a range as small as one degree. One example of this use is a sheet of liquid crystal material that can be used medically as a diagnostic tool (Figure 3.15). When spread over the part of the body to be investigated, it pinpoints any unusually warm areas, often a signal of some abnormality such as a tumour near the surface of the skin. Another rather more aesthetic use is as a fashion feature (Figure 3.16). Liquid crystal materials incorporated into clothes change colour when worn, depending on one's activities!

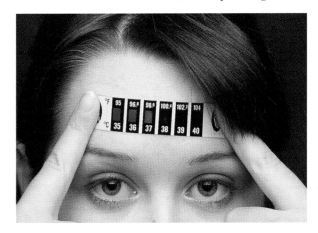

Figure 3.14
Liquid crystal thermometer.

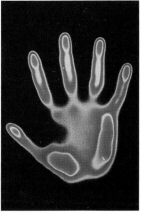

Figure 3.15
Thermogram. The different colours show parts of the hand at different temperatures.

Figure 3.16
Clothes made from cloth incorporating liquid crystal materials.

All of these applications make use of the fact that chiral nematic liquid crystals selectively reflect certain wavelengths of light. If white light shines on such a chiral nematic material, most of the wavelengths will be transmitted. However, for light with a wavelength equal to the pitch (the degree of twist of the director) the light is selectively reflected. Because of this the liquid crystal will appear to be coloured. For certain chiral nematic liquid crystal materials, the pitch changes drastically with temperature, and hence so does its colour.

Question 8 Which of the molecules **A** to **E** are most likely to form liquid crystals?

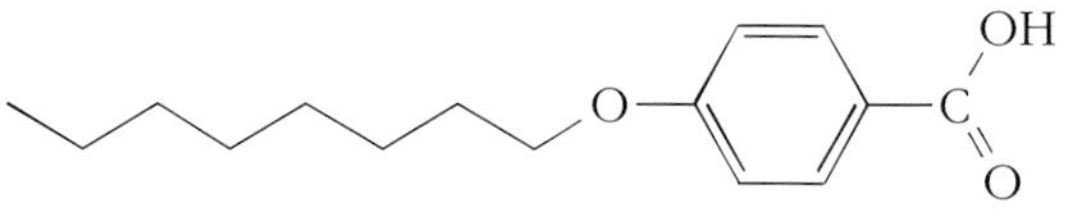

A

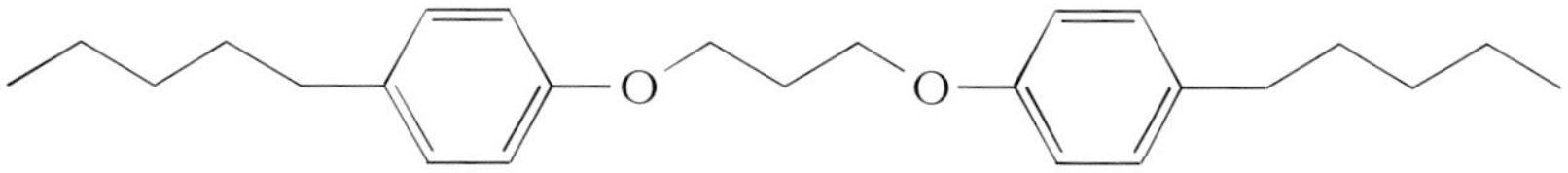

B

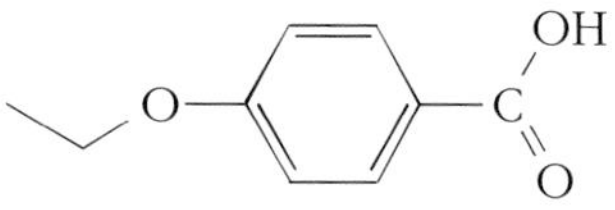

C

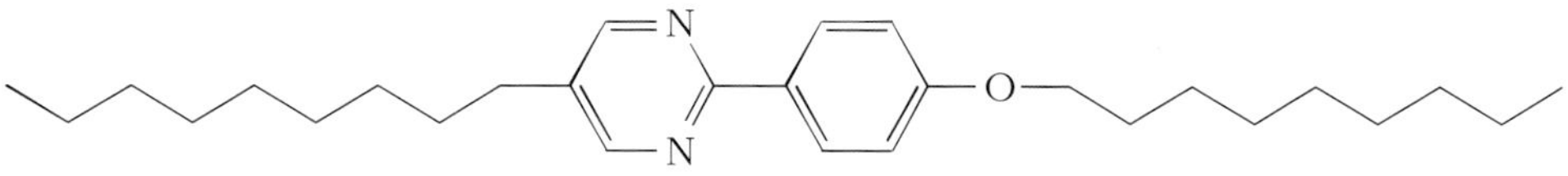

D

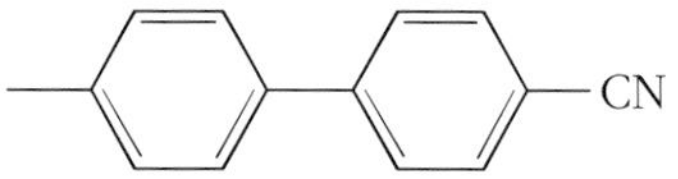

E

Question 9 What is the essential difference between the mode of action of an LCD and the use of liquid crystals in a thermometer strip?

3.3 Superpolymers

Perhaps the most pervasive and versatile group of synthetic materials are the polymers. You have seen earlier in the Course (Book 2 Part 1) that bulk thermoplastics such as polyethene, poly(vinyl chloride) (PVC) and polystyrene have many uses in our everyday lives. They have largely replaced traditional materials, such as wood or paper, for some applications, and for others their unique properties allow uses for which there is no analogous natural material. Synthetic fibres, such as nylon, have not totally replaced their natural counterparts, such as cotton or silk, but they are frequently used to supplement them. Cloth made from a mixture of natural and synthetic fibres combines the desirable features of both types of material.

However, there are increasingly applications for which the properties of the older polymers are not suited: for example, stronger fibres may be needed for applications involving extreme conditions, or new plastics with greater toughness and durability are required for engineering uses in the building of cars. There are other uses for which totally new polymers are being devised. Our much improved understanding of the way in which molecular structure influences bulk properties, together with state-of-the-art techniques such as computer-based molecular modelling, means that the process of discovering new polymeric materials is now more the result of a rational design process and less based on trial and error.

The design of new polymers is guided by a number of principles that have been developed over a period of years.

The strength, toughness or elasticity of a polymeric material depends on the presence of long molecules. These typically have 1000 atoms or more connected in a chain. Smaller molecules, even if in the regular array found in a crystal, do not confer on the material these properties.

The nature of the backbone structure has a dramatic effect on properties.

- The replacement of every sixth $-CH_2-$ group by an amide group converts polyethene (**3.1**) into a type of nylon called nylon-6 (**3.2**), a material with quite different properties.

3.1 polyethene

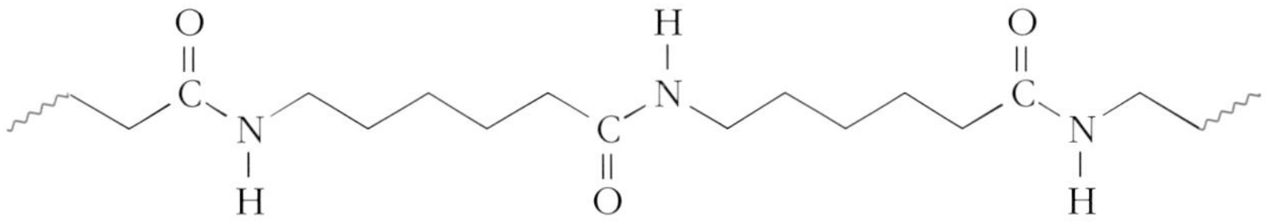

3.2 nylon-6

- The replacement of each $-CH_2-CH_2-$ unit by a $-CH=CH-$ unit converts polyethene, an insulator, into polyethyne (**3.3**), a silver-coloured material that conducts electricity.

3.3 polyethyne

- The replacement of every other $-CH_2-CH_2-$ unit by a $-CH=CH-$ unit converts polyethene into polybutadiene (**3.4**), a synthetic rubber used in tyres.

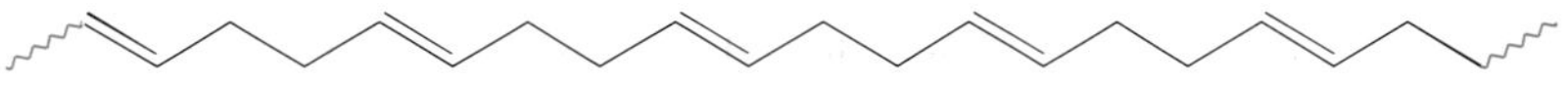

3.4 polybutadiene

- The replacement of the flexible $-CH_2-CH_2-CH_2-CH_2-$ groups in poly(ethylene adipate) (**3.5**) by rigid benzene rings in poly(ethylene terephthalate) (PET, **3.6**) shows the effect of rigidity on melting temperature: **3.5** melts at around 50 °C, **3.6** at around 265 °C.

3.5 poly(ethylene adipate)

3.6 poly(ethylene terephthalate)

- The replacement of the $-CH_2-CH_2-$ groups in PET (**3.6**) by benzene rings in poly(phenylene terephthalate) (**3.7**) shows a further enhancement of this effect of rigidity on melting temperature: **3.7** melts at around 600 °C compared with **3.6** at around 265 °C.

3.7 poly(phenylene terephthalate)

The properties of a polymer also depend markedly on the nature and size of any side-groups attached to the polymer chain. For example, the hydroxyl groups attached to the chain in poly(vinyl alcohol) (PVA, **3.8**) make the polymer soluble in water whereas poly(vinyl chloride) (PVC, **3.9**) is not. Attaching a long rigid group via a flexible chain gives rise to polymers that form liquid crystals, as in **3.10**.

OH   OH   OH   OH   OH   OH   OH   OH   OH   OH
3.8 poly(vinyl alcohol)

Cl   Cl   Cl   Cl   Cl   Cl   Cl   Cl   Cl   Cl
3.9 poly(vinyl chloride)

3.10 liquid crystal polymer

Despite their many useful properties, saying something is 'just plastic' remains a derogatory term. But plastics are beginning to be viewed with greater respect for their intrinsic value rather than as fragile, throwaway substitutes for costlier materials.

▨   Look around you and see if you can identify examples of 'high-value' applications for plastics as opposed to more mundane uses such as for plastic bags.

■   Some possible uses you may have identified are as computer disks; optical disks for uses such as CD-ROM or as audio CDs; tape for audio and video; contact lenses; and an increasing number of components in your car. One use that may be regarded as mundane, but actually requires a tough plastic, is for bottles containing carbonated drinks.

Increasingly, the motor industry is looking to replace traditionally metal components with plastics, although, because of the inferior connotation of the term 'plastic', these materials are now often referred to as 'resins'. Cars with plastic bodies are lighter and less likely to corrode than ones with steel bodies. The resins used are as often mixtures or composite materials made from existing polymers as they are completely new polymeric compounds.

In the 1960s, the very useful properties of the various polyamides (nylons) coupled with their limitations in terms of toughness and heat resistance led scientists to search for new 'superpolymers' that would provide materials for uses for which existing polymers were simply inadequate. A group at the chemical company Du Pont explicitly set themselves the goal to discover a (thermoplastic) polymer fibre that would have the heat resistance of asbestos coupled with the stiffness of glass.

▨   From the rules set out above and what you know about the binding
      forces between molecules, what type of structure would you think is
      likely to possess high heat resistance?

■   For a structural material to be heat resistant it must have a high melting
      temperature. Accordingly the polymer needs strong forces between
      molecules.

In the absence of cross-linking (Book 2 Part 1), the strongest type of force
between molecules is provided by hydrogen bonds, as found in polyamides.
Polyesters might also be candidates, as the dipole–dipole forces between
polyester molecules can also be strong (see **3.5** and **3.6**).

What type of structure is likely to give rise to a stiff material? Polymers are
relatively flexible for two reasons: (a) the molecules that make up the
material are flexible; and (b) the molecules are often tangled up and not
ordered as they are in a crystal. If a more rigid molecule could be devised,
this might solve both problems at once.

▨   What type of molecular grouping have you come across that is rigid?

■   Aromatic groups such as benzene rings are rigid.

In 1965, a research scientist, working at the Du
Pont Experimental Station in Wilmington,
Delaware, made a key discovery that was to lead
eventually to the discovery of a new aromatic
polyamide with just the properties sought. Until
then, it had been the conventional wisdom that
such materials were far too insoluble for
manufacture to be feasible. But StephAnie Kwolek
(Figure 3.17) was able to prove that assumption to
be wrong. She managed to polymerize *para*-
aminobenzoic acid (**3.11**) in a condensation
reaction to produce a polyamide with the structure
3.12, the first so-called **aramid polymer**.
Furthermore, she was able to find a solvent that
would dissolve the polymer and so allow fibres to
be produced by the conventional method of
spinning while extruding through a spinneret
(Figure 3.18). Initially, because the solutions were
cloudy, it was thought that they contained
insoluble material that would clog the holes in the
spinneret. In fact, it proved possible to produce
fibres without any problems. It was later
discovered that the cloudiness was due to the fact
that the polymer solution formed a liquid crystal
phase.

3.11 *para*-aminobenzoic acid

Figure 3.17
StephAnie Kwolek, the Du Pont scientist who discovered a
new series of aromatic polyamides.

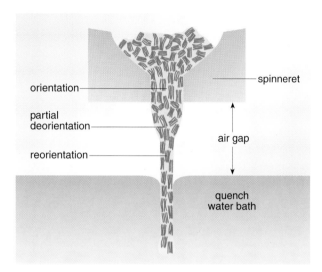

3.12 the first aramid polymer

Figure 3.18
Schematic diagram of a
spinneret for the production
of aramid fibres.

However, the monomer *para*-aminobenzoic acid was too expensive to scale
up. The structure of **3.12** is akin to that of nylon-6 (**3.2**), because the
monomer molecule has the amino group and the carboxyl group in the same
molecule. The 6 in the name nylon-6 refers to the fact that the monomer
contains six carbon atoms; other nylons are known in which the monomer
has a different number of carbon atoms, for example nylon-11, which gives
rise to a nylon with different properties. However, there is another type of
nylon which is made from two different monomers, one containing two
carboxyl groups, and the other containing two amino groups. A well-known
example is nylon-6,6 (**3.13**). The two 6s in nylon-6,6 indicates that the two
monomers both have six carbon atoms; other nylons are known in which the
monomers have different numbers of carbon atoms, for example nylon-6,10.

3.13 nylon-6,6

Analogy with nylon-6,6 led to the realization that another aramid polymer could in principle be formed between two different monomers, one containing two carboxyl groups, and the other containing two amino groups. The first, terephthalic acid (**3.14**), was already used to make PET (polyester) and the second, *para*-phenylenediamine (**3.15**), could be manufactured at an economic cost. In due course, the polymer (**3.16**) was synthesized and spun into a fibre. It was given the trade name Kevlar™ (Book 2 Part 1).

3.14 terephthalic acid

3.15 *para*-phenylenediamine

3.16 Kevlar

At this point, the entire programme almost came to a complete halt because of a very significant obstacle. When the researchers talked to the chemical engineers about operating the process on a commercial scale, the latter had the shock of their lives to learn that the only solvent that dissolved the polymer was 100% sulfuric acid! Furthermore, the polymer seemed to dissolve only to a small extent so a very large amount of sulfuric acid would be needed. Fortunately, another scientist, Herbert Blades, made a crucial discovery, that the polymer could be persuaded to form a crystalline compound with the sulfuric acid at a polymer concentration of 20% (by mass). The compound melted at 70 °C, low enough to allow spinning to be carried out. But the use of sulfuric acid did present the company with a waste disposal problem. The best solution turned out to be converting the waste acid into calcium sulfate (gypsum): for every 1 kg of Kevlar manufactured, 7 kg of gypsum are produced. Fortunately, gypsum has commercial value for turning into plasterboard and cement.

By 1972, a plant was built to produce over 450 000 kg of Kevlar per year for development uses, for example to allow potential customers to undertake trials for particular applications. By 1982, full commercialization had been achieved with a plant capable of producing 20 000 000 kg per year in the USA. In 1988, a second plant was started up in Northern Ireland and, in 1991, a third opened in Japan.

Kevlar is immensely strong, mainly because its fibres are almost totally ordered, with extensive hydrogen bonding (Figure 3.19). Mass for mass it is much stronger than steel. And immersed in water, of course, it does not rust. Because of these highly desirable properties, Kevlar is used extensively in ropes and cables, for example for tethering equipment on offshore oil drilling platforms, and even as mooring lines for the platforms themselves. It has found many uses, as varied as cords for tyre reinforcement, cut-resistant gloves for handling glass and other sharp objects, bullet-proof vests and composite materials for use in light-weight canoes (Figure 3.20) and aircraft construction, and it still has unfulfilled potential.

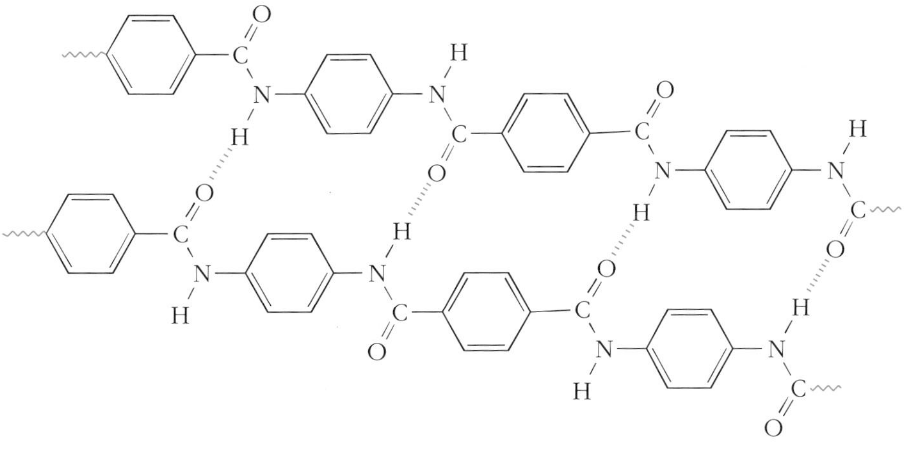

Figure 3.19
Hydrogen bonding between
Kevlar molecules.

Figure 3.20
A canoe made from Kevlar.

Question 10 In the late 1970s, it was discovered that polyethene made with very long molecules could be made to produce extremely strong fibres provided that the polymer was spun from a very concentrated jelly-like solution, akin to the spinning of Kevlar. Why should polyethene in this form be so strong? Do you think the strength is likely to be maintained at higher temperatures?

Question 11 Another aramid polymer called Nomex™ has the structure shown (**3.17**). (a) By identifying the monomer unit, and by analogy with the reaction that forms Kevlar, determine the monomers needed to manufacture Nomex. (b) By comparing its molecular structure with that of Kevlar, do you think Nomex would form stronger or weaker fibres than Kevlar?

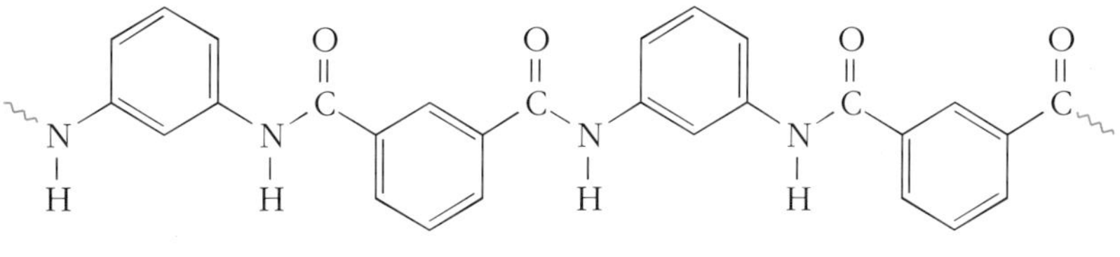

3.17 Nomex

3.4 Disappearing polymers

In the Course so far, most of the applications of synthetic polymers have been as structural materials to replace more traditional materials, such as metal, wood, paper, cotton or silk. For these applications, it has been improvements in the strength, toughness and durability of the polymer that have been the aim of most polymer research. Recently, however, there has been a great deal of interest in polymers that are designed to self-destruct. One such area is the use of biodegradable plastics for such uses as carrier bags: once these have fulfilled their use, and are disposed of in landfill sites, the object is for bacteria and/or light to cause relatively rapid decomposition (Book 2 Part 1). Another, perhaps surprising, use is in delivering medicine specifically to a particular site in the body or where controlled release is required over a long period, for example with certain types of contraceptive drug.

One of the chief disadvantages of administering medicines as tablets or by injection is the variation this causes in concentration over time. Ideally, the concentration in the body should be kept at some optimum value: too high can be dangerous, and too low is less effective. With the more traditional methods of taking medicines, the concentration will be highest shortly after each dose, and will then steadily decline until the next dose (the so-called 'rollercoaster' effect, Figure 3.21). In order to ensure that a sufficient amount reaches the target site, high doses are necessary because of the dilution effect and because the drug is metabolized to a greater or lesser extent before it gets there. The result is an increased risk of undesirable side-effects.

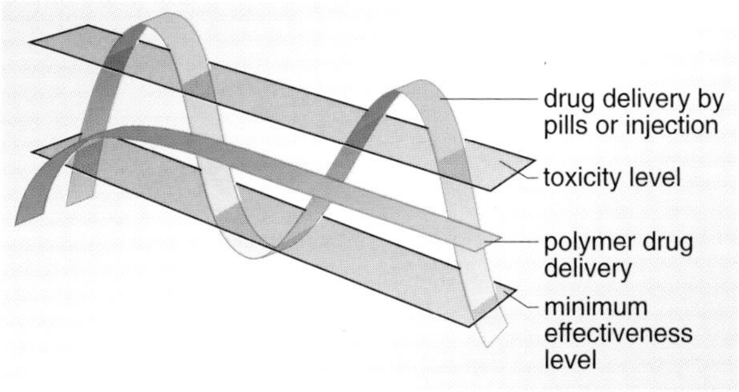

drug delivery by pills or injection

toxicity level

polymer drug delivery

minimum effectiveness level

Figure 3.21
'Rollercoaster' effect of traditional method of administering drugs compared with the constant dose delivered by a drug-impregnated dissolving polymer.

A method of releasing drugs that gets around both these problems has been under development for some years. It involves the use of tablets in which a special type of polymer is impregnated with the drug. The polymer is designed to be harmlessly biodegradable. In use, a small pellet of the drug-impregnated material is implanted under the skin. As the polymer slowly dissolves away, a constant dose of the drug seeps out (Figure 3.21). By tailoring the structure of the polymer appropriately, the time that the polymer takes to dissolve can be varied and hence the rate at which the drug is released can be controlled. By placing the implant near the diseased organ or target site, much lower doses can be used and the 'rollercoaster' effect is avoided. The result is much more effective use of (often expensive) drugs, and fewer side-effects.

One type of tablet makes use of polymers containing the **anhydride** functional group (**3.18**). Anhydrides are formed by the joining together of two carboxylic acids with the loss of a molecule of water. Polyanhydrides (**3.19**) have been known for many years. They were first discovered in the 1930s by Du Pont scientists led by Wallace Carothers, the discoverer of nylon. Polyanhydrides were tested for use in textiles but, because the molecules readily react with water and break down, the Du Pont scientists lost interest. Polyanhydrides were largely ignored until the 1980s, when scientists became interested in them *because* of their propensity to break down in the presence of water. This is just the property needed for a biodegradable polymer. Once it had been shown that the polyanhydrides and their breakdown products were harmless, the way was open for developing the dissolving polymer tablet.

3.18 anhydride group

3.19 a polyanhydride

For each application there is a different requirement for the length of time over which the polymer tablet erodes. By varying the monomer used to make the polymer, it is possible to alter the rate of degradation over a very wide range. The time taken for complete erosion varies from around one week for a tablet made from monomer **3.20**, to more than two years for a polymer made from **3.21**. A polymer made from a mixture of both types of monomer in varying proportions erodes over a period intermediate between the two extremes, for example around three weeks for one made from 80% of monomer **3.20** and 20% of monomer **3.21**. Incorporating the drug is straightforward. It simply involves grinding the appropriate polymer into a powder, mixing in the drug and then moulding the resulting mixture into a wafer or tablet.

3.20

3.21

One initial application is to treat cancer of the brain. Unlike most cancers, brain cancers do not spread to other organs. So, provided that it is detected early enough, it can be removed surgically with a fair degree of success. If this is followed by drug therapy to prevent a recurrence, the chances of survival are substantially increased. Unfortunately, one of the anti-tumour agents used for this purpose, called BCNU (**3.22**), is metabolized very quickly in the body and is also toxic to other tissues. Only 15 minutes after injection, half of the BCNU has been broken down. Raising the dosage to counteract this may give rise to side-effects such as lung damage and lowered resistance to infection.

3.22 BCNU

Figure 3.22
Henry Brem of Johns Hopkins University, one of the surgeons involved, holds a wafer of the type used in the BCNU implant trial.

Using the dissolving polymer method could greatly increase the effectiveness of the drug and also reduce the dosage needed. The pharmaceutical company Nova, together with scientists at the Massachusetts Institute of Technology in Boston and Johns Hopkins University in Baltimore, mounted a trial in which polymers impregnated with BCNU were implanted in the brains of patients following surgery (Figure 3.22). The wafers can deliver up to 1000 times more BCNU than could be delivered by injection. The polymer tablets last for about three weeks, releasing a more or less constant level of BCNU.

The patients who volunteered for the trial all suffered from a type of brain tumour that is particularly difficult to treat. Even with surgery and chemotherapy, the average survival time is only 50 weeks. So even a remote possibility that using dissolving polymer tablets could be much more effective was clearly worth investigating. Results from an initial trial involving 21 patients showed a significantly increased survival time compared with conventional treatment. A much larger trial involving 222 patients has recently been completed but the results have still to be published.

The development of biodegradable polymers for use in drug delivery provides a textbook example of how a polymer can be designed for a specific purpose. Although various polyanhydrides were already known, the specific molecules used for controlled release purposes were tailor-made to have the combination of properties required. The trials already carried out have shown sufficient promise to indicate that this method has great potential for treating diseases of the brain and indeed localized diseases in general.

> **Question 12** Identify two advantages of the use of a drug-impregnated polymer implant over taking the same drug orally. What disadvantage does this method have?

3.5 New ceramics

Of the various types of material, ceramics (Book 2 Part 1) are the ones that seem to have realized the least of the potential that materials scientists promise. The development of new ceramic materials is being hotly pursued by both industrial and academic research laboratories across the world yet, as we shall see, a number of crucial weaknesses have so far prevented their full exploitation.

Most of the ceramics in general use are the traditional ones that have been used for hundreds of years.

Figure 3.23
Two cooking vessels made of the ceramic material variously known as Pyroceram, Pyrosil or Corningware. This tough, heat-resistant material was discovered by accident when an object made of a special type of glass was left in an oven overnight at a higher than normal temperature. Next morning, the glass was no longer clear but looked like porcelain. A controlled crystallization process had occurred, giving smaller, more uniform crystals than those in conventional ceramics.

◻   From the knowledge gained from Book 2 and your general knowledge, list some of the ceramic materials that are currently in common use.

◼   Some possible ones are china and porcelain, glass, cements, enamels, and refractory materials used to line kilns in steel-making, where very high temperatures are used.

Another type of ceramic, which is much more recent, is the white material used by the Corning glass company to make certain types of saucepan and other cooking vessels (Figure 3.23). Other uses that capitalize on the hardness and wear-resistance of ceramics include materials such as tungsten carbide or silicon nitride for making drill tips for drilling brick, glass and rock.

◻   What distinguishes ceramics chemically from other materials?

◼   Ceramics are non-metallic inorganic solids.

The fact that ceramics are said to be non-metallic does not mean that they do not contain elements that are themselves metals, simply that in the ceramic form they do not have the properties of a typical metal. The term inorganic is used to distinguish them from organic materials, such as polymers.

■ What do you think are the advantages of traditional ceramics and what disadvantages do they have as materials?

■ Ceramics are generally hard and hard-wearing. They are also thermally very inert and so can be subjected to very high temperatures without degradation. They do have the disadvantages that they are generally brittle and tend to be susceptible to thermal shock, in other words sudden changes in temperature lead to fracture.

For many applications, the choice of a particular material depends on its strength in a given situation. But what do we mean by strength? It is actually a rather subtle and complex concept. If we relate the strength of a material to the forces between its constituent atoms, then the strongest material should be the one with the strongest chemical bond. But one of the strongest bonds is that between nitrogen atoms in the molecule N_2, and that is a gas at normal temperatures!

■ Why are these two facts not incompatible?

■ Though nitrogen atoms in a molecule are held very tightly, the forces between nitrogen molecules are much weaker.

So for a strong material, we need to have strong forces between the atoms throughout the structure.

■ What types of material have such a structure?

■ Metals and materials with a giant molecular structure.

One criterion we have used to indicate strong forces between the constituent atoms of a material is its melting temperature. So materials with a very high melting temperature might be expected to be strong. Some obvious examples are concrete and brick. But these materials tend to crack readily; they are very brittle. Indeed, concrete often has metal reinforcing rods embedded in the interior to provide additional strength. We recognize a material as being brittle by its total lack of plasticity; it can only be deformed elastically or else it fractures. By **plasticity** we mean the ability to undergo a permanent change of shape without a substantial loss of structural integrity; **elasticity** means that any change of shape is reversed as soon as the deforming forces are removed.

What about metals themselves? Consider two otherwise identical objects, say two tankards, but one made of glass and the other of pewter. If they were dropped onto the floor, the glass one would break, but the pewter one would simply be dented. Yet the glass fragments would be able to scratch the pewter. So the pewter is softer than the glass, yet we would normally regard it as being stronger. It is stronger because it is in some ways weaker than glass! But consider what happens if you do scratch the two materials: there is essentially no effect on the strength of a metal such as pewter, but as you probably know, glass will easily fracture along the scratch: this is the method used to cut glass for windows and picture frames.

Mechanical strength is actually a combination of three different properties: hardness, stiffness and resistance to cracks. By hardness is meant lack of plasticity; by stiffness is meant lack of elasticity; and the third property is self-explanatory. Unfortunately, these three properties are to some extent mutually incompatible. It is not difficult for a material to have two of the three, but rarely all three. For example, steel is stiff and resistant to cracks but can be bent, whereas ceramics are hard and stiff but not resistant to cracks; steel is said to be tough whereas ceramics are brittle. It is finding the best compromise between the requirements for the three different properties in any given application that provides the challenge, and fascination, of the study of materials.

Many of the newer ceramic materials are prepared chemically from simpler raw materials, or sometimes from specially purified grades of naturally-occurring materials. This distinguishes them from traditional materials such as pottery, which is made by baking naturally occurring clay. They are sometimes also referred to as 'engineering' or 'technical' ceramics.

As an example of the development of novel ceramics we shall take the materials called **sialons**. These derive their name from the fact that they contain the elements silicon (Si), aluminium (Al), oxygen (O), and nitrogen (N). They were discovered during investigations into the ceramic material silicon nitride. In the early 1970s, silicon nitride was regarded as the 'ceramic of the decade'. Here was a material with an unusual combination of properties: high-temperature strength combined with resistance to wear, oxidation, corrosion and temperature shock. It seemed bound to become the material of choice where these properties were demanded, for example inside motor car and aircraft engines (Figure 3.24). However, problems associated with fabrication have meant that this material has not entirely fulfilled its early promise. The problem is that these properties are fully developed only in a single ideal crystal and in practice this cannot be achieved.

Figure 3.24
Turbine blades made from silicon nitride for use in a helicopter engine.

Ceramics have giant molecular structures with very high melting temperatures. Indeed, the molecular framework often begins to break down before melting. Consequently, the traditional method has been to 'fire' components made from powder or slurry of the material in question, that is to heat it to a temperature high enough that the atoms begin to move around, breaking and remaking bonds to form a solid object. Unfortunately, silicon nitride begins to degrade before a high enough temperature is reached.

Another method often used, akin to the formation of an alloy in modifying the properties of a metal, is to use an additive that melts at a lower temperature. The required object is then produced by sintering, a method involving high pressure and heat in which the particles fuse together, with the additive acting as a kind of 'glue'. The first successful additive was magnesium oxide. It was while investigating other such additives that the sialons were discovered. It turned out that if aluminium oxide was used, not only did this act as a glue, it altered the molecular structure of the silicon nitride and some of the silicon atoms were replaced by aluminium, and some of the nitrogen atoms by oxygen.

As you may recall from Book 2, one of the components of many traditional ceramics is sand, which is largely silicon dioxide (silica). This ends up in the form of a silicate in which the structural unit is the SiO_4 tetrahedron (Figure 3.25). Now, although silicon is at least partially covalently bonded in silicates, in terms of counting electrons it can be thought of as being Si^{4+}. Likewise, the oxygen in the silicate ion can be regarded as O^{2-}.

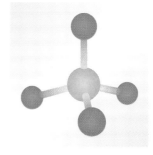

Figure 3.25
The silicate unit found in most traditional ceramics.

Figure 3.26
The mineral phenacite.

■ What is the overall charge on the silicate group?

■ The silicate ion has an overall charge of 4– (4+ from the silicon and (4 × 2–) from the oxygen).

These silicate tetrahedra are linked by sharing corners, edges or faces to form the many structures found in nature. One example of such a structure is the mineral phenacite (Figure 3.26), beryllium silicate, Be_2SiO_4, in which the silicate tetrahedra share corners (Figure 3.27). Silicon nitride is also built up from tetrahedral units, but in this case SiN_4 units. Silicon nitride has the empirical formula Si_3N_4, since the 3 × 4+ charges on the silicon are then formally balanced by the 4 × 3– charges on the nitride ion. One form of silicon nitride, the β-form (Figure 3.28), has a similar arrangement of atoms to beryllium silicate (Figure 3.27) where the two additional silicon atoms occupy the same positions as beryllium and nitrogen occupies the same positions as oxygen.

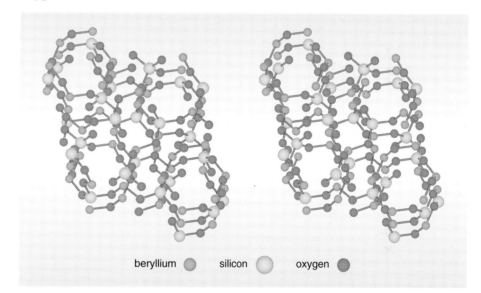

Figure 3.27
Stereoscopic model of the structure of beryllium silicate.

beryllium ● silicon ○ oxygen ●

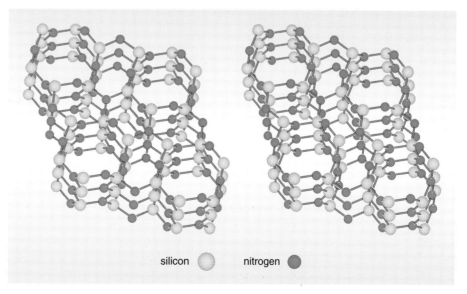

Figure 3.28
Stereoscopic model of the structure of β-silicon nitride.

silicon ○ nitrogen ●

In the formation of sialons, reaction with aluminium oxide (alumina) replaces some of the silicon atoms by aluminium atoms.

▨   Given that aluminium in alumina is in the form of Al^{3+} ions, what effect would this have on the overall charge of the modified silicon nitride?

▧   There will be an excess of electrons from the nitride ions.

▨   What would the overall charge be if exactly the same number of O^{2-} ions replaced nitride ions as Al^{3+} ions replaced Si^{4+} ions?

▧   Since each oxygen has one charge fewer than each nitrogen in silicon nitride, neutrality would be restored.

This is exactly what happens. By sintering silicon nitride and alumina together, up to two-thirds of the silicon can be replaced by aluminium, and an equivalent quantity of nitrogen is replaced by oxygen. The resulting sialon has an analogous relationship to the starting silicon nitride as brass does to copper. Pure copper is relatively soft, but up to 40% of copper atoms can be replaced by zinc without altering the structure. The result is an alloy that is both harder than the pure metal and has a lower melting temperature that enables objects to be fabricated more easily. An example of the superiority of the sialon is in its use to make cutting tips for machine tools (Figure 3.29). Because it retains its hardness when hot much better than conventional materials, such as silicon carbide, it can be used for cutting at very high speeds where temperatures exceeding 1000 °C can be reached. Sialon-tipped cutting tools are thereby able to work at three or four times the cutting rate of silicon carbide-tipped tools.

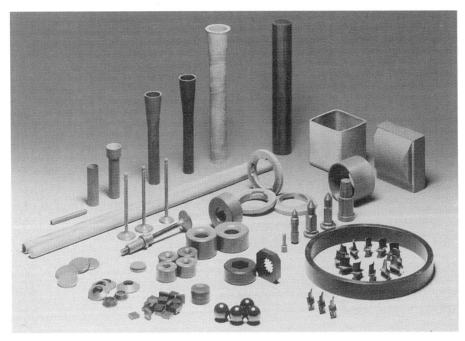

Figure 3.29
A selection of objects made from sialon, ranging from tips for cutting tools through engine valves to ball bearings.

Many other types of sialon material have been investigated. Other additives, in addition to alumina, can have a beneficial effect on the properties. The use of yttrium oxide seems to be particularly effective in producing a tougher material by producing a strong glass-like material between the grains of the sialon. Sialons formed from α-silicon nitride (the other crystalline form) are even harder than those formed using the β-form. Composite sialons consisting of mixtures of both α and β have particularly good properties and all sialon cutting tips for machine tools are now made of composite αβ-sialons.

Interest in new ceramic materials arises from their possible use in a number of areas. One is in engines where the ability of ceramics to withstand high temperatures in a hostile environment is needed (Figure 3.29). Engines of all types – petrol, diesel, gas turbine and jet engines – work more efficiently at high temperatures. The use of ceramics for key components allows the working temperatures to be raised above that achievable with all-metal engines. Most existing car engines are fitted with cooling systems to ensure that the temperature is kept within the limits set by the metal components and the oils necessary to lubricate the moving parts. Experimental ceramic-based engines are quite different. They are smaller, do not need a cooling system, and are more efficient because they can run at higher temperatures. Also, because of their better wear characteristics, they should last much longer.

Question 13 Using information from this section and your own general knowledge, fill in Table 3.1, comparing the properties of ceramics and metals, by putting high or low as appropriate.

Table 3.1 Relative properties of ceramics and metals

Property	Ceramics	Metals
hardness		
fracture toughness		
density		
ductility[a]		
thermal conductivity		
electrical conductivity		

[a]Ability to be drawn out into a thinner form such as wire.

3.6 The future

It is probably in the area of materials that it is easiest to make predictions about likely future developments. As you have seen from Book 2 Part 1 and earlier in this Chapter, metals are gradually being replaced by polymers and ceramics for a whole variety of uses. It is tempting to think of this as a new development, but in fact polymers and ceramics constituted a large proportion of the materials used before metals found widespread use. This can be seen in Figure 3.30. It is clear that the use of metals reached its peak in the 1950s. Since then, the application of polymers, ceramics and composites has steadily increased. The likelihood is that this trend will continue.

Figure 3.30
The evolution in use of different types of material for structural purposes.

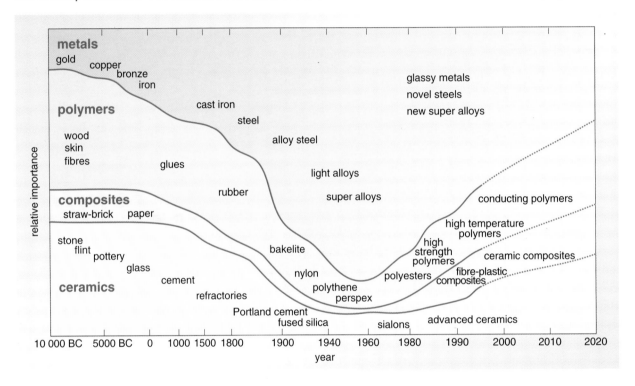

But Figure 3.30, which deals with structural materials, tells only part of the story. There are many other novel materials under development, particularly in the fields of electronics and optics. This is typified by the development of better, and cheaper, flat-panel displays. Although the liquid crystal materials currently available have a good range of properties, the search continues for new and better compounds; for example, liquid crystals have been discovered with disc-shaped molecules, rather than the rod-shaped molecules of those currently in use. The need for improved dyes, together with more economic methods of manufacture, means that research into active colour displays will continue. It is predicted that improvements in technology will allow the economic production of large wall-hung screens within a decade.

There have been rapid advances in recent years in our understanding of the relationship between the structure of polymers at the molecular level and their macroscopic properties. In the area of polymers as elsewhere, as discussed in Chapter 2, our understanding has been aided by the advances in computing power that allow more realistic molecular modelling. This has enabled scientists to become true molecular engineers, to design polymeric materials with a particular range of properties in mind.

One example is in linking liquid crystals with polymers. The incorporation in the polymer chain of rigid groups that form liquid crystals gives rise to polymers such as Kevlar (Section 3.2), which can be orientated mechanically and thereby produce fibres with superior mechanical strength. Attaching the rigid groups as side-chains gives rise to materials that can be used in displays; another possible use arousing a great deal of interest is for erasable optical storage devices capable of storing vast amounts of information.

The polyanhydrides are just one of a whole range of polymers under investigation for drug delivery purposes. They exemplify the process mentioned above of designing polymers from scratch based on a desirable set of properties, namely bioerosion at a controlled rate combined with lack of toxicity. Perhaps most exciting of all is the prospect of combining our knowledge of biology and chemistry to design specific biological activities into polymers to give a new generation of materials that can actually promote desired medical responses.

There is also much activity in the study of novel ceramic materials, but a complete solution to the fundamental problem of their brittleness remains elusive. The main reason why ceramics are brittle is the presence of defects or impurities resulting from the method of manufacture. With most metals, the raw material is produced in a molten state which allows any impurities to be dispersed evenly throughout, and gives a uniform material. Further, because the metal atoms are held together by a sea of electrons involving forces that are not very directional, they can be induced to move relative to one another without losing strength.

In contrast, as we mentioned earlier, ceramics are often made by a process of sintering in which only partial melting occurs. As a result, impurities are often concentrated at the boundary between the constituent particles, which weakens the material. Consequently, ceramic components are much less uniform in their properties than those made from metals. Further, the types of force between the constituent atoms, and the fact that several different elements are involved, mean that it is much more difficult to deform a ceramic without causing it to weaken dramatically.

There are several methods being investigated to improve the resistance to fracture and uniformity of ceramic components. One is to make sure that any residual pores are as small as possible. This can be achieved by the use of pure raw materials in the form of a very fine powder, with particles that are even in size and spherical in shape. These are able to pack together tightly and ensure a much more homogeneous material. Even a material as humble as cement can have its properties transformed by this approach (Figure 3.31).

Figure 3.31
A spring made from defect-free cement. This involves a different approach in which the cement powder is mixed with a polymer to form a material rather like Plasticine, which can then be moulded before setting. This greatly reduces the number and size of residual pores.

A second method is to form the ceramic by a chemical reaction between appropriate substances. This method is called the **sol–gel process**. These terms derive from the study of colloids (Book 1): a sol is a colloidal solution and a gel is a jelly-like state. An example is gelatine dissolved in hot water (a sol), and after it has set (a gel). In the sol–gel process, the raw materials are compounds that react together to form the desired ceramic material.

As an example, take the ceramic magnesium aluminium oxide, $MgAl_2O_4$ (spinel). By the conventional route, this would be made by firing an equimolar mixture of magnesium oxide (MgO) and aluminium oxide (Al_2O_3) powders. In the sol–gel process, compounds called metal alkoxides are used. These are derivatives of alcohols (Book 3 Part 1) in which the hydroxyl hydrogen is replaced by a metal. In this case the alkoxides used are $Mg(OR)_2$ and $Al(OR)_3$, where R is a small hydrocarbon group such as methyl (CH_3), ethyl (CH_3CH_2) or propyl ($CH_3CH_2CH_2$). The alkoxide mixture is first dissolved in a suitable solvent, often the corresponding alcohol. Water is then added, which reacts with the alkoxide. Usually a catalyst is added to speed up the reaction. On reaction with water, the alkoxy groups in alkoxides are replaced one at a time by hydroxyl groups:

$$Mg(OR)_2 + H_2O = Mg(OR)(OH) + ROH$$

$$Al(OR)_3 + H_2O = Al(OR)_2(OH) + ROH$$

As reaction proceeds, the molecules begin to join up with the loss of a molecule of water in a condensation polymerization process:

$$Al(OR)_2(OH) + Al(OR)_2(OH) = (RO)_2Al{-}O{-}Al(OR)_2 + H_2O$$

$$Mg(OR)(OH) + Al(OR)_2(OH) = ROMg{-}O{-}Al(OR)_2 + H_2O$$

$$Mg(OR)(OH) + Mg(OR)(OH) = ROMg{-}O{-}MgOR + H_2O$$

This leads initially to polymer clusters (the sol), which then join together to give a jelly-like mass (the gel). The gel is then heated to a temperature of a few hundred degrees Celsius to complete the process. This contrasts with temperatures of 1500 °C or so that are required for sintering.

The sol–gel process is still in its infancy, but the technology has considerable promise. It is versatile and energy-efficient, and allows the production of materials with compositions or structures not easily achieved by conventional methods. Ceramics made by this method are much more homogeneous, with more reproducible properties (Figure 3.32). For some materials, the sol–gel process and the conventional route have been combined: the raw materials for the latter are produced as fine even powders by the sol–gel process, allowing the production of ceramics with only small imperfections (see above).

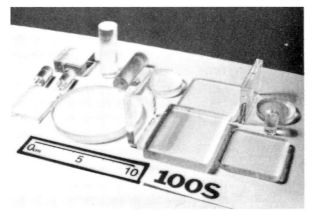

Figure 3.32
Sol–gel ceramics.

Another solution to many of the problems associated with existing materials is to make use of composites. These consist of strong fibres (e.g. carbon or ceramic fibres) in a matrix of some other material, such as a thermoplastic or a ceramic. The resulting composites have properties that are superior to those of the individual materials. They are much stronger than homogeneous materials because, if one fibre begins to fail, as soon as the fracture reaches the matrix, it is unable to propagate any further because of the relative softness of the matrix. The development of novel composite materials is likely to be a major area of growth.

As you will know from Book 2 Part 1, there is much current interest in the phenomenon of superconductivity (Figure 3.33), stimulated by the surprising discovery in 1986 that certain ceramics are superconductors. This was rapidly followed in 1987 by the discovery of a ceramic that was superconducting at substantially higher temperatures than any substance previously known. Until these two discoveries, all the superconductors known were metals and none was a superconductor above about −250 °C.

(a)

(b)

Figure 3.33
(a) Demonstration of magnetic levitation of one of the new high temperature superconductors, yttrium–barium–copper oxide. The photograph shows a small cylindrical magnet floating freely above a nitrogen-cooled cylindrical specimen of the superconducting ceramic. The vapour is from liquid nitrogen, which maintains the ceramic within its superconducting temperature range. Superconductors have the property of repelling magnets; this is called the Meissner effect. (b) One application of the Meissner effect is for trains that rely on magnetic levitation (MAGLEV) for support rather than wheels: such trains, like this experimental MAGLEV train in Japan, would experience little friction and so be highly energy efficient.

A practical 'high-temperature' superconductor material would offer advantages in almost every facet of our lives: more efficient electricity transmission; the potential for storing huge quantities of electricity in a superconducting 'battery'; more efficient methods of transport; computers so powerful that present-day machines would look like pocket calculators by comparison; and medical diagnostic systems with much greater capabilities than current scanners (Book 2 Part 1 Figure 4.53).

At present, the record is held by a ceramic containing five elements, mercury (Hg), barium (Ba), calcium (Ca), copper (Cu), and oxygen (O), with the formula $HgBa_2Ca_2Cu_3O_8$ (Figure 3.34). It remains superconducting up to a temperature of $-138\ °C$. Already ceramic superconducting materials are being marketed in the forms suitable for making a range of electrical instruments and appliances. The 1987 publication stimulated frantic activity in laboratories around the world as scientists race each other in the search for the 'holy grail' of a room temperature superconductor. With the huge prizes awaiting this discovery, the recent high level of activity looks set to continue into the foreseeable future.

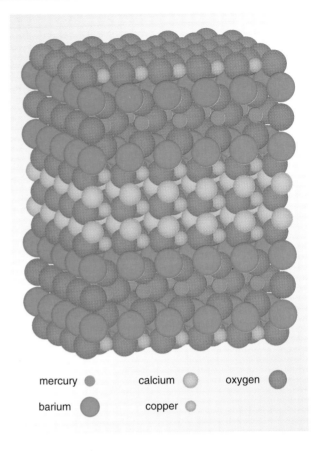

mercury ●   calcium ●   oxygen ●

barium ●   copper ●

Question 14 Silica (SiO_2) fibres can be made by the sol–gel process from tetraethoxysilane, $Si(OCH_2CH_3)_4$, by reaction with water. Silicon hydroxide ($Si(OH)_4$) is formed as an intermediate. Write two balanced equations to represent the overall reactions of the two stages in which $Si(OCH_2CH_3)_4$ is converted into $Si(OH)_4$ and then $Si(OH)_4$ is transformed into SiO_2.

Figure 3.34
The crystal structure of the ceramic material with formula $HgBa_2Ca_2Cu_3O_8$, which has the highest recorded superconducting transition temperature to date.

Summary of Chapter 3

The vital role of materials for technological developments is now widely recognized. The importance of materials has been realized throughout history. What has changed in recent times is the range of materials that are now available. These include liquid crystals, polymers and ceramics.

Liquid crystal materials are used for displays in electronic calculators, information boards, digital watches and laptop computers, to name just a small selection. The liquid crystal state has properties intermediate between a crystalline solid and a liquid. In energy terms, liquid crystals are more 'liquid-like' than 'crystal-like'.

Many liquid crystal materials have three features in common: (a) the molecules are elongated; (b) the molecules have a rigid part; (c) there are groups at one or both ends that are long and fairly flexible. The presence of a polar group at one end seems to enhance liquid crystal formation.

Liquid crystals can form a number of different types of phase: the two most important are the nematic phase and the smectic phase. Liquid crystals have the property of rotating polarized light.

The most common type of display for laptop computers is based on nematic liquid crystals. They rely on the rotation of polarized light for their operation. Passive LCDs appear rather dull and suffer from leakage from one pixel to adjacent ones; active LCDs are brighter and sharper, but much more expensive.

The rational design of new polymers is now guided by a number of basic principles: (a) the strength or toughness of a polymeric material depends on the presence of long molecules; (b) the nature of the backbone structure has a dramatic effect on properties; (c) the properties also depend markedly on the nature and size of any side-groups attached to the polymer chain.

Application of these principles led to the discovery of Kevlar, the first commercially available aramid polymer. Kevlar is immensely strong due to extensive hydrogen bonding between the polymer molecules, and has found a wide range of uses, including ropes to tether oil platforms, tyre reinforcement, and bullet-proof vests.

Polyanhydrides have the property of slowly reacting with water to revert to the monomer substance. This has been applied to the delivery of certain drugs to specific sites within the body. One trial application has been to treat brain cancer. Indications are that patients treated this way survive longer than those undergoing traditional therapy.

Of the various types of material, ceramics are the ones that seem to have realized the least of the potential that materials scientists promise. This is because a number of crucial weaknesses have so far prevented their full exploitation: they are brittle, and are difficult to manufacture uniformly.

The search for new ceramics has encompassed a variety of different approaches. One is to make use of specially purified raw materials with a more controllable particle size. Another is to use mixtures akin to metallic alloys. These two approaches were used to develop the family of ceramics called sialons.

Sialons are related to the ceramic material silicon nitride, regarded in the 1970s as the 'ceramic of the decade'. However, its very high melting temperature and its propensity to decompose at the high temperatures needed to 'fire' components led to the investigation of various additives. One of the most successful was aluminium oxide. This gave rise to a range of materials in which a significant number of silicon atoms were replaced by aluminium, and an equivalent number of nitrogen atoms by oxygen. Sialons have been made from each of the two crystalline forms of silicon nitride. Composites of the two types have particularly good properties.

For the future, the trend away from the use of metals to other materials looks set to continue. Advances in our understanding of the relationship between the molecular structure of polymers and their macroscopic properties allows scientists to custom-design new polymeric materials, for example polymers that are liquid crystals. One of the most exciting possibilities is to be able to design specific biological activities into polymeric materials.

Much effort is being expended in finding methods of manufacturing ceramics that are not brittle and have greater uniformity. One way is to make sure that any residual pores are as small as possible; a second is to form the ceramic by a chemical reaction between appropriate substances by the sol–gel method; a third is to make use of composites, namely strong fibres (e.g. carbon or ceramic fibres) in a matrix of some other material, such as a thermoplastic or a ceramic.

The discovery in 1987 that certain ceramics are superconductors up to temperatures much higher than previously (the highest at the time of writing being −138 °C) triggered frantic activity around the world in the search for a room temperature superconductor.

Chapter 4
Power to the people

4.1 Energy sources

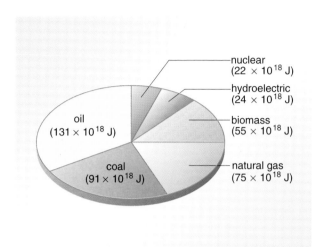

Figure 4.1
Estimated world primary energy consumption in 1992 by source ; the total was about 4×10^{20} J. (Note: the total given here differs from the estimate given in Book 2 Part 2.)

As you will already know from Book 2 Part 2, modern society, and particularly the industrialized world, is totally dependent on a continuous supply of energy. What you still may not fully appreciate is the truly enormous quantity of energy used by human activities. The estimated global energy consumption from primary sources, mostly fossil fuels, for 1992 was approximately 4×10^{20} joules (Figure 4.1). This is equivalent to a continuous power of 1.3×10^{13} watts (joules per second); that represents the output of 26 000 power stations operating continuously, each with a capacity of 500 MW (megawatts or 10^6 watts).

Fossil fuels (coal, oil, and natural gas) account for by far the largest proportion of all energy sources. Clearly the Earth has only a finite quantity of these fuels. Sufficient new reserves of fossil fuels have been found to maintain the current level of consumption in the short term. However, there remains the long-term problem of finding replacement energy resources.

Among the medium-term options are the discovery of further resources of coal, oil and natural gas; the development of practicable methods of exploiting low grade reserves such as tar sands and oil shales without unacceptable levels of pollution or energy input; and nuclear energy. However, following the Chernobyl disaster, public opinion has turned against this last option.

Longer term options come down to essentially two possibilities: one of these is the large scale use of solar energy, of which more below, and the other is the development of a practical power source based on nuclear fusion. Current nuclear reactors depend on the phenomenon of nuclear fission, which involves the splitting of atoms of radioactive elements, such as uranium or plutonium, with the release of huge amounts of energy. One consequence of nuclear fission reactors is the creation of a great deal of radioactive waste that, even with reprocessing, still represents a substantial disposal problem.

In contrast, a fusion reactor (Book 2 Part 2) would involve the combination of very light nuclei – such as those of deuterium, an isotope of hydrogen, to produce helium – with the release of huge amounts of energy. It is likely that this process would involve much less radioactive waste than fission, and the necessary deuterium could be obtained in almost unlimited quantities from seawater. Unfortunately, despite the expenditure of considerable amounts of money and research effort (Book 2 Part 2 Figure 9.3), progress has been very slow and a workable fusion reactor is unlikely to be feasible until well into the 21st century. Furthermore, many people argue that we have no need to develop a fusion reactor on Earth as we benefit from a steady flow of energy from an existing fusion reactor that is reliable, needs no upkeep, and will continue to function far into the foreseeable future, namely the Sun!

Solar energy may be converted *directly* into end-use energy or it may be converted *indirectly*, via one or more intermediate forms of energy.

▨   Can you think of an example of the direct use of solar energy and an example of indirect use?

◼   Examples of direct uses would be solar heating and the generation of electricity using solar cells; indirect uses would be the harnessing of wind energy to generate electricity or the conversion of solar energy into a chemical fuel such as hydrogen.

The various conversion paths are shown in Figure 4.2. All of these have been demonstrated on a small scale; the greater challenge comes in developing methods of using solar energy on a large scale. Of these, hydroelectric energy is at present by far the largest indirect source. However, the number of suitable sites for hydroelectric generation is limited. Three of the more successful among the other options are direct solar energy conversion to heat (for space and water heating), wind power using modern wind turbines (often grouped in 'wind farms'), and solar driven thermo-electric power stations (Book 2 Part 2 Chapter 9).

Figure 4.2
Methods of solar energy conversion. The top two paths are direct and the others are indirect.

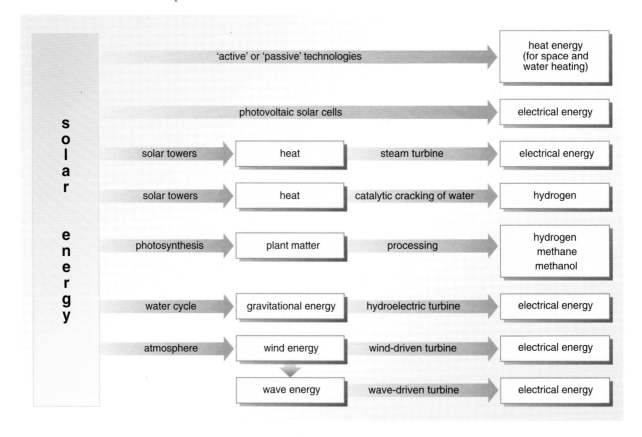

Of these various methods of using solar energy, which ones are likely to require the application of chemical knowledge and expertise to develop them for use on a large scale? Of the direct methods, the use of solar cells to generate electricity certainly would: the production of solar cells on a large scale at an economic price has still to be achieved, and chemists are heavily involved both in developing better methods for producing currently used materials (largely silicon-based) and in searching for suitable new materials. Among the indirect methods, the production of fuels, both hydrogen from water and carbon-based fuels from plants, clearly require the skills of the chemist. We shall look at prospects for both these methods, beginning with solar cells.

4.2 Solar electricity

In order to understand how solar cells (the technical term for which is **photovoltaic cells**) work, we need to understand why some materials are electrical conductors, some are insulators and others are semiconductors.

▨   Think of the materials you know that are electrical conductors: what do most of them have in common?

▪   The great majority of electrical conductors are metals.

The most commonly used metal for electrical conductors is copper, though aluminium is used for power transmission lines. Sometimes, where good electrical contact is essential, as in computers and satellite applications, gold plating is used for its excellent electrical conductivity and its resistance to oxidation or corrosion. The best known conductor that is not a metal is graphite, one of the forms of the element carbon (Book 1, Section 10.3).

What then makes a substance an electrical conductor? Indeed, what is electrical conduction? Essentially, it simply involves the movement of electrons through the conductor from one location to another; such a movement constitutes an electric current (Book 2 Part 1). To understand why some substances allow such free movement of electrons and others do not, in other words why some substances are conductors and others are insulators, we need to take a closer look at the energies of electrons in solids.

As you know from earlier in the Course, electrons in individual atoms have certain fixed energies. They are said to occupy energy levels (Book 4 Part 1). Now let's consider what happens in a metal. As with other crystalline solids, metals consist of atoms arranged in a regular array, called a lattice (Book 1 Chapter 7). When many atoms are combined in a solid, there are many energy levels, so many in fact that they form a **band** in which each level is extremely close in energy to the next (Figure 4.3, overleaf).

Suppose we consider the element copper. Remember, we are interested only in the outermost electrons, as it is only these that are involved in bonding. Copper has a single electron in its outermost (valence) shell, which resides in a particular energy level. Let's consider what happens in a fragment of solid copper containing n atoms.

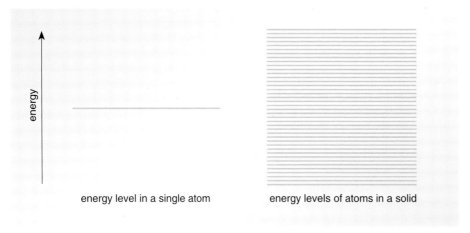

Figure 4.3
Formation of a band of energy levels in a solid.

◻ For n copper atoms, how many energy levels associated with the outermost shell will there be in total?

◼ Since each atom has a single electron in the outermost shell in an energy level, for n atoms there will be a total of n energy levels.

Now it turns out that for each individual energy level, the maximum number of electrons that it can hold is two.

◻ So for n copper atoms, how many of the n energy levels associated with the outermost shell will be occupied?

◼ Since each energy level can hold two electrons, n electrons will occupy $n/2$ energy levels, just half the total available (Figure 4.4).

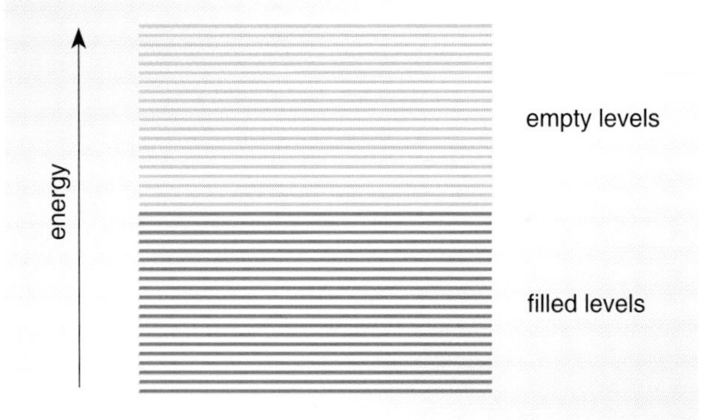

empty levels

filled levels

Figure 4.4
The energy levels of copper metal showing the band structure. The filled levels are coloured red and the unfilled ones are grey.

The result, then, is a half-filled band. Now, because the energy levels are so close together, it requires only a small amount of extra energy for one of the electrons near the top of the filled levels to move up to one a little higher in energy. If that happens, this electron can move to another part of the lattice. Because a vacancy remains in the slightly lower energy level, another electron can fall into that level. This constant exchange of energies allows the electrons to move freely through the lattice, and hence the copper can act as an electrical conductor. If the copper is part of an electrical circuit, this movement constitutes an electric current. Of course, with the many electrons in a metal (billions and billions!) more than one electron will be promoted at any one time, so the process makes for very easy movement of electrons through the lattice.

Why are only some substances metals, and others not? Let's think about diamond as an example. Diamond does not conduct electricity; it is an insulator. It turns out that because each carbon atom in diamond has relatively few nearest neighbours (each atom is bonded to only four others) compared with copper (each atom has twelve nearest neighbours), the energy levels do not form a continuous band. Instead, they form two bands,

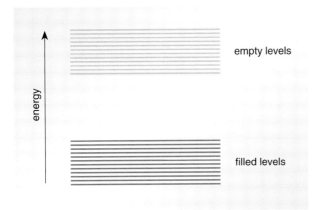

Figure 4.5
The energy levels of diamond.

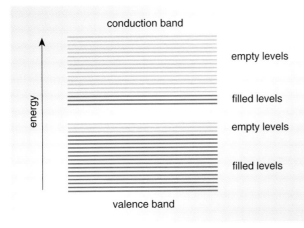

Figure 4.6
The energy levels of silicon, with some electrons promoted to the conduction band.

separated by a **band gap** (Figure 4.5). The valence electrons just fill the lower band. Because of the band gap, this means that for any electron to get into the upper band, a substantial amount of energy is needed, more than is available from the thermal motion of the electrons under normal conditions. Because of this, the electrons remain localized and are unable to travel readily through the lattice. The result is that diamond is an insulator at normal temperatures.

Certain elements and compounds have the property of behaving as insulators under some sets of conditions and as conductors in other circumstances. Such substances are called **semiconductors**. Semiconductors have the property that their conductivity increases as the temperature is increased. Perhaps the best known semiconductor is silicon. Because silicon is in the same group of the Periodic Table as carbon, its band structure might be expected to be very similar. The band structure for silicon is shown in Figure 4.6. The feature that differentiates it from carbon is that the gap between the upper and lower bands of energy levels (the band gap) is much smaller than in carbon. This means that by heating silicon, or more usefully for our purposes, shining light on it, enough energy can be given to the electrons so that some of them are promoted to the upper band and the silicon becomes conducting. The upper band of energy levels is therefore called the **conduction band**; the lower band is called the **valence band**.

An analogy may make this clearer. Consider the occupied levels as the lower floor of a car park with two storeys. If the lower floor is full up, with cars parked nose to tail, it is no longer possible to move a car from one place to another (Figure 4.7a). However, if a car is transferred by lift to the upper floor, that car can move around freely, and the resulting 'hole' allows the cars on the lower floor to be moved around (Figure 4.7b). So, when some of the electrons in the valence band of silicon are excited to the conduction band by light, they are free to move and hence to conduct electricity. At the same time, for each electron promoted, a positive **hole** (or vacancy) is left, which allows other electrons in the valence band to move around also.

Figure 4.7
The car park analogy for conduction in a solid.

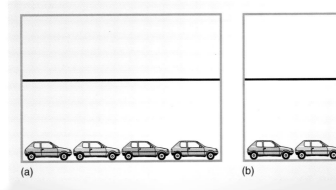

(a)　　　　　(b)

In the construction of photovoltaic cells, it has been found that the efficiency is greatly enhanced if the silicon is 'doped' with a small amount of another element. Suppose some of the silicon atoms are replaced by phosphorus atoms. Phosphorus has one more valence electron than silicon, so for each silicon atom replaced by a phosphorus, there would be one extra electron.

▨   Where would the extra electrons be located?

■   They would have to occupy the lower part of the conduction band.

▨   What effect would this have on the conductivity of the phosphorus-doped material compared with pure silicon?

■   It would be greater because the electrons in the conduction band would be able to carry some current.

In contrast, consider what happens if some of the silicon atoms are replaced by boron atoms. In this case, because boron has one valence electron fewer than silicon, for each silicon atom replaced by a boron, there would be one (negative) electron fewer. Put another way, for each boron atom present, there would be a (positive) hole created.

▨   What would the effect be on the occupation of the two bands?

■   The valence band would no longer be completely full.

▨   What effect would this have on the conductivity of the boron-doped material compared with pure silicon?

■   It would also be greater because the holes in the valence band would allow some of these electrons to move through the lattice and hence carry some current (remember the car park analogy!).

Such doped materials are called impurity semiconductors: the phosphorus-doped silicon is an n-type semiconductor (the n stands for negative because it has more electrons than pure silicon); the boron-doped silicon is a p-type semiconductor (p stands for positive).

You may be wondering why these doped semiconductor materials are so useful. The reason becomes apparent if we make up a device in which thin layers of the two are placed in electrical contact to make a solar cell (Figure 4.8). Before being joined, the two semiconductors are electrically neutral because the number of electrons balances the number of positive charges on the nuclei. The energy levels are essentially the same in each (Figure 4.9a). However, when the two are in contact, because the n-type semiconductor has electrons in the conduction band and the p-type semiconductor has holes in the valence band, some of the electrons move from the n-type to the p-type material. This leaves the n-type semiconductor with an excess of positive charge and the p-type semiconductor with an excess of negative charge.

▨   What effect will the development of excess charge have on further transfer of electrons from the n-type material to the p-type?

■   The increasing negative charge will repel the incoming electrons.

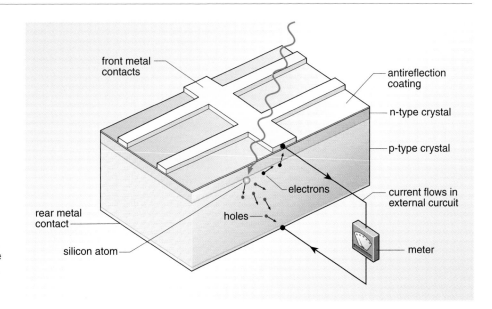

Figure 4.8
A solar cell made of a thin layer of n-type silicon on a wafer of p-type silicon. The red wavy line represents a photon, striking a silicon atom at the junction.

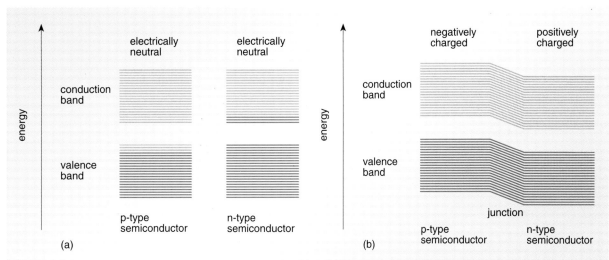

Figure 4.9
Energy levels in doped n-type and p-type semiconductors (a) before and (b) after being placed in contact.

The build-up of charge eventually stops any further transfer of electrons across the junction. This build-up of charge has another important consequence: it alters the energies of the valence and conduction bands on either side of the junction (Figure 4.9b). This is because the electrons in the n-type semiconductor, which now has excess positive charge, have a lower energy and conversely the electrons in the p-type semiconductor, which now has excess negative charge, have a higher energy. The result is an energy gradient between one layer and the other.

If a photon with the right energy now strikes the junction where the two materials are in contact, electrons will be promoted into the conduction band. Because of the charges on the two layers and the associated energy gradient, the electrons promoted to the conduction band will be attracted towards the positively charged side of the junction, that is towards the n-type semiconductor. As a consequence, more electrons will flow from the p-type semiconductor toward the junction, so that the effect is as if the holes migrate towards the negative charge on the p-type semiconductor. If the two layers of the cell are connected through an external circuit, the electrons will flow through the circuit and recombine with the holes in the valence band of the p-type semiconductor, giving rise to an electric current (Figure 4.8).

■ Above, we said that the photon that produces the electric current has to have the right energy. What energy is needed for this to happen?

■ At least the energy of the band gap.

Until recently, most silicon solar cells were made from single crystals of extremely pure silicon (Figure 4.10) of the type used for computer chips (Figure 4.11). This expense was one of the main barriers to their widespread use for electricity generation. However, use of a slightly less pure 'solar' grade reduces the cost substantially without greatly affecting the efficiency (Figure 4.12a). The use of the much cheaper polycrystalline silicon has reduced the cost of manufacture of photovoltaic cells still further without an unacceptably large loss in efficiency (Figure 4.12b). Another, even cheaper, form of silicon, called amorphous silicon, is also looking very promising.

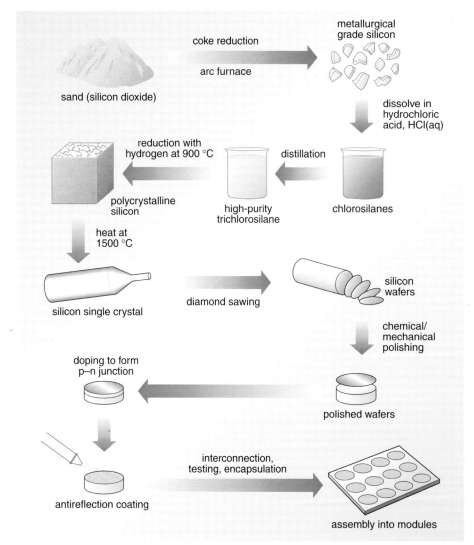

Figure 4.10
The process used for making monocrystalline silicon photovoltaic cells. The most expensive part of the process is growing the silicon single crystal by very slowly pulling a seed crystal from molten silicon.

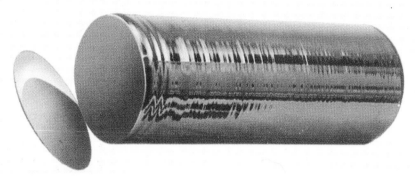

Figure 4.11
Ultra-pure silicon used for making computer chips.

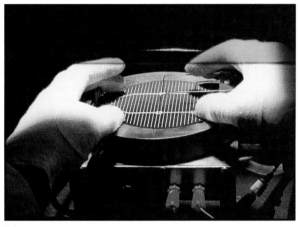

(a)

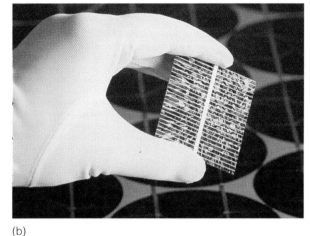

(b)

Figure 4.12
(a) A solar cell made from impurity-doped single-crystal silicon. The current is picked up and transmitted by the grid of fine wires which covers the cell's surface. (b) A solar cell made from polycrystalline silicon. The individual silicon crystals can be clearly seen. (c) A solar cell made from gallium arsenide The use of gallium arsenide in place of conventional silicon means that the cell may be up to ten times smaller for the same output.

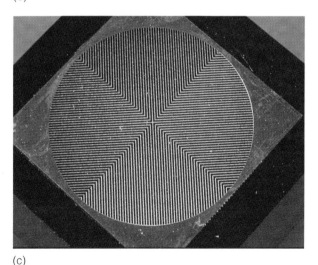

(c)

Other semiconducting materials, such as gallium arsenide, and cadmium telluride, are also used to make solar cells. Gallium arsenide is even more efficient than monocrystalline silicon, but is also more expensive (Figure 4.12c). Cadmium telluride cells are cheap to manufacture but only moderately efficient; also cadmium is highly toxic, so its use on a large scale requires stringent controls on manufacture, use and eventual disposal. Some of the relative advantages and disadvantages together with typical uses of the various types of solar cell are given in Table 4.1.

Table 4.1 Characteristics of various types of solar cell

Cell type	Advantages	Disadvantages	Uses
monocrystalline silicon	high efficiency	expensive; round shape, so creates 'inactive' area or waste silicon	remote areas, buildings, power stations
polycrystalline silicon	moderately cheap; can be made square for maximum use of space	lower efficiency	prototype units
amorphous silicon	inexpensive; better absorber of light so thinner films; less energy required in manufacture	low efficiency; efficiency rapidly degrades	pocket calculators
gallium arsenide	higher efficiency than silicon; better light absorber so thinner films needed; can operate at higher temperatures	more expensive	satellites, other 'cost-no-object' uses
cadmium telluride	simple and cheap to manufacture	cadmium toxic; moderate efficiency	prototype units

A single silicon cell typically produces about 2.5 amperes of current at 0.5 volts, that is about 1.25 watts (Figure 4.12a). So, to generate significant amounts of electrical power, the cells are combined as modules made up of 30 or more cells connected together (Figure 4.13).

Production of electricity using photovoltaic systems is becoming increasingly widespread. Photovoltaic generation in remote areas is already being widely used (Figure 4.14). A 40 kW photovoltaic array is in use at the University of Northumbria (Figure 4.15). There are also large photovoltaic power stations connected to the grid already in use in the USA (Figure 1.3) and Europe. One of the largest European systems, with a peak capacity of around 340 kW, is located on the banks of the Moselle river in Germany.

The production of electricity is a direct method of using solar energy. However, although it can be readily transmitted over large distances, it has the great disadvantage that the period of peak production does not match well the cycle of demand over the year. Further, unless there is some means of storing the electricity, it is not available during the hours of darkness. Fortunately, there are a number of possible ways of storing electrical energy by converting it into other forms, such as chemical energy. For use in transport, this is necessary regardless of the time or the season. The two main methods of storing electrical energy for use in vehicles are the production of fuels such as hydrogen, or storage in batteries. We shall look at the first of these methods in the next Section, along with other possible fuels from renewable sources, before going on to look at batteries in the following Section.

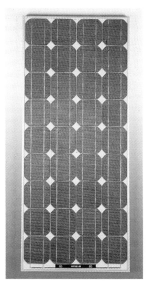

Figure 4.13
A solar module sold by BP Solar made up of 36 monocrystalline silicon cells. This module is capable of producing 65 watts of power.

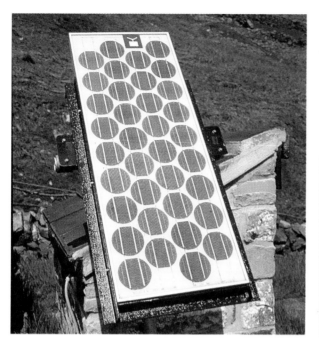

Figure 4.14
An array of photovoltaic cells, which are used to drive an electric water pump at Healaugh in the Yorkshire Dales National Park.

Figure 4.15
The Computer Sciences building at the University of Northumbria in Newcastle. One complete side of the building is covered with solar modules. The cells convert around 17% of the energy of sunlight into electricity.

Question 15 In a photovoltaic cell, what happens if (a) a photon with too small an energy (that is with an energy less than the band gap), and (b) a photon with greater energy than necessary, strikes the semiconductor?

4.3 Chemical fuels from the Sun

Fuels are used for a number of purposes, chiefly electricity generation, space heating and transport. Clearly, electricity produced by solar cells does not require the direct use of any fuels. The need for fuels for space heating could be much reduced by energy conservation measures, such as improved insulation and the use of passive solar heating. This leaves transport, which requires either the use of a fuel or batteries to provide motive power. We shall consider the possibilities for battery-powered vehicles in the next Section.

Perhaps the fuel that has the greatest attraction is hydrogen. The possibility of using hydrogen as a fuel was discussed in some detail in Book 2 Part 2.

■ Can you recall some of the advantages of using hydrogen as a fuel?

■ When hydrogen is burned it produces just water as a product (though the high temperatures give rise to some nitrogen oxides as well). It can be produced from water (available in abundance!) by electrolysis and therefore represents a convenient method of converting electrical energy into chemical energy. Because solar-produced hydrogen is formed from water in the first place, there is no net addition of water to the environment. Consequently the use of hydrogen does not pollute the atmosphere or add significantly to the greenhouse effect.

This is the basis of the experimental 'Hysolar' collaborative project between Germany and Saudi Arabia, where a 350 kW photovoltaic power plant in the Saudi desert is coupled to an electrolysis plant to produce hydrogen as a fuel.

Hydrogen can, in principle, be transported by pipeline more cheaply than electricity can be transmitted through power lines, so it would make sense for the hydrogen production to take place as close to the source of electricity as possible. For example, if photovoltaic generation is used, the best place for this would be in the desert areas of the world, where the solar intensity is high and where the environmental effects of the need for large areas of land are minimized. This is one of the considerations behind the Hysolar project. Hydrogen could then readily be used by industry or as a domestic fuel.

■   What is the main problem associated with the use of hydrogen as a fuel for transport?

■   The fact that hydrogen is a gas means that it occupies a very large volume at ordinary pressures. In order to use it as a fuel for transport, it needs to be stored either as a liquid, which requires very low temperatures, or by adsorption in a suitable metal, which adds to the cost and weight. Its flammability also has potential safety implications (Book 2 Figure 6.11).

This is a considerable disadvantage. However, tests in Japan have shown that running cars on hydrogen is feasible. One demonstration by the car company Nissan involved storage of the hydrogen in a stainless steel Dewar flask (essentially a giant Thermos vacuum flask); the car covered 200 miles on 100 litres of liquid hydrogen. The car had a diesel engine that had been modified so that it would burn hydrogen at high pressure (around 100 bars).

It is also possible to make use of the property of certain alloys to absorb large amounts of hydrogen: titanium/iron or magnesium/nickel alloys can absorb up to 1 000 times their own volume of hydrogen. The hydrogen molecule splits into atoms on absorption and, because these are so small, they can pack in the interstices between the metal atoms. Mazda have developed a prototype car that uses hydrogen stored in this fashion, although in this case the hydrogen is not burned, but used in a fuel cell (see Box 4.1). Unfortunately, after a few cycles of storing then using the hydrogen, the alloys tend to become brittle and disintegrate. Also they are very sensitive to moisture.

Photovoltaic cells at present are less than 20% efficient in converting solar energy into electricity. Furthermore, it is estimated that only around 50% of the electrical energy used to produce hydrogen by electrolysis of water is recoverable. The overall efficiency of this process is not that much greater than the efficiency of green plants converting solar energy via photosynthesis. So an alternative approach to producing renewable fuels would be to obtain them from plants. One example that you have already

Box 4.1 Fuel cells

The fuel cell, one of the oldest electrical devices, was invented in 1839 by Sir William Grove at the Royal Institution in London, where Michael Faraday had carried out his famous researches into electricity. However, it lay largely forgotten for many years until the British scientist/engineer Francis Bacon came across it in 1932 and realized its potential. It is simple in concept, being the reverse of electrolysis. Instead of electricity being used to split a compound into simpler substances, electricity is produced by the direct reaction together of a fuel, such as hydrogen or methanol, with oxygen (Figure 4.16). To provide a constant flow of electricity, the process needs a continuous supply of fuel and oxygen. In order for the reaction to proceed at an adequate rate, a catalyst is needed.

Despite its apparent simplicity, it took many years of work before Bacon was able to demonstrate a successful fuel cell unit (capable of producing 6 kW) in 1959. Shortly after, the American aerospace company Pratt & Whitney (now United Technologies) decided to use his design in the Apollo space programme. This provided the resources

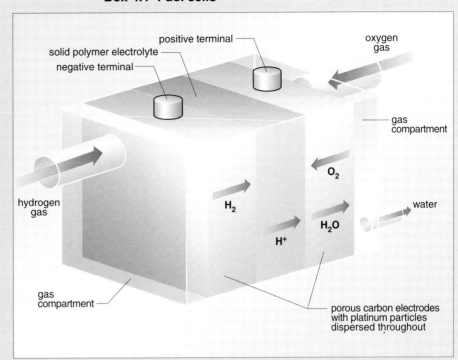

necessary to produce a reliable and efficient device able to make use of the hydrogen and oxygen available as propulsion fuel for the space capsules. The fuel cells were a great success, providing both electricity and drinking water (you will recall that the 'waste' product when hydrogen is the fuel is pure water).

Since then, after a great deal of research and development work, the efficiency of fuel cells in converting fuel into electricity has been raised to 80%. One of the barriers to their widespread use has been

Figure 4.16
A schematic diagram of a fuel cell powered by hydrogen and oxygen.

their high cost. However, a new polymer has recently been developed for use as the electrolyte, which it is claimed will cut the cost by 80%. Because the fuel is not burned, the cells operate at relatively low temperatures and so there is no pollution by oxides of nitrogen or sulfur. The only waste products are water, carbon dioxide if carbon-based fuels are used, and heat. The heat can be used for heating vehicles (or buildings, depending on the location of the fuel cell). This makes them very attractive in the light of California's legislation that requires 2% of all new vehicles to have zero

emission of NO_x or SO_x by 1998.

Although the fuel cell was invented in the UK, it is other countries, notably Japan and the USA, that have now taken the lead. Prototype buses and cars powered by fuel cells are on trial in Canada, Holland and the USA. The UK has its own programme for developing a car powered by fuel cells. Fuel cell power stations have been constructed in Canada, Scandinavia, Italy, Germany, the USA and Japan; the largest such power stations currently have a capacity of around 10 MW.

met is the use of oil derived from rape seed (Figure 4.17) as a replacement for diesel (Book 1 Chapter 4). The oil extracted from the rape seed is an ester of glycerol ('glycerine') and is too viscous to be used directly. To convert this into a usable fuel, it is treated with methanol in the presence of a catalyst to produce the corresponding methyl ester and glycerol as a by-product:

Figure 4.17
A field of rape.

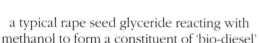

a typical rape seed glyceride reacting with methanol to form a constituent of 'bio-diesel'

Historically, wood has for centuries been the most important source of stored solar energy available to humanity, and in many poorer countries it still is. Wood is only part of the enormous volume of plant matter produced by photosynthesis. The most fuel-starved regions of the world happen also to be the tropical regions of high rainfall and high solar energy flux. World-wide, photosynthesis stores around 3×10^{21} J per year in plant matter, roughly ten times as much energy as is being converted by combustion of fossil fuels. Of course, only a small fraction of this large source of energy could be used without serious risk to the environment. But, even if only a small fraction of the biomass accumulated by photosynthesis could be converted into convenient fuels, we would have a potential renewable energy source of major importance.

▨   Would the carbon dioxide released on combustion of such fuels contribute to the greenhouse effect?

▧   If the plants used were part of a sustainable planting programme, the answer would be no. The process of photosynthesis during the plants' growth would consume, on balance, an equivalent amount of carbon dioxide from the atmosphere to that produced subsequently by combustion.

One of the best known examples of the production of a fuel from plants is the production of ethanol (CH_3CH_2OH) in Brazil and the USA (Book 2 Part 2). In Brazil, some cars have been converted to run on pure ethanol, others on a mixture called *gasohol*, which consists of 80% petrol (gasoline or 'gas' in American English) and 20% ethanol. However, with the price of oil having declined in real terms from its high point of the 1970s and early 1980s, ethanol is no longer competitive. The cost of producing ethanol from sugar cane is greater than the cost of imported oil. Of course, the effect on Brazil's balance of payments and hence her debt burden is quite different for the two fuels, as well as there being the ecological argument in favour of ethanol. Because of this change in the economics of ethanol, Brazil is considering abandoning the twenty-year-old experiment despite the tremendous cost of converting cars back again to be able to use petrol.

Similar considerations are affecting the production of ethanol in the USA. There, corn (maize) rather than sugar cane is used to produce the alcohol, which is used only in the form of gasohol containing 10% ethanol. Ethanol is not only advantageous in that it is a renewable resource and so the carbon dioxide produced does not contribute to the greenhouse effect, but it gives rise to reduced emission of nitrogen oxides as well. Its use is being proposed primarily for those areas where pollution is high as a means of reducing it to within the required limits. Unfortunately, the fact that gasohol is more volatile than petrol means that more of the fuel escapes to the atmosphere, giving rise to a different sort of pollution. Until the situation has been resolved, much of the current (1993) capacity (in excess of 3.5×10^9 litres) is on hold.

Methanol (CH_3OH) is another fuel much talked about, particularly for use in transport (Book 2 Part 2). It can be produced both from coal and from waste plant products; carbon dioxide produced by burning methanol from the former source could exacerbate global warming whereas that obtained from biomass would not. Unfortunately, because the waste materials are spread over a large area, only small, less efficient, generators of the conventional type can be used. However, calculations indicate that the electricity produced from methanol using efficient gas turbine generators is competitive with that produced with conventional large-scale power stations, be they coal-fired, nuclear or hydroelectric.

> **Question 16** Compare the advantages and disadvantages of hydrogen generated electrolytically and fuels such as bio-diesel or ethanol produced from plants.

4.4 Advanced batteries

Instead of using an intermediate fuel to store surplus electricity for times of peak demand or for use by cars and other vehicles, another approach has been to use batteries as a storage medium (Box 4.2, overleaf). The driving force for the development of a practical electric car is the same as that for the use of alternative fuels discussed in the previous Section, namely environmental concerns coupled with the finite nature of fossil fuel reserves. The main problem with the traditional lead–acid battery for motive power (as opposed to its normal use for starting vehicles) has been the adverse ratio of performance to mass and its relatively low recharge rate.

The search for the ideal battery system has involved a world-wide research effort over many years with the expenditure of huge amounts of money. The major car manufacturers have recognized the need for electrically powered vehicles, and so, in collaboration with battery manufacturers, have mounted programmes to develop prototype vehicles using a variety of different types of battery. These include alkaline, nickel–cadmium (NiCad), nickel–metal hydride, aluminium–air, sodium–sulfur, zinc–air, zinc–bromine, and various types of lithium batteries. They all have their different advantages and disadvantages, so none has yet emerged as the ideal power system. Some of the problems encountered are expense, short life, inadequate power, the need for high temperatures, and the use of materials that are toxic or potentially dangerous if exposed to the atmosphere.

Box 4.2 Batteries

Modern life could not function without batteries. They are essential components of cars, laptop computers, mobile phones, calculators, cameras, camera flash units, many clocks and watches, and flashlights, to name but a few examples. How do they work and what distinguishes rechargeable batteries from the type known as 'dry cells', which cannot be successfully recharged?

The process that goes on in a battery is essentially the reverse of electrolysis, and so batteries are similar to fuel cells. However, whereas in the fuel cell the reactants are continuously added, in a battery these are not added to once the battery has been constructed. All batteries rely on the variation in the reactivities of different elements (usually metals). You recall from Book 2 Part 1 that elements can be arranged in an activity series, with elements such as caesium and potassium at the top, and mercury and gold at the bottom. You also carried out an

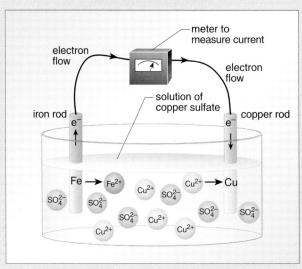

Figure 4.18
A schematic diagram of an iron–copper battery.

experiment showing this by placing a piece of iron in a solution of copper sulfate. A deposit of metallic copper appeared on the iron. This results from iron atoms passing into solution as Fe^{2+} ions, and Cu^{2+} ions coming out of solution as copper atoms.

If the experiment had been carried out in a different way (Figure 4.18), a deposit of copper could once again have been observed, but this time on the copper rather than on the iron rod. At the same time an electric current would have registered on the meter.

What happens is simply understood by considering the two metals individually. At the iron rod, iron atoms lose electrons and pass into solution as Fe^{2+} ions as before:

$$Fe(s) = Fe^{2+}(aq) + 2e^-$$

Because the iron and copper rods are connected by a wire, the electrons can pass from the iron to the copper. At the copper rod, the electrons can combine with Cu^{2+} ions in solution to form copper atoms, which are deposited on the copper rod:

$$Cu^{2+}(aq) + 2e^- = Cu(s)$$

The passage of the electrons is recorded as an electric current.

These reactions take place because of the difference in reactivity between iron and copper: iron atoms go into solution and copper atoms are deposited rather than the opposite because of the greater reactivity of iron. This is the basis of the operation of all batteries. The potential difference between the two electrodes (commonly called the 'voltage') depends on how far apart the two elements are in the activity series: the further apart, the greater the potential difference. Because of the similarity with electrolysis, the two rods are called electrodes and the solution in which they are immersed is called the electrolyte. Note that in this case the iron rod will be the negative electrode (the electrode that supplies electrons to the external circuit) and the copper will be the positive electrode.

The common 'dry cell' was invented by George Leclanché in 1866. Although it has been refined greatly in the detail of its construction, the principles involved remain the same. It is based on the elements zinc and manganese. The negative electrode is the zinc inner casing of the battery (Figure 4.19). The positive electrode is a carbon rod immersed in a paste of manganese dioxide, MnO_2, moistened by a solution of ammonium chloride, NH_4Cl, which acts as the electrolyte. The two electrode reactions are as follows:

negative electrode

$$Zn(s) = Zn^{2+}(aq) + 2e^-$$

positive electrode

$$MnO_2(s) + 4H^+(aq) + 2e^- = Mn^{2+}(aq) + H_2O(l)$$

At the positive electrode it is the MnO_2 that undergoes reaction rather than the carbon; the hydrogen ions, H^+, are supplied by the ammonium chloride. In practice the reaction is more complex than this and it cannot be reversed by recharging (that is by electrolysis). Consequently, once discharged, this type of battery has to be discarded.

The most common type of rechargeable battery is the lead–acid type found in the majority of vehicles (Figure 4.20). The negative electrode is made of lead, Pb, and the positive electrode is made of lead dioxide, PbO_2. The electrolyte is an aqueous solution of sulfuric acid, H_2SO_4.

The reactions involved are as follows:

negative electrode

$$Pb(s) + SO_4^{2-}(aq) = PbSO_4(s) + 2e^-$$

positive electrode

$$PbO_2(s) + 2H^+(aq) + H_2SO_4(aq) + 2e^- = PbSO_4(s) + 2H_2O(l)$$

Essentially, the reaction at the negative electrode involves oxidation of Pb metal to Pb^{2+}, and the one at the positive electrode involves reduction of Pb^{4+} (in PbO_2) to Pb^{2+}. In both cases, lead sulfate, $PbSO_4$, is formed on the electrode. These reactions *can* be reversed by electrolysis, and the lead–acid battery has proved a valuable workhorse for many years.

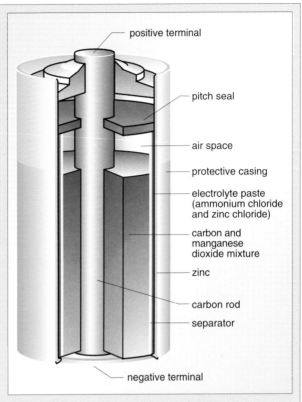

Figure 4.19
A cut-away schematic diagram of a 'dry cell' battery.

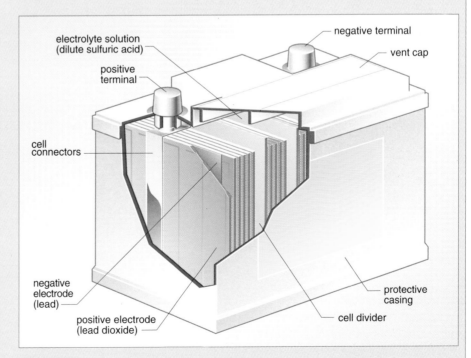

Figure 4.20
A cut-away schematic diagram of a lead–acid car battery.

In addition to financial and safety considerations, there are several technical parameters that need to be optimized for a battery to be a success:

- Cycle efficiency – this is the ratio of the energy obtainable from the battery to that required to charge the battery;
- Energy and power densities – these are the energy and power per litre, important because the battery needs to be as small as possible; the specific energy and specific power (the energy and power per kilogram of battery mass) are also important;
- Cycle life – the number of times the battery can be charged and discharged before the performance falls below an acceptable value;
- Charge retention – resistance to self-discharge, essentially a long 'shelf-life'.

Two of the leading contenders are the sodium–sulfur battery and the nickel–metal hydride battery. The former is unusual in that it involves molten electrodes and a solid electrolyte, the opposite to the normal situation (Figure 4.21). The overall reactions involved in the discharge process are as follows:

negative electrode

$$2Na(l) = 2Na^+(soln) + 2e^-$$

positive electrode

$$S(l) + 2e^- = S^{2-}(soln)$$

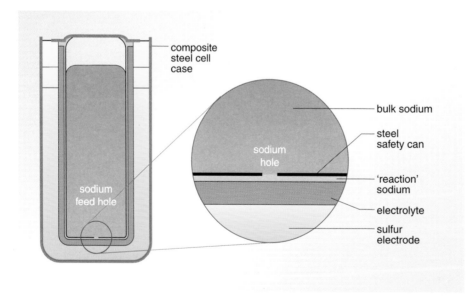

Figure 4.21
A schematic diagram of a sodium–sulfur battery. The electrodes are molten sodium and molten sulfur; the electrolyte is solid aluminium oxide.

In order for the sodium and sulfur to remain in the molten state, the battery has to be operated at a high temperature, about 320 °C. It has the advantage of cheap chemical components and a high specific energy (typically 400 kJ per kg, compared with around 90 kJ per kg for a lead–acid battery). It is highly efficient, with a cycle efficiency close to 100%, and discharges of its own accord only very slowly. A further advantage is that no 'memory effect' is observed if the battery is recharged before being fully discharged. This is one of the major disadvantages of the NiCad (nickel–cadmium) battery, which has a powerful memory effect. For example, if a NiCad battery is recharged after only 50% discharge, it only has 50% of the energy density previously available.

■ What apparent major disadvantage does the sodium–sulfur battery have?

■ The presence of molten sodium and molten sulfur is potentially hazardous if the battery is fractured in a crash.

To minimize the hazard, the sodium–sulfur batteries produced by the Silent Power battery company are made from small cells about the size of a standard dry cell; these are then connected together to give batteries containing up to 2 000 cells (Figure 4.22). Because only small amounts of sodium and sulfur are contained in each cell, any spillage would be minimized. Other disadvantages are a relatively low rate of charge, requiring up to 9 hours, and possible corrosion, which has been a problem in limiting the life of some prototype batteries.

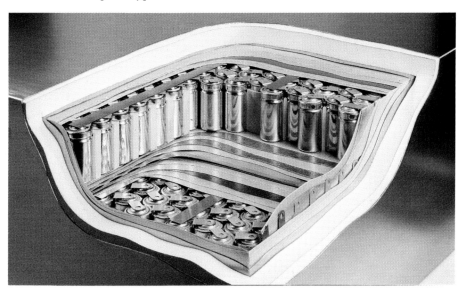

Figure 4.22
A cutaway view of a sodium-sulfur battery made of a large number of individual cells connected together.

The other leading contender is the nickel–metal hydride battery (abbreviated as NiMH). For the negative electrode, it makes use of the ability, referred to earlier, of certain alloys to absorb hydrogen. This allows storage and release of hydrogen during the charging and discharging processes. The positive electrode consists of solid nickel hydroxide, $Ni(OH)_2$, which on charging is converted into nickel oxyhydroxide, $Ni(O)OH$, by oxidation of Ni^{2+} to Ni^{3+}. The electrolyte is a 30% solution of potassium hydroxide, KOH, in water.

The reactions involved in the discharge process can be written as follows:

negative electrode

$$MH(s) + OH^-(aq) = M(s) + H_2O(l) + e^-$$

positive electrode

$$Ni(O)OH(s) + H_2O(l) + e^- = Ni(OH)_2(s) + OH^-(aq)$$

In the first equation, M stands for a mixture of metals with the property of absorbing hydrogen. In use, at the negative electrode, hydrogen atoms from the metal hydride release electrons to the external circuit, forming hydrogen ions. These react with hydroxide ions in the electrolyte to form water. At the positive electrode, nickel oxyhydroxide and water, together with electrons from the external circuit, give nickel hydroxide and hydroxide ions.

NiMH batteries have been known for some time and indeed are now commercially available for high-value uses such as powering laptop computers. Their advantages over the NiCad batteries more commonly used are lighter weight, greater power capacity (longer time between charges), and, of course, the environmental impact is much less because there is no need to use toxic cadmium as one of the materials.

An intensive programme of research was mounted by the Ovonics Battery Company (OBC) on behalf of a consortium of USA car manufacturers to see if the NiMH battery was a practical proposition for use in vehicles. The breakthrough that OBC achieved with their NiMH battery was greatly to improve its performance. The key was the nature of the metal hydride electrode. It turned out that the requisite properties were not to be found in any one, single metal. However, by using a complex alloy it proved possible to make electrodes with the desired properties. The solution was not, as is usually the case, to make a homogeneous alloy, but one with small domains of the various metals. The OBC MH electrodes vary in composition depending on the precise requirements. A typical electrode includes the elements vanadium, titanium, zirconium, nickel, and chromium.

The OBC NiMH battery has some advantages over the sodium–sulfur battery. It has a very long cycle life and can be recharged in less than one hour. And, of course, it contains much less hazardous materials. However, comparing the Silent Power sodium–sulfur battery with the OBC NiMH battery shows the former to have significantly better power and energy characteristics on a mass basis, although the latter is better if size is the more important criterion (Figure 4.23).

Figure 4.23
Comparison of the Silent Power sodium–sulfur battery with the OBC NiMH battery. The US Advanced Battery Consortium (USABC) performance goals are also shown.

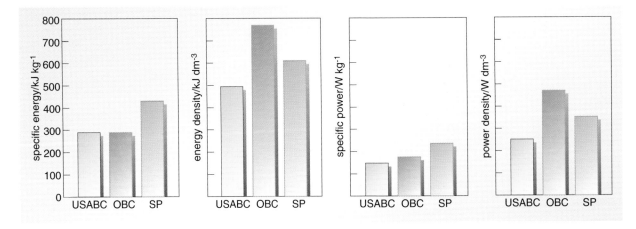

Question 17 Briefly describe what happens in the NiMH battery at each electrode during the charging process.

4.5 The future

Making predictions about the nature of future energy sources is, in some ways, easier and in other respects more difficult than for other topics. In the long term, there will have to be either a workable fusion reactor, or much greater use of renewable sources. In the shorter term, it is the latter that is closer to realization. The question mark is more political than scientific or technological in nature, and relates to taxation policies and international relations. Even so, developments are in the pipeline that promise to make some renewable sources economic in the reasonably near future.

The widespread use of photovoltaic devices, allied with the storage of electricity either as hydrogen or in batteries, seems to offer a sensible strategy for the production of at least a part of our future energy requirements. Such a scenario has a number of advantages. The main two are that it relies on a renewable primary energy source, namely solar radiation, and it both produces less atmospheric pollution and reduces the contribution to the greenhouse effect caused by burning more fossil fuels. However, there are still some technological problems, and the costs need to be reduced even further to become truly competitive.

One prototype system currently under development (1995) seems to offer solar-powered electricity at a fraction of the cost of present systems. One reason for the low cost is that it makes use of waste silicon from the electronics industry. Particles of silicon are embedded in defect-free cement (Section 3.6), which is then cast in the form of ultra-thin sheets. These could be used as roof tiles, or cladding for walls. At present, the efficiency is low, around 1%, but the developers are optimistic that this can be improved to 10% in the near future.

What cannot be predicted with any certainty at present is whether the best system for providing motive power for vehicles will be batteries, fuel cells powered by hydrogen, fuel cells powered by methane or methanol obtained from biomass, or the direct combustion of fuels such as hydrogen, methane or methanol. Whichever eventually comes out on top, the chemist will have a major part to play: in searching for new, more efficient, semiconductor materials, in seeking new methods of hydrogen formation and improving existing ones, and in continuing the development of more efficient batteries. Compared with the situation even ten years ago great strides have been made, and this success gives grounds for optimism that the remaining problems will, given time and effort, eventually be solved.

Summary of Chapter 4

The industrialized world is totally dependent on a continuous supply of fossil fuels. However, there is only a finite quantity of these available, and so alternative sources of energy must be found.

In the longer term, two options present themselves: nuclear fusion and solar energy in all its forms. Nuclear fusion is still at the research stage and a workable fusion reactor is unlikely to feasible until well into the 21st century. Many believe that it is more sensible anyway to make use of the energy already available from the Sun.

Examples of solar energy use are conversion into heat at relatively low temperatures for space heating, conversion into heat at much higher temperatures for use in turbines to generate electricity, and wind power. The methods likely to require an input of chemical knowledge are the photovoltaic generation of electricity, the production of alternative fuels such as hydrogen obtained by electrolysis of water or methane and ethanol obtained from biomass, and the development of advanced batteries for the storage of electricity.

Photovoltaic cells are made from semiconductor materials. The majority of solar cells use various forms of silicon; others use semiconductors such as gallium arsenide and cadmium telluride. Each type has advantages and disadvantages, and at present solar electricity is more expensive than that produced in conventional power stations.

In order to match the production with demand, some means of storing electrical energy is needed. The two most promising are the electrolytic production of a fuel and storage in batteries. One of the most popular ideas is to generate hydrogen by the electrolysis of water. Hydrogen is a relatively clean fuel and would cause only a small addition to the greenhouse effect. However, its transport and use pose a number of problems.

It is possible to use hydrogen in fuel cells to drive electric motors for vehicles. Fuel cells can also make use of other fuels, such as methane and methanol, obtained from biomass. These fuels do not make any net contribution to the greenhouse effect either, because the amount of carbon dioxide released exactly matches the amount taken up by the plants used for their production. Methane and methanol, along with ethanol produced from sugar cane and corn, can also be burned as conventional fuels.

The use of batteries is also under active investigation. They work by reversibly converting electrical energy into chemical energy: they comprise two electrodes of different materials and an electrolyte. The traditional lead–acid battery has an adverse performance:mass ratio, and efforts are being made to develop new batteries suitable for use in vehicles. Of the various types under active investigation, two of the most promising are the sodium–sulfur and the nickel–metal hydride batteries.

For the future, as much depends on politics as on science and technology. However, it seems highly likely that some combination of photovoltaic cells, batteries and renewable fuels will provide us with a significant fraction of our energy needs in the medium term.

Chapter 5
The strange world of nanotechnology

5.1 Small is beautiful

A very wide range of materials is available for a multitude of purposes, and to a considerable extent the properties of a given polymer, alloy or ceramic can be tailored to suit a particular purpose. Increasingly, demands are being made of materials scientists for more thermally stable polymers, stronger alloys and less brittle ceramics. In many instances the properties of a particular material do not approach those of an ideal material made up of polymers of a given length and composition, alloys of uniform crystalline structure, or a ceramic of uniform composition. The problem arises because all such materials made by manipulating bulk raw materials have defects of one sort or another. The control that can be exerted on the structure of such materials with current methods of manufacture is limited.

Some 30 or more years ago, the Nobel Prize winning physicist, Richard Feynman, predicted that, in the not-too-distant future, scientists would be able to control the arrangement of matter on a minute scale, and thereby give rise to new materials with a much richer variety of properties. It is only in the past few years that materials scientists have been able to exert such delicate control. As a result a new field, called **nanotechnology**, has opened up with the development of what have been variously termed **nanostructured**, **nanophase** or **nanoscale** materials.

Nanostructured materials are so called because they are made up of building blocks that have sizes of the order of nanometres or tens of nanometres. As a working definition, any material made up of grains or particles between 1 nm and 100 nm can be considered nanostructured. Above 100 nm, the grains begin to approach the size found in conventional materials; below 1 nm, the grains approach the sizes of individual atoms.

Nanostructured materials have quite unusual properties. The extremely small size of the constituent particles means that many such materials are transparent. A polymer containing nanometre-size iron particles is not just transparent but magnetic as well, and when melted gives rise to a magnetic liquid. At normal temperatures, nanophase ceramics are much tougher than those with a coarser grain structure made by more traditional methods. And nanophase titanium dioxide is a much better catalyst than the normal forms of the material.

Nanostructured materials have created a great deal of interest for a number of reasons.

- Many nanophase materials have atomic structures that differ significantly from those of normal crystalline solids or glasses of the same chemical composition; because many properties of solid materials depend on the precise arrangement of atoms, particularly the nearest-neighbour ones, it is to be expected that nanostructured materials should exhibit quite novel properties.

- Nanostructured materials can be made that involve the alloying of components that otherwise do not mix, again leading to quite novel properties.

- By varying the method of preparation, the composition and hence properties of the resulting solid material can be 'tuned' much more precisely. For example, nanometre-sized particles can be embedded in or between larger grains, or they can be coated with a monatomic layer of a different element.

The greatest flexibility is obtained with **nanocomposite** materials. There are several types of composite possible: ceramic/ceramic, ceramic/metal, ceramic/polymer, metal/polymer, and metal/metal. Each of these can be one of a number of different types, as shown for ceramic/ceramic composites (Figure 5.1). One nanocomposite form of silicon carbide has nanoscale silicon carbide particles dispersed between larger grains of silicon carbide: this behaves quite differently from conventional silicon carbide, a very hard material, and can be machined like a metal. The very fine nanoscale particles, possibly with traces of carbon at the interfaces, seem to act as a lubricant. When nanoscale silicon carbide is combined in a composite with nanoscale silicon nitride the resulting material, when heated to 1 600 °C, is no longer rigid but becomes 'superplastic', which means it can be stretched like chewing gum.

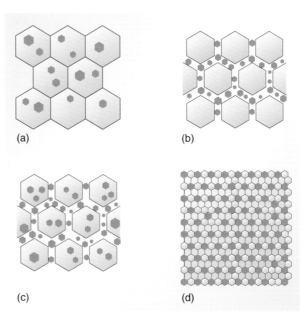

(a)   (b)   (c)   (d)

Figure 5.1
Four different types of ceramic/ceramic nanocomposite: (a) nanoscale particles of one ceramic embedded within larger grains of another; (b) nanoscale particles of one ceramic between larger grains of another; (c) nanoscale particles of one ceramic embedded within and between larger grains of another; (d) both components are present as nanoscale particles.

Similar dramatic changes in properties are seen when the two components are different types of material, for example as in ceramic/plastic nanocomposites (Figure 5.2). When single polymer chains are dispersed between sheets of a layered silicate, the result is a material with properties intermediate between plastic and ceramic: it melts at a higher temperature than would the corresponding conventional plastic, and the polymer chains are less susceptible to degradation. If single nanometre-thick silicate sheets are dispersed through a plastic matrix, the material is much stronger yet can be processed similarly to conventional plastics. A nanocomposite reinforced using just 6% ceramic behaves similarly to conventional composite material containing 60 or 70% ceramic. There is much interest in composites in which so-called 'buckytubes' (Figure 5.3), tubular versions of buckminsterfullerene (see Book 1 Chapter 10), are used to reinforce materials in a way similar to the silicate layers just described.

Some of the most exciting types of nanophase composite are those involving iron as one of the components. These have been found to have exceptional magnetic properties, such as an unusually high cooling effect when placed in a magnetic field that is cycled on and off. This has given rise to suggestions that such materials might one day replace conventional refrigerants in domestic refrigerators and freezers.

Enough work has been undertaken in the relatively short time since nanostructured materials were first discovered to show the immense promise

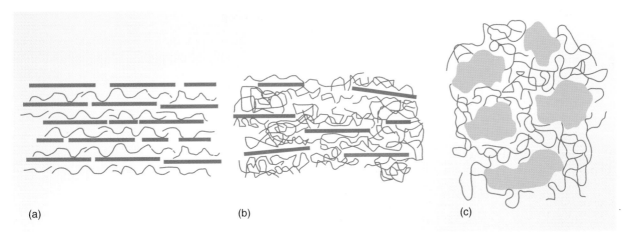

(a)　　　　　　　　　　　(b)　　　　　　　　　　　(c)

Figure 5.2
Examples of ceramic/plastic nanocomposites: (a) single polymer chains dispersed between sheets of silicate; (b) single silicate sheets dispersed through the bulk of the plastic; (c) larger particles of silicate dispersed through the plastic produces much less dramatic improvements in properties.

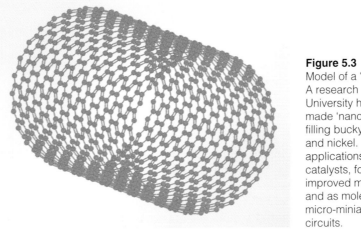

Figure 5.3
Model of a 'buckytube'. A research group at Oxford University have recently made 'nanomagnets' by filling buckytubes with iron and nickel. Possible applications are as catalysts, for making improved magnetic tape, and as molecular wires in micro-miniature electrical circuits.

for a wide variety of applications. The control that can be achieved, allied to the very wide range of possible structures, means that they have great potential. Already there are several companies that have been set up to exploit the unique properties exhibited by nanophase materials.

The main hurdle to large-scale use of such materials is their method of manufacture. Nearly all the methods used are painstaking and expensive, and generally not very suitable for adapting to an industrial scale. None the less, for certain applications, the unique advantages presented by nanophase materials justifies their large premium in cost. With improvements in manufacturing methods, the sky's the limit: who is to say that, sometime in the future, the long-sought room-temperature superconductor may not turn out to be a composite involving nanophase materials!

Question 18 What advantages do nanophase ceramics have over conventionally manufactured ceramics?

5.2 Seeing atoms

Ever since the Greeks first proposed that matter was composed of particles that they called atoms, the possibility of seeing such microscopic entities has been envisaged but, until recently, thought to be an impossible dream. Some might argue that it is still an impossible dream to see an atom, but to the extent that an image of atomic dimensions can be obtained, the development of the **scanning tunnelling microscope** (STM) warranted the Nobel prize that was awarded to its inventors in 1986.

Figure 5.4 shows a simplified diagram of a scanning tunnelling microscope. The measuring device consists of a probe with a conical tip, which is positioned very close (within a few tenths of a nanometre) to the sample surface. The mechanism used for moving the probe depends on the **piezoelectric effect**; this is the property of certain crystals to change size when subjected to a potential difference. The probe is attached to a mount made of three piezoelectric crystal elements, two for moving across the surface, and the third for moving towards or away from the surface. By applying steadily increasing voltages to the crystal, the probe can be moved by minute amounts (as little as a few tens of picometres at a time) over the surface of the sample. Because such small movements are involved, the measuring device has to be mounted on a special vibration-free table. The scanning is controlled electronically, and the probe tip can be moved over distances of from less than a nanometre to hundreds of micrometres.

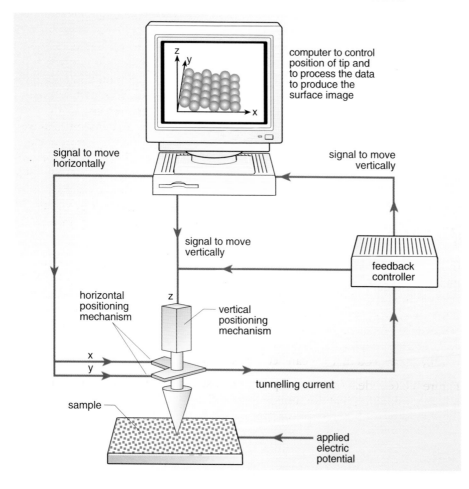

Figure 5.4
A schematic illustration of a scanning tunnelling microscope.

The principle behind the operation of the STM is the observation that an electric current flows between two conductors with a potential difference between them even when they are separated, provided the separation is very small, typically around 0.1 nm. This current is known as the tunnelling current, because it tunnels through the intervening insulating layer between the two conductors, which can be a vacuum, air or a liquid. The tunnelling current depends on the applied voltage and the distance apart of the two conductors, which in the STM are the tip of the probe and the surface of the sample. The current decreases rapidly as the distance between the two conductors increases. It is this strong dependence of the tunnelling current on the separation distance that enables such a clear image of the surface structure to be obtained. As the tip is scanned over the surface, a very localized stream of electrons flows between the surface and the tip of the probe.

- Do you think that this means the probe tip must be sharpened so that the tip is made up of a single atom, or at most a very small group of atoms?

- The answer is yes and no! It is not possible to form such a fine tip reproducibly. However, there is almost invariably a small protuberance present which does indeed terminate in just a few atoms.

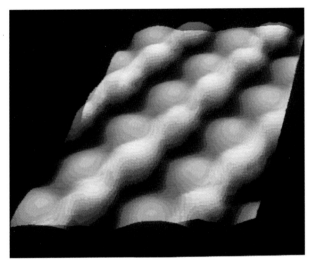

As the tip is passed over the surface, it is moved closer or further away so as to maintain the tunnelling current at a constant value. This is achieved by feedback of the tunnelling current signal via a control device to the piezoelectric translator on which the tip is mounted. By recording the voltage applied to the piezoelectric mount as it scans over a given area and using a computer to process the data, an electronic image of the surface is obtained: atoms appear as peaks, and the areas between atoms appear as troughs. In plotting the images, an arbitrarily chosen scale of a series of shades of grey or a range of colours indicates the size of the measured current, with peaks being indicated by lighter shades and troughs by darker shades.

Figure 5.5
The surface of the semiconductor material gallium arsenide, as revealed by scanning tunnelling microscopy. Simulated colours are used to distinguish the two types of atom: gallium atoms are shown as blue and the arsenic atoms as orange.

In addition to the probe and its piezoelectric mount, the STM workstation includes hardware and software to control the scanning process, and to process the data. Simulated colours are sometimes used to make data from different types of atom or molecular entity readily distinguishable by the eye (Figure 5.5). In this amazing picture, even allowing for the fact that simulated colours are used, the appearance of the image is such that one could be readily convinced that we can actually 'see' atoms.

Figure 5.6 (overleaf) shows a top view of a silicon crystal, together with a 3D rendition showing that the surface is not a flat plane but has steps of varying heights, with each a multiple of the spacing between the atomic layers.

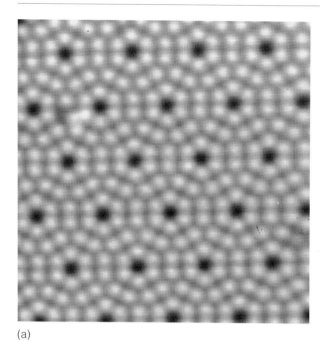

(a)

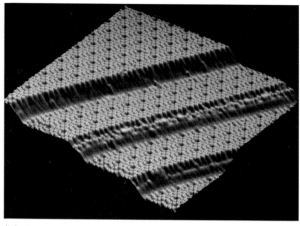

(b)

Figure 5.6
STM images of silicon: (a) top view; the image measures
12.6 nm × 14.2 nm; (b) 3D view; the image measures
32 nm × 36 nm; the steps are 1.25 nm deep, which
corresponds to four atomic double layers.

A related technique called atomic force microscopy (AFM) works similarly to
STM, but instead of an electric current being measured, the changes in force
experienced by the tip as it is dragged over the surface are measured. By its
nature, AFM is less sensitive than STM, but it has the advantage that the
material being investigated does not need to conduct electricity.

Organic and biological molecules, such as DNA (Figure 1.4), can be imaged
by STM, provided they are adsorbed on a conducting surface. This is not
particularly difficult to achieve because the probe simply pushes aside and
ignores those molecules not adsorbed as they do not sustain a tunnelling
current. One of the most studied classes of organic molecules is liquid
crystals. An example of such an image is shown in Figure 5.7a, in which
molecules of the liquid crystal compound shown in Figure 5.7b are adsorbed
on a graphite surface.

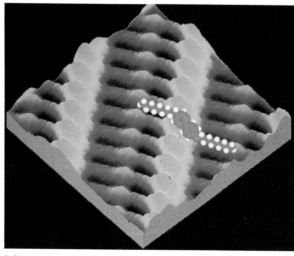

(a)

(b)

Figure 5.7
(a) STM image of the liquid crystal material shown in (b).

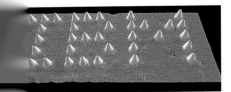

Figure 5.8
The letters 'IBM' produced using STM techniques.

Figure 5.9
A ring of 48 iron atoms on a copper surface produced using STM techniques.

Not only does STM enable images of matter at the atomic and molecular level to be obtained, but it can also be used to manipulate individual atoms. One of the best known examples is the image of the letters 'IBM' formed by scientists at one of IBM's research laboratories from individual xenon atoms on the surface of a nickel crystal (Figure 5.8). Another beautiful example is a group of iron atoms placed in a ring on a copper surface (Figure 5.9). In addition to showing the iron atoms themselves, a standing wave can be seen within the circle. Theoretical models suggest that this arises from electrons trapped in the ring, demonstrating in a spectacular fashion their wave-like properties (Book 1 Chapter 7). More practical applications of this technique potentially include custom fabrication of computer chips, information storage and selective formation of catalysts.

To make it easier to visualize the images, the ARM remote manipulator used for molecular modelling (Chapter 2) has also been attached to a scanning tunnelling microscope. The use of a head-mounted display or active 3D glasses enables the operator to get the feeling of walking across the surface of the material (Frontispiece). The effect is unbelievably stunning. In this image, the individual hexagonal units of carbon atoms are easily seen.

This combination of the ability to observe matter and events at the molecular level, together with the facility to manipulate individual atoms, opens up a whole new range of possible applications that are only now being thought about. There seems little doubt that we have only just begun to scratch the surface of what is possible, and that the technique of scanning tunnelling microscopy will have a major influence on scientific discoveries and technological innovation well into the 21st century.

Question 19 What is the chief difference between the technique of STM (or AFM) and X-ray crystallography for obtaining images of atoms and molecules?

5.3 The future

Attempting to give an idea as to the direction that
nanotechnology will take over the next ten or
twenty years is perhaps the most difficult feat of
crystal-ball gazing of all the topics outlined here.
Some of the developments touched on in the
previous two Sections, if predicted just twenty
years ago, would have sounded more like science
fiction. So it is difficult to assess whether the
predictions of those who say that nanotechnology
will revolutionize our lives (Box 5.1 and Figure
5.10) are likely to be fact or fantasy.

Certainly many of the most dramatic discoveries in
recent years have been the result of joint efforts by
interdisciplinary teams of scientists and
technologists from a wide range of subject areas.
Developments in genetic engineering have been
the result of biologists and chemists coming
together and combining techniques and methods
to give the new science of molecular biology. So
when K. Eric Drexler, one of the world's foremost
crusaders for nanotechnology, predicts that even
greater discoveries are not just possible but
inevitable through the application of this new
science, in which the methods and techniques of
mechanical engineering are applied to the
molecular level (Figure 5.11), it would be short-
sighted in the extreme to dismiss such forecasts
out of hand.

*A very readable summary of some of Drexler's
ideas is given in the Offprints for Book 4: Martin
Pearson, The Age of Miracles, The Independent
Magazine, 18 March 1995, pp. 32-7.*

'This molecule is so smart, not only does it assemble
itself, but it writes up the paper and then submits it for
publication'

Figure 5.10

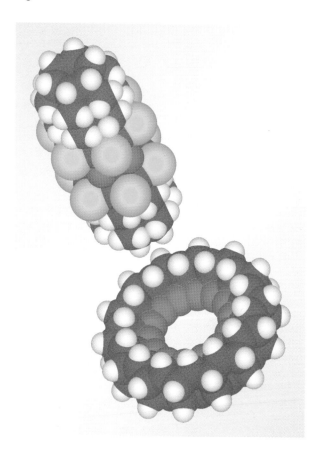

Figure 5.11
A proposed molecular ball-bearing, one of a whole range
of molecular devices envisaged by Drexler as providing
the means for constructing a 'molecular assembler',
necessary for carrying out molecular engineering.

Box 5.1 The chemistry of tomorrow takes its cue from nature

Article by Nina Hall, *The Observer*, 14 August 1994.

New age chemistry is almost upon us, and it will be cleaner, greener and cleverer than its predecessor. Research chemists are now designing radically different methods for making advanced materials that will use up less energy and raw materials, and produce minimum waste.

Since the 1970s, when the environmental movement took off, the chemical industry has been a PR nightmare. Chemical plants have been regarded as breweries from hell where Satan's servants (they are called scientists) commit unnatural acts, creating artificial molecules that were never meant to be.

Traditionally, the industry has depended on bulk transformations of raw materials, employing energy-hungry processes and often requiring intense heat and pressure, whether to make plastic from the simple constituents of petroleum or a complex drug compound which is the result of a long series of carefully designed reactions. Inevitably there is waste, which may be difficult to prevent.

But the old image of chemistry is undergoing a dramatic sea change.

One of the most ingenious new approaches, which is currently the talk of the chemistry labs, is to take a leaf out of nature by mimicking the way large biological molecules self-assemble from smaller units.

Requiring only normal temperatures and pressures, molecular self-assembly would allow chemists to grow chemicals with elaborate structures at the scale of nanometres (billionths of a metre). These might operate as tiny electronic devices or even miniature medical repair kits, so achieving a level of microscopic complexity to rival that of life itself.

Most of us forget that biology is nothing more than intelligent chemistry – self-organising machinery made of thousands of different molecular cogs and wheels working in concert, doing what comes naturally.

Take the kingpin of life, DNA, for example. Its famous helical structure consists of two complementary strands built from four smaller units called bases, arranged in sequences – genes – that encode all the information needed to make a living organism. DNA replicates with ease by unwinding and unzipping, each separate strand acting as a template for the self-assembly of a new complementary partner from a pool of single bases.

One of the most striking examples of biological self-assembly emerged in virus studies in the 1950s. The tobacco mosaic virus, which resembles a sausage roll, consists of a single strand of RNA (which is similar to DNA) encased in a tube of protein made of over 2,000 identical units. If you break open the virus so that RNA and the protein units separate, and then bring all the components back together again, the sausage roll reconstitutes to form the active virus.

How does such self-assembly operate? The chemist's buzz term here is 'molecular recognition'. Weak but precisely arranged electrostatic forces between the molecular components pull them together and lock them into a tight 3D configuration like a Lego toy. A glance at the structure of DNA or a virus reveals the elegance of the results.

Chemists are already fabricating simple structures that work on the same basis. Professor

Fraser Stoddart and Dr. David Amabilino of the University of Birmingham have created molecules built of interlocked rings by programming the individual links with the right chemical information so they naturally encircle each other. Their latest triumph is a five-ring molecule which they have dubbed Olympiadane, for obvious reasons.

The chances of forming such a molecule by the usual chemical reactions, says Amabilino 'must be a million to one'. This said, the researchers concede that the molecules they have so far made are of no use. But they hope that they will pave the way for larger, more complex structures.

An American researcher, Professor Julius Rebek of Massachusetts Institute of Technology, has created another molecule with sporting connotations.
(continued overleaf)

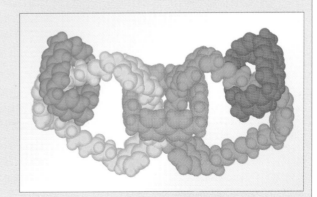

Olympiadane

It self-assembles from components that look like two halves of a tennis ball to form a hollow sphere. Rebek's aim is to mimic in the simplest possible way the outer shell of a virus; the resulting molecule could then act as a delivery vehicle for drugs by sneaking into cells in the same way as a virus would.

Viruses, of course, contain self-replicating DNA or RNA. Rebek's ultimate goal is to take the analogy further by creating drug molecules that can replicate themselves from raw materials available in the cells, so increasing the drug dose where it was needed.

Although this strategy is a long way from becoming a reality, with self-assembly we have had a sneak preview of the chemistry of the future.

Question 20 K. E. Drexler envisages that it will be possible in the foreseeable future to make new materials by constructing individual molecules on a molecular assembly line. You can get an idea of how fast molecules would need to be synthesized to make this feasible by considering the growth of a single wool fibre on a sheep. Wool grows at about 1 mm per day, and a typical wool fibre has a diameter of 30 μm. By assuming that wool is made up of atoms occupying a cube 150 pm each side, calculate approximately how many atoms per second are organized into the keratin molecules that make up a wool fibre.

Summary of Chapter 5

Nanostructured materials are made up of building blocks with sizes of the order of nanometres. Such materials have quite unusual properties. They often have atomic structures that differ from those of normal crystalline solids or glasses of the same chemical composition. Nanostructured materials can be made which involve the alloying of components that otherwise do not mix. And the composition and hence properties of the resulting solid material can be 'tuned' much more precisely.

The greatest flexibility is obtained with nanocomposite materials, that is materials made from nanoscale particles of one or both components. The main hurdle to large-scale use of such materials is their painstaking and expensive methods of manufacture. None the less, for certain applications, the unique advantages presented by nanophase materials justifies their extra cost.

Scanning tunnelling microscopy and atomic force microscopy have enabled images to be produced at the atomic scale. STM involves measuring the variations in electrical current as a probe is passed over the surface of a material. AFM involves the measurement of the change in force under similar circumstances.

STM and AFM enable the surfaces of bulk materials to be imaged. Molecules adsorbed on the surface can also be seen. Atoms can be placed individually on a surface opening up the possibility of custom fabrication of atomic-scale computer chips and the production of selective catalysts.

Future developments in nanotechnology are probably the most difficult to predict. What has already been achieved would twenty years ago have been thought impossible. Accordingly, it would be short-sighted to dismiss out of hand some of the more extravagant forecasts about the future possibilities for true molecular engineering.

Postscript

As we remarked at the beginning of Part 2, predicting the future is an uncertain activity at the best of times, and some of the topics we have chosen may turn out to be blind alleys. Perhaps the most difficult area to predict is the one of nanotechnology. Each day seems to bring news of some new development concerned with miniaturization, and there are many examples of experiments involving devices that, potentially, are on the molecular scale.

Yet, some of the scenarios depicted by those who champion the power of molecular nanotechnology or molecular manufacturing appear to be in the realms of science fiction. But, then, many of the developments that are now in everyday use, such as lasers, satellite telephones and television, and laptop computers, would have seemed similarly fantastic at the beginning of the 20th century. It seems that not only are the dreams of the early Greek philosophers, of being able to see atoms, essentially now a reality, but the ability to manipulate individual atoms and molecules at will is close to realization.

Whatever the directions that science and technology take us in these and other areas, what is much more of a certainty is that molecular science will have a very significant, and probably increasing role. We hope that this Course has provided you with the necessary skills as a foundation to enable you to appreciate such developments as they occur and to assess their potential impact on your own environment. More than that, we hope that we have demonstrated the fascination of molecular science so that we have not only aroused your curiosity to want to know more, but have managed to convey something of the excitement that knowledge and understanding of new discoveries can bring.

Objectives for Book 4 Part 2

After you have studied Book 4 Part 2 you should be able to do the following:

1   Understand the meaning of the words emboldened in the text.

2   Apply concepts and ideas from earlier in the Course at an appropriate level to understanding (i) new developments in molecular science and (ii) proposed solutions to particular problems that have a partial or wholly chemical basis.

3   Outline the extent to which examples of research and development in each of the topics covered are promoted by (i) pressures from society, (ii) human curiosity about fundamental chemical principles, or (iii) human curiosity about other phenomena.

4   (a) Recognize the strengths and limitations of computer-based molecular modelling; (b) describe the application of molecular modelling to the design of new drugs.

5   (a) Outline relationships between the molecular structure of polymers and their bulk properties; (b) give examples of applications where advanced polymers are required, explaining the properties that suit them for a particular purpose; (c) outline the special requirements for biodegradable polymers for use in medical applications.

6   (a) Give examples of applications where ceramics are being investigated for possible use; (b) identify the potential advantages and disadvantages of ceramics over existing materials in these cases.

7   Describe possible chemically based solutions to the quest for renewable energy sources, and compare these with other energy sources.

8   (a) Compare the atomic/molecular structure of nanophase materials with that of the crystalline and glassy states; (b) describe the operation of the scanning tunnelling microscope.

9   Give an informed opinion concerning prospects for future developments in the areas of computer-based molecular modelling, polymers, ceramics, solar-derived fuels, solar electricity, advanced batteries, semiconductors and nanoscale materials.

Answers to Questions

Question 1 Particularly for large molecules, physical models are not easy to manipulate and they are prone to falling apart. Computer-drawn models do not have such limitations. Another advantage is that the same molecule can be represented on screen in different ways: each representation has its own advantages and disadvantages and so it is very useful to be able to switch from one to another at will. Computer-drawn models can have very precise bond lengths and bond angles, whereas physical models use standardized values. Another limitation of physical models is that it is not obvious which particular conformation is the one adopted by the molecule in reality. Molecular graphics systems can calculate the lowest energy conformation. The way in which molecules interact can also be calculated, and the preferred way in which a molecule 'docks' into a receptor molecule can be predicted.

One advantage of physical models is that they are eminently portable, and don't need a computer – they can be used anywhere, anytime. Another advantage of a physical model is that being able to handle and look at it from any angle gives an immediacy that may be lacking on a screen. However, as we shall see in Section 2.4, new methods of displaying models by computer are under development that should give computer models similar attributes.

Question 2 In modelling complex three-dimensional objects such as molecules, a great deal of information needs to be processed. To manipulate a realistic looking model, it is necessary to carry out the calculations sufficiently quickly to produce detailed images with appropriate colours and realistic looking shapes without any perceptible delay (often described as 'in real time'). Desktop computers have become powerful enough to do this only relatively recently.

Question 3 First, influenza is caused by a virus. Viruses operate by taking over the genetic material of the host. As a consequence, targeting just the virus without also harming the patient is much more difficult than treating diseases that are caused by bacteria. Secondly, the influenza virus seems to have an unusual ability even among viruses to mutate to give different strains. Each strain differs to a greater or lesser extent in the proteins that are the key to the action of the virus. As a result, it is even more difficult to find molecules that are active against all strains.

Question 4 Sialidase has a particular function in releasing replicated influenza virus particles from cells. The natural substrate is bound sialic acid, which is cleaved off as part of this process. A molecule that interfered with the action of sialidase would bind to the enzyme without itself being changed. Once bound, it would prevent the sialic acid from having access to the sialidase active site, and so block this key step in the propagation process.

Question 5 The first step would be to isolate the enzyme ACE, and to produce crystals for X-ray diffraction. This in itself is no easy task. Once crystals are available, the structure of the enzyme can be determined from a combination of the X-ray data and a knowledge of the amino acid sequence in the enzyme, obtained from separate measurements. To see how captopril binds to the ACE receptor, an X-ray study of an ACE crystal soaked in a solution of the inhibitor would be highly advantageous. Once the ACE structure had been determined, GRID calculations would provide an indication of the various 'hot-spots' for different types of functional group. A comparison of these results with the position of the captopril attached to the receptor would then provide a check on the GRID calculations. Finally, the binding site would be examined to see if there are (a) unoccupied spaces in the active site and (b) suitably placed functional groups that could interact with additional groups added to the captopril template. New molecular structures could then be designed and synthesized. Tests *in vitro* and *in vivo* would then follow to see if the predictions were borne out in practice.

Question 6 It is less likely that significant improvement in activity would be possible than in the case of the sialidase inhibitor. The lead compound in that case was only weakly active *in vitro*, inactive *in vivo*, and not very selective, so there was a lot of room for improvement. In contrast, captopril is an existing drug and so is highly active itself. It would seem that there is less scope for improvement in this case.

Question 7 This is obviously a matter of opinion, but the balance of argument would seem to favour the improved display. A force feedback arm would allow you to feel the interactions involved in docking two molecules together. However, being able to see clearly and with full stereoscopic vision the molecules themselves, and how they are oriented one with another, is crucial to being able to manipulate them effectively. Further, the size of the forces involved could be displayed on screen giving some indication of the extent of attraction or repulsion, even in the absence of force feedback.

Question 8 Molecules **A** and **D** are most likely to form liquid crystals; **B**, **C** and **E** are unlikely to form liquid crystals. Molecule **A** is elongated with a rigid part, a long flexible group at one end and a polar group at the other. Molecule **B** is elongated and has two rigid benzene rings, with long flexible groups at the ends; however, it has a flexible chain in the centre, which is likely to prevent liquid crystal formation. Molecule **C** has a rigid central part with a polar group at one end; however, it is not elongated and the other end has a group that is short and hence not very flexible. Molecule **D** is elongated with a rigid part, long flexible groups at each end, and a polar group attached to the rigid central group. Molecule **E** is elongated with a rigid central group to which is attached a polar group at one end; however, attached at the other end is only a short methyl group.

Question 9 A liquid crystal display operates by using an electric charge to orient a nematic liquid crystal in a particular direction. Liquid crystal thermometers rely on the change of reflecting properties of a chiral nematic liquid crystal as the temperature varies.

Question 10 By analogy with Kevlar, the spinning process would have the effect of aligning the polyethene molecules, giving a very ordered structure. This would mean that the forces between the molecules would be much stronger than for normal polyethene. Although these are the relatively weak London forces, and not the stronger hydrogen bonding found in Kevlar, the extreme length of the molecules means that the total forces between the molecules make the material very strong. However, in contrast to Kevlar, there are no rigid groups present, and as the temperature is increased, the increased motion of the molecules would rapidly lead to a decrease in the strength of the London forces as the molecules move apart. Indeed, above about 100 °C, this type of polyethene loses much of its strength.

Question 11 The two monomers needed to make Nomex are structures **A1** and **A2**. They are isomers of the monomers used to make Kevlar: in each case the two substituents are not on opposite ends of the benzene ring but one position closer together. The effect is that the polymer molecules have a zig-zag shape, in contrast to the straight rod-like shape of the molecules of Kevlar. Consequently, though the molecules are rigid, they are unable to line up quite so well, and the forces between the molecules are not as strong in Nomex as in Kevlar, and so the Nomex fibres are weaker.

A1   **A2**

Question 12 Some advantages are: (a) a more precise dose can be administered because the degree to which drugs administered orally are metabolized before reaching the target site is often unknown; (b) a more even dose can be administered, avoiding the rollercoaster effect; (c) the drug can be specifically administered at its target site. A disadvantage is that minor surgery is required to implant the drug-impregnated polymer tablets.

Question 13

Relative properties of ceramics and metals

Property	Ceramics	Metals
hardness	high	low
fracture toughness	low	high
density	low	high
ductility	low	high
thermal conductivity	low	high
electrical conductivity	low	high

This comparison is a gross generalization and is purely relative. It ignores wide variations, and some metals, for example, are very hard.

Question 14

$$Si(OCH_2CH_3)_4 + 4H_2O = Si(OH)_4 + 4CH_3CH_2OH$$

$$Si(OH)_4 = SiO_2 + 2H_2O$$

Question 15 If the energy of the photon is less than the energy of the band gap, electrons will not be promoted to the conduction band because no absorption will take place; the light will either pass straight through or be reflected. If the photon has an energy greater than that of the band gap, then it will be absorbed and the photoelectric current will be observed. However, the electrons will initially be in an energy level higher up the conduction band. They will then drop to a lower level, and their excess energy will be dissipated as heat.

Question 16 Hydrogen is a clean fuel, giving rise to water as its main product on combustion. However, as with any internal combustion engine, the high temperatures also cause the formation of nitrogen oxides. Further, as it is a gas, carrying it as a fuel for cars and other vehicles poses problems. Liquefaction is possible but requires the use of insulated containers, rather like giant Thermos flasks, so adding to the expense.

Fuels obtained from plants require large areas of fertile land to produce the necessary crops. There is an obvious conflict with the need to plant crops for food. However, because the fuels are liquid they are easily stored and carried in a conventional fuel tank on vehicles.

For the generation of electricity in power stations, the problems associated with handling hydrogen are less of a disadvantage. However, both fuels are handicapped by the economics of generation compared with the current price of petroleum-based fuels.

Question 17 During charging, the opposite reactions to the discharging process take place. At the negative electrode, electrons from the charging source cause the conversion of hydrogen cations (from water molecules) into hydrogen atoms, which then enter the metal alloy (represented as M) to form the metal hydride. At the same time, hydroxide anions are formed. At the positive electrode, hydroxide anions from the electrolyte react with the nickel hydroxide electrode to form nickel oxyhydroxide and water, and electrons are fed back to the charging source to complete the circuit.

Question 18 Nanophase ceramics are more uniform in structure than bulk ceramics, and can be made from components that otherwise do not mix. Their composition can be controlled much more precisely. They have a range of unusual properties, such as exceptional magnetic properties, transparency, and the ability to be stretched like chewing gum at high temperatures rather than fracturing as conventional ceramics do. They are often better catalysts. Nanocomposite ceramics have exceptional strength because the grains are so small that cracks are unable to propagate.

Question 19 Scanning tunnelling microscopy and atomic force microscopy are different from X-ray crystallography because the data are obtained from individual atoms, rather than from a very large number. The latter type of technique therefore gives an average picture whereas STM and AFM look at particular sites, and so can detect not just the regularity of the crystal lattice but also imperfections and atoms or molecules attached to the surface.

Question 20 To make the calculation easier, it is best to work in a consistent set of units, say nanometres (nm). So the volume of a wool fibre grown in a day is obtained by multiplying the length of fibre grown, 1 000 000 nm (1 mm), or 10^6 nm, by its cross-sectional area. Assuming the cross-section is circular, the area is given by the formula πr^2. The radius is 15 μm, that is 15 000 nm, so the cross-sectional area is $3.142 \times 15\,000 \times 15\,000$, which equals approximately 7.1×10^8 nm^2. The volume per day is therefore approximately 7.1×10^{14} nm^3. There are $24 \times 60 \times 60$ seconds in a day, that is 86 400. So the volume per second is about 8.2×10^9 nm^3.

The volume of an atom is $0.15 \times 0.15 \times 0.15$ nm^3, which equals 0.003 4 nm^3. So this means that the number of atoms organized per second is 8.2×10^9 nm^3 divided by 0.003 4 nm^3, which is approximately 2.4×10^{12}! And that's just for one fibre! This gives an idea of the size of the task with which a molecular assembly process of the kind envisaged by Drexler would have to be able to cope.

Acknowledgements

Grateful acknowledgement is made to the following sources for permission to reproduce material in this part of Book 4:

Text

Box 5.1 Hall. N. (1994) 'Science', *Observer Life Magazine*, 14 August 1994. Illustration: courtesy of Dr B. Amabilino, Laboratoire de Chimie Organo-Minerale.

Figures

Cover photo and Figure 4.17 Dr R.R. Hill; *Frontispiece and Figure 2.28* Alex Treml photography; *Figure 1.1* cover painting by Tomo Narashima, accompanying the article 'Solid acid catalysts', by Sir John Meurig Thomas. copyright © 1992 by Scientific American Inc. All rights reserved; *Figure 1.2* James L. Amos; *Figure 1.3* courtesy of Donald E. Osborn, Sacramento Municipal Utility District; *Figure 1.4* Lawrence Berkeley Laboratory/Science Photo Library; *Figure 2.2* courtesy of Cray Research Ltd; *Figure 2.3a* Antony Barrington Brown; *Figure 2.3b* Oxford Molecular Biophysics Laboratory/ Science Photo Library; *Figure 2.5* photo courtesy of Shell Research Lab, Amsterdam; *Figures 2.6, 2.7, 2.9, 3.33b, and 4.12* Science Photo Library; *Figure 2.8* McNamara, S. (1993) 'Under the influenza', *Sunday Times*, 14 November 1993, © Times Newspapers Ltd, 1993, graphic by Chris Sargent; *Figure 2.10* Kaplan, M. M. and Webster, R. G. 'The epidemiology of influenza', *Scientific American*, December 1977, Vol. 237, no. 6, copyright © 1977 by Scientific American, Inc. All rights reserved; *Figure 2.24* reprinted with permission from *Nature*, 'Rational design of potent sialidase-based inhibitors of influenza virus replication', von Itzstein, M., *et al.*, Vol. 363, copyright 1993 Macmillan Magazines Ltd; *Figure 2.27* Division Ltd; *Figure 3.1* courtesy of Goodfellow Cambridge Ltd; *Figure 3.3a* NEC; *Figure 3.3b* Sharp Electronics; *Figures 3.7, 3.10, 3.11, 3.15 and 3.16* Merck Ltd; *Figures 3.17 and 3.20* Dupont Advanced Fibers Systems; *Figures 3.21 and 3.22* Johns Hopkins Magazine; *Figure 3.24* Rolls-Royce; *Figure 3.26* The Natural History Museum, London; *Figure 3.29* International Syalons, Newcastle; *Figure 3.30* Ashby, M. F. (1987) 'Technology in the 1990s: advanced materials and predictive design', in Hondros, E. D. and Kelly, A. (eds) *The Promise of Advanced Materials*, Fig. 1, The Royal Society, London; *Figure 3.31* Prof. J.D. Birchall; *Figure 3.32* from Wallace, S. and Hench, L.L. 'The processing and characterization of DCCA modified gel-derived silica', *Materials Research Society Symposia Proceedings*, 1984, Vol. 32, p.47; *Figure 3.33a* David Parker/Science Photo Library; *Figure 4.7* Green, M. (1982) *Solar Cells*, Prentice-Hall; *Figure 4.8* from *Scientific American*, October 1976, Vol. 235, no. 4, copyright © 1976 by Scientific American, Inc. All rights reserved; *Figure 4.11* Intel; *Figures 4.13 and 4.15* BP Solar Ltd; *Figure 4.14* Jeremy Burgess/Science Photo Library; *Figures 4.21 and 4.22* Silent Power Ltd; *Figure 5.1* courtesy of Koichi Niihara, Institute of Scientific and Industrial Research, Osaka University, Japan; *Figure 5.2* courtesy of E. P. Giannelis, Cornell University, Ithaca, USA; *Figure 5.5* courtesy of Randall M. Feenstra and Joseph A. Stroscio, IBM Corporation; *Figure 5.6* courtesy of Dr D.E. Bürger, Institut für Physik, University of Basel; *Figure 5.7a* courtesy of Jane E. Frommer, IBM Almaden Research Center; *Figure 5.8* IBM Corporation, Research Division, Almaden Research Center; *Figure 5.9* courtesy of Michael Crommie, Christopher Lutz and Donald Eigler, IBM Almaden Research Center; *Figure 5.10* Ward, M. (1994) 'Chemistry for life - 75th anniversary of IUPAC', *Chemistry International*, Vol. 16, no. 5, Blackwell Science Ltd; *frontispiece for Part 1* Matthew Gladstone.

Offprints attached to Book 4

Pearson, M. (1995) 'The age of miracles', *Independent Magazine*, 18 March 1995, © Martin Pearson. Figure: courtesy of Hitachi.

Index